Buddhist Aesthetics and Ethics

BUDDHIST AESTHETICS AND ETHICS

H Prasad

MD PUBLICATIONS PVT LTD
NEW DELHI
www.mdppl.com

Published by :

MD Publications Pvt Ltd
"MD House", 11, Darya Ganj,
New Delhi - 110 002
Phone : +91-11- 45355555
E-mail : contact@mdppl.com
Website: www.mdppl.com

ISBN : 978-81-7533-348-2

Published and Printed by Mr. Pranav Gupta on behalf of **MD Publications Pvt Ltd** at Repro India Limited.

Preface

Aesthetics is a branch of philosophy dealing with what is beauty. It studies the qualities of nature of the beautiful and makes judgments concerning beauty. Beauty is visual pleasantness of a person, animal, object or scene, and also pleasantness of sound, especially music that gives pleasure to the senses or pleasurably exalts the mind or spirit. For instances, the flowing rivers and streams, thick wood, mountain peaks, starry midnight sky and the imaginative and creative pieces of work produced by artists, poets, authors and musicians, etc. However, in the Buddhist concept of the beautiful there is an attitudinal as well as an objective aspect in what is beautiful.

Buddhist concept of aesthetic is a beauty of things imperfect, impermanent, and incomplete. According to Buddhism, the cultivation of the right attitude to aesthetic is very important. A beautiful object itself is not goodness or rightness per se. Similarly, perception as it is neither good nor evil but the judgement based upon it turned to be good or evil. Buddhism advocates aesthetic experience congenial to a higher mode of living; it should be instrumental for moral development. Subjective evaluation of beautiful things and nature which are viewed with desire and attachment as perceived by the five senses and the unthoughtful reflection usually result in lust. Thus it is the distortion of perception which has to be got rid of by perceiving objects as impermanent, unsatisfactory, repulsive and non-substantial. The primary aesthetic concept at the heart of Buddhist culture is the aspiration of leading a holy life. In Buddhism, beauty is not for beauty's sake. It has been viewed as an incentive for those who aspire to the holy life.

Ethics in Buddhism are traditionally based on what Buddhists view as the enlightened perspective of the Buddha, or other enlightened beings that followed him. Moral instructions are included in Buddhist scriptures or handed down through tradition. Most scholars of Buddhist ethics thus rely on the examination of Buddhist scriptures, and the use of anthropological evidence from traditional Buddhist societies, to justify claims about the nature of Buddhist ethics.

According to traditional Buddhism, the foundation of Buddhist ethics for lay people is the Pancasila: no killing, stealing, lying, sexual misconduct, or intoxicants. In becoming a Buddhist, or affirming one's commitment to Buddhism, a layperson is encouraged to vow to abstain from these negative actions. The precepts are not formulated as imperatives, but as training rules that laypeople undertake voluntarily to facilitate practice. In Buddhist thought, the cultivation of dana and ethical conduct will themselves refine consciousness to such a level that rebirth in one of the lower heavens is likely, even if there is no further Buddhist practice. There is nothing improper or un-Buddhist about limiting one's aims to this level of attainment. Buddhist monks and nuns take hundreds more such vows.

I am very grateful to Mr. Pranav Gupta, Director of MD Publications Pvt Ltd, New Delhi, for his kind cooperation and support for this book.

H Prasad

CONTENTS

1

Buddhism and the Virtues

Buddhism's success in the West is most likely if Buddhist ethics is specifically grafted to and enriched by the "ethics of virtue" approaches of Western tradition, approaches recently revived in Christian thinkers like MacIntyre and Hauerwas. This second guess is more specific, tentative, and provocative, and, therefore, more interesting, so it will be my dominant theme. Viewing Buddhist morality and ethics in the light of virtues theory is true to the central core of Buddhism. The virtues approach also generates a wide range of analytical comparisons with Western philosophical and theological tradition, and helps us foresee and plan for the limits of Buddhism's Western pilgrimage.

Returning for a moment to my first and most general hypothesis, that Buddhism is on the threshold of a more significant future in the West. It will increasingly play practical, heuristic, balancing, and liberating roles in the lives of Western people and their societies.

But, in order for this to happen, philosophers, Buddhist and non-Buddhist, must help more to clarify the moral and ethical terms of Buddhism's soteriological project, in ways coordinate with Western intellectual tradition. For more than two decades, Buddhist philosophical talent in the West has been focused almost exclusively on ontology and hermeneutics. One result is that Buddhist philosophy in the West has ballooned off into the clouds of "s*u*nyata-focused dialectics.

Our philosophical soaring needs the ballast of Buddhist moral practices and the landmarks of a refreshed Buddhist ethics to bring Buddhist philosophy more into a practical relationship with the on-the-ground, everyday realities of people's lives. I am moved to this recommendation by my deductive understanding of Buddhist teaching, but also by the fact that American Buddhists, since the early 1980's, have increasingly puzzled over moral and/or political choices and issues, without much help from Buddhist philosophers and scholars who are also well-grounded in Western moral and political thought. When Christians translated their Gospel into Chinese contexts, the Greek "Logos" became the Chinese "Tao," a daring and radical translation, transmuting the Gospel as it transmitted it.

A similar translation problematique faces us now as Buddhism transmits the "Dharma" to the West. But, in the matter of that part of the Dharma which can be called "Buddhist ethics," no proposal in Western philosophical terms on the shape of Buddhist ethics currently commands wide attention, much less agreement. As a result, the legitimization of the Buddhist Dharma as a whole is at risk in the West, for no religious or soteriological philosophy without a developed ethic can be fully and widely legitimized in Western culture. A variety of philosophical proposals relevant to the Western shaping of Buddhist ethics can be seen across the spectrum of Buddhist thinkers. Happily, no one argues that Buddhist ethics or moralities are *sui generis*, a unique and inviolate form of Buddhist tradition to be transplanted whole and entire into Western cultural soil.

Also, few are suggesting that Buddhist morality and ethics are so much embedded in Asian cultures that they cannot be transplanted. Both in theory and in practice, most Western Buddhists appear to look for and accept a grafting or hybridizing process, assimilating Buddhist moral stock to a plausible, compatible Western moral root. Some are tempted to confuse this process, by reversing it, as if the task is to graft Western moral concerns to a Buddhist root of compassion or, worse, transcendental wisdom. This confusion is like "growing a lotus without planting it in the mud," or "putting the spiritual cart before the moral horse." More simply, this confusion assumes that ethics follows spirit or theory, a rather un-Buddhist notion, given the Buddha's existential impatience with metaphysical gymnastics. In the 1960's, Buddhist ethical reflection, and morality in the broad sense of "a way of life," was grafted by Western apologists to the stem of existentialism and to some branches of the human potential movement.

These early efforts fell short of a satisfactory ethical development of Western Buddhism, in my opinion, because they failed to include much critical, communal, or practical guidance for would-be Buddhist existentialists (or existentialist Buddhists?) and other Aquarians. Recently, more politically relevant splicings have been attempted by several Buddhists within the peace, environmental, and feminist movements. Only a few Western philosophers have attempted grafting work recently in Buddhist ethics, usually by asserting and working out conceptual analogies between Buddhist ethics in general and particular Western philosophers and theologians.

Examples of this comparative work include David Kalupahana's proposal that Buddhist ethics melds interestingly with William James' pragmatism, and Christopher Ives' explorations of opportunities to develop a Zen Buddhist social ethic in contrast with Reinhold Niebuhr's Christian social ethics. Also noteworthy, if less comparative in its analysis, is Robert Thurman's proposal to find a relevant recipe for contemporary social activism in a specific text of Nagarjuna. While I do not find these proposals sufficiently developed to be compelling to Western ethicists, they are thought-experiments that address some issues of interest to Western philosophical and theological ethics, while taking interpretive risks for the sake of Buddhist relevance.

None of the proposals can withstand the kind of friendly critique that comes quickly and easily from ethicists grounded in Christian and Western ethical studies; Winston King, for example, has long been helpful in raising a variety of critical and disturbing questions about the strengths and weaknesses of Buddhist philosophy in a Western ethical milieu dominated by demands for human rights and individual autonomy.

Assuming the under-developed condition of the domain of Buddhist ethics in Western context, I now address at length my second, more tentative conjecture on the future prospect of Western Buddhism. I propose that the most appropriate analogy, the most fruitful grafting prospect for a Western Buddhist ethics, will be with the Western tradition of the "ethics of virtue." By "ethics of virtue" I mean simply an ethics that is character-based (rather than principle-driven or act-focused), praxis-oriented, teleological, and community-specific. More fully, I mean the complex tradition of ethics that stretches in the West from Socrates and Aristotle to Alasdair MacIntyre, Philippa Foot, and other contemporary virtues theorists increasing notice."

This proposal does not originate with me. The conceptual and heuristic linkage of Buddhist ethics with Aristotle's is a key to Damien Keown's approach in his well-argued, revisionist view of Buddhist ethics, The Nature of Buddhist Ethics. Earlier, Robert Bellah favored grafting Buddhism to the virtues approach as a possible path to meet his concern to renew an American ethic of community. Specifically, Bellah has called for a "cultural symbiosis" of Zen and modern Aristotelianism as a way of re-asserting "a teleological understanding of the order of human life" and bringing about "the creation of actual communities" that can resist:

> A modern Western culture that is destroying the natural habitat, undermining any kind of social solidarity, and creating a conception of the individual person which is utterly self-destructive.

The utopian spirit of his call for Buddhist-like communities of personal and civic virtue suggests that these communities would almost certainly be "marginalized," growing only at the edges of the dominant socio-cultural structures of Western individualism or bureaucratic nation-states. Its utopian character does not seem to dissuade Bellah from making his recommendation. Nor am I. Indeed, such "contrast" communities already exist, however tenuous their rooting in the Western "soul and soil." Before taking up this proposal, that Buddhist "morality" and "ethics" can be appropriately transplanted in the West by assimilating them to our own virtues tradition, I need to define Buddhist morality more precisely, in the terms of "awakened virtue."

"Awakened, compassionate virtue-cultivation" is a more accurate phrasing of what I mean, but, for simplicity's sake, I will avoid using it. "Awakened virtue" usefully describes the process and goal of Buddhist morality. It affirms the intertwined correspondence of the moral and the spiritual, in fresh language, by referring to Buddhist moral vision and praxis in the language of virtues theory, and by retaining the Buddhist insistence on spiritual awakening as a necessary, although not sufficient, condition of moral maturity. Second, I will simply define Buddhist ethics as "philosophical reflection upon Buddhist morality, including descriptive, normative and meta-ethical reflections." My purpose in this chapter about "awakened virtue" is not to engage in historical and textual analysis. I will not exegete the comparative analogies of "*sîla* or the *paramitas* to *phronesis, arete,* or *virtus*.

My aim is more philosophical, practical, and even policy-oriented: to probe constructively the implications of "awakened virtue," the goal of Buddhist morality and the object of Buddhist ethics, in connection with the future prospects of Western Buddhism. The effort to construct a Western Buddhist ethics by means of a virtues approach is not without exemplars. For example, Robert Aitken relies on it often in his homiletical text, The Mind of Clover: Essays in Zen Buddhist Ethics. Aitken fashions refreshing sermons on Buddhist ethics, with a Zen twist, framing most of his chapters as expositions of "The Ten Grave Precepts" of Buddhist morality. He also writes briefly about the Six Perfections, the six *paramitas* of generosity, morality, patience, vigor, meditation, and self-realization, and discusses "virtue" as a way of understanding the Zen life.

Aitken opens his chapter, "The Way and Its Virtue," with a saying of his teacher, Yamada Koun Roshi: "The purpose of Zen practice is the perfection of character." Aitken proceeds to discuss briefly but provocatively the six *paramitas*, relating them to contemporary experience and applications. But his teacher's saying is overlooked and the focus on virtue collapses as, in the perennial fashion of most Zen interpreters, he concludes that:

> At the same time, "virtue," "the Six *Paramitas*," "perfection of character"-these are simply labels for an organic process. Breathing in and out, you let go of poisons and establish the serene ground of the precepts.

Aitken here falls into a common pitfall in the path of ancient and contemporary Zen interpreters, what I call "the transcendence trap." The trap misleads them and us into portraying the perfected moral life as a non-rational expressiveness, something natural, spontaneous, non-linguistic, and uncalculating. This is a "Taoist-like" view of virtue as "natural, intuitive, skill/power" (Chin., te; Jap. toku), a view Aitken shares with some influential, but late Mahayana *sutras*. This ethical conception results in the kind of ontological dismissal of morality and ethics preached by Aitken at the end of his chapter: "Thus, in the world, too, there is nothing to be called virtue."

The common corollary, "there is also nothing to be called character," is unstated by Aitken, although it is part of the same syllogistic net of claims deduced ostensibly from "no-ego" and "sunyata axioms. The net is true and helpful only within the "deconstructive" mood and context of *sunyata* dialectics and metaphysics. When the net of "no-self" is thrown to catch truth in an ethical context, villains laugh and demons thrive. A good beginning by Aitken, in taking a virtues approach to interpreting Buddhist ethics, is later swamped by the "sunyata-weighted dialectical anamorphisms of Mahayana and Zen thought. Aitken is enmeshed in what I have called "the satori perspective" in Zen philosophy, the position most clearly seen in D.T. Suzuki's vigorous anti-rationalism and antinomianism.

The "satori perspective" characteristically over-emphasizes the "awakening" dimensions of Buddhist soteriology, to the detriment of the moral, "virtuous" dimensions. Consequently, a view of the Buddhist virtues from this standpoint tends insistently to relativize and diminish the "virtue" in the summum bonum of "awakened virtue," until there is only the "awakened One," beyond good and evil. A clear and egregious example of this spiritualizing over-emphasis on "awakening," comes to us in the writings of Gerta Ital, in her book, *On the Way to Satori*, where she offers us this advice:

This is something that cannot be repeated often enough: no one who has not completely erased themselves as an ego can do anything to help liberate anyone else, and the attainment of the goal is not easy. The journey is very long.... Until one is liberated oneself one is simply not capable of helping anyone else.

This is not a complete Buddhism, I believe, and certainly not one that can expect a significant future in the West, except as an individualistic, private, and mainly "therapeutic" mysticism. Buddhism is far more and other than that. A fuller and more finely articulated virtues approach to Buddhist ethics guides Ken Jones' The Social Face of Buddhism. I consider this the best available ethical manual on Buddhist social ethics by a Westerner. I recommend it, convinced that it is a touchstone philosophical text in Buddhist ethics. It is unlike Aitken's, because Jones' seriously pays attention to key philosophical, moral, and psychological issues. Regrettably, Jones, like Aitken, walks into "the transcendence trap," by devaluing the roles of will and deliberation in the life of awakened virtue.

Jones affirms in good virtues theory fashion that Buddhist morality is a matter of character and cultivation, and that it focuses on cultivating character rather than evaluating particular acts. But quickly he slides toward "the transcendence trap," beginning with a too casual substitution of the word "personality" for "character":

The emphasis in Buddhist morality is therefore on the cultivation of a personality which cannot but be moral, rather than focusing upon the morality of particular choices and acts. But, to repeat, it is not the will that can create such a personality, no more than I can pick myself up from the ground by my collar. It is to the training that the will must be applied, from which virtue will naturally flow [emphasis mine].

Jones's disclaimer on the power of will may only be a rejection of Nietzchean or Sartrean voluntarism. If so, he would be correct from a Buddhist point of view, which dialectically affirms both the deterministic weight of karma or character dispositions and our freedom from them in the concomitant "emptiness" of "*su*nyata. And he is certainly correct to assert that the will in Buddhist practice, rather than serving a "creative" role in free self-creation, serves mainly to restrain and hold oneself in the various forms of moral and intellectual practice.

However, the fuzziness of the phrase, "from which virtue will naturally flow," places Jones on the lip of the "transcendence trap." He later falls in by constructing virtue as a kind of natural "grace," emergent from the forms of moral discipline and repetition, yet different from them, somehow transcendent, natural and free. As Robert Scharf suggests, this transcendent view of virtuous activity is a mystification of what in Buddhist practice is simply a repetitive and normal process of learning to perform in certain ways with skill; Hee-jin Kim, discussing what he calls the "heart of Dogen's thought," refers to the process of Buddhist practice as essentially something prosaic, "the ritualization of morality."

More than Jones can or will admit, schooling in the forms of virtue is a social, emotional, and cognitive process. Becoming good is hardly a natural process in the sense suggested, of being the non-voluntary, non-deliberative unfolding of a natural goodness. Aristotle would agree: "While it is Nature that gives us our faculties, it is not Nature that makes us good or bad." The goal of ethics is to become a person who does good or virtuous things freely from the ground of a well-tempered character, supported by a matured, resolute, and reasonable knowledge of what one is doing. The path of

Buddhism does not dissolve character (which is different from ego and personality).

It awakens and illuminates moral character and establishes a "noble" selfhood in the wide, deep, expressive freedom of creative forms of life and its perfections. Jones's view of virtue echoes the Christian moral doctrine of "infused virtue," but without dependence on St. Thomas Aquinas' transcendent, theistic assumptions and absent his clear sense of the endurance of the "natural" virtues in the perfected saints. I venture the guess that, like Alan Watts and others who fall into "the transcendence trap," Jones devalues the will in preferring "natural expressiveness" (in the sense of what we are born with, *natus*), in his beliefs about learning to be good, because of things that have little to do with Buddhism, the Diamond S*u*tra, and Mahayana dialectics. I suspect that many a Westerner's "Taoist-like" misreading of Buddhist ethics, as a form of individualistic naturalism, is mostly and often a reaction to the West's residual Victorian morality-a morality characterized by and hated for its conceived overemphasis on individual, rational self-discipline, strength of will, rigidity of personality, and psychophysical repressions-and from which middle-aged and older Western Buddhists seem to be still trying to make their escape.

In their desire to escape, they share in a broader, late 20th century Western shift to a moral outlook that prizes a rather passive, non-judgmental tolerance of others, combined with a preference for the spontaneous or ecstatic expression of impulses... at least and especially in contrast with the much maligned Victorians. To disdain the necessary roles of will and reason in the Buddhist moral process is to overlook the importance of both in early Buddhism. Early Buddhism did not abandon reason, although it did not rely on reason alone. Neither did early Buddhists overlook the necessity of a steady will, even in the stages of Buddhist meditation training.

That will and reason were requisite accompaniments of the good person is also evident in later additions to the six *paramitas* list, namely, the *paramitas* of resolution, determination, strength, and skillful means. Obviously, strength of will is necessary even in samadhi exercises, in making the *Bodhisattva* vow, or in responding to exhortations of the Zen masters to throw one's whole self and attention into zazen or koan. Buddhist cultivation requires a constant dose of what William James called "animal spirits" and doing the difficult thing against our inclinations. Now, having bypassed the "transcendence trap" on the way to a Buddhist virtues perspective, I wish briefly to describe what I mean by Buddhist "awakened virtue" in the context of general virtues theory, distinguishing it somewhat from traditional Western views. Following this description, I will conclude by exploring some implications for the West of viewing Buddhist ethics and the Buddhist "way of life" in a virtues perspective.

BUDDHIST MORALITY AS AWAKENED VIRTUE

The Buddha's Dharma or teaching was authoritatively divided in early times into three groups, but they were interdependent facets of one process leading to deliverance *(vimutti)*. The Buddhist investigated and cultivated *sîla* (morality), *samadhi* (deep meditation), and *prajña* (transcendental wisdom). Each of the three facets of self-cultivation evolved appropriate practices... of moral intention, behavior, and correction; of meditation method and mapping; of transformative shifts of consciousness. We may speak of these practices as the moral, contemplative, and transformative *paramitas*. The last, the transformative *paramitas*, are concerned with practices that alter consciousness on a transcendental, "Nirvanic" level, while the contemplative *paramitas* have to do with the development of powers of concentration, stability, and tranquilization in meditation. The moral *paramitas* involve practices in which good intentions are aroused and acted upon in the light of a right understanding of the good and of situations.

With repetition and correction these practices severally and together nurtured the dispositions, both karmic and salvific, that together constitute Buddhist character. Why these *paramitas* as the specific Buddhist virtues, rather than others, invites a fuller treatment. The *paramitas* as methods of attending, energizing, pacifying and relates the self to others, work together to wean the self from egocentricity. Beyond ego-weaning, the goal of the *paramitas* is positive: to foster a character that increasingly encounters each moment, each space, each being, as a "mother" enjoys and protects her only child... to use a traditional simile attributed to the Buddha. Since moral intentions are always elastic, they need shaping by forms and disciplines, taught by teachers and learned in communities.

The virtuous practices that in Buddhism characterize a good person were often defined as at least the six *paramitas* of generosity or gift-giving (*dana*), morality or the Five Precepts (*sîla*), patience and forgiveness (*ksanti*), courage and vigor (*vîrya*), concentration (*dhyana*), and wisdom (*prajña*). Some held that the six *paramitas* constituted a progressive order of training in virtue, from generosity to wisdom. These may be said to be the necessary moral, mental, and spiritual touchstones of the Buddhist virtues tradition, notwithstanding later additions to and analytical divisions of the six. Enrichment of virtue-like practices beyond the *paramitas* is seen in the development of the well-known Four Immeasurables (the *Brahmaviharas* or "divine abodes") of Buddhist friendliness, compassion, joy, and peace, which further mapped out, stimulated, and idealized Buddhist moral praxis.

These practices, moral and otherwise, were more often than not "methodologized," that is, formalized, ritualized and institutionalized in ways to promote habitual performances in a general program of self-cultivation and character development, conceived to stretch over many aeons of time (thus requiring the *paramita* of patience!). Methods would differ somewhat between monk and layperson, and from culture to culture. Some practices were Buddhist adaptations of pre-existing practices and rituals in the surrounding non-Buddhist culture, as Nath shows in her study of the Buddhist transformations of Hindu *dana*, gift-giving rites.

Buddhist moral self-cultivation tends to encompass not only the formation of good intentions in the heart and mind (reminding us of Kant). Practices also include physical postures and breath-speech techniques. This holistic "psycho-pneumo-physical" approach to moral self-cultivation results, for example, in attention to helping others not only by forming a good will, but also by expressing kind words and offering the material things that they also need. A more holistic self-training also opens a way to fuse moral practice with aesthetic practice, as an early concern in Buddhism with how gracefully to give gifts demonstrates. Practice of the moral *paramitas* is said to create and accumulate "merit," or favorable karma dispositions within the psyche, that lead to a better life and higher rebirth.

The "ethics of karma," focused upon by Melford Spiro and Winston King as the key to understanding Theravadin Buddhist societies, is when looked at closely but an "ethics of karma-cultivating virtues and practices." Spiro and King, reflecting an interpretation within the Theravadin tradition, highlight the ostensibly traditional split between the karmic and the Nibbanic motives in Buddhist life, one for goodness and reward, the other for salvation and transformative liberation. The two motives are personalized in layperson and monk, respectively. The tension between moral and religious motives appears also in Mahayana Buddhism.

At one point the tension was reconciled in the *bodhisattva* image of a virtuous layman-sage, Vimalakîrti. The *Vimalakîrti Sutra* affirms that a breach between moral effort and spiritual awakening constitutes bondage and delusion. The center of Buddhist tradition affirms that moral effort, mainly through practicing the *paramitas*, must be conjoined with meditative and transformative practices to be ultimately effective for one and for others. It also affirms that the practices of awakening have little foundation and less result, for oneself or others, without the frame, skills, and habit of moral practice. Moral virtue without *sunyata*, or transforming liberation, may be shallow and weak; but *sunyata* without moral virtue is blind and dangerous.

She who has accomplished awakened virtue, the merging of skilled, well-disposed, rational moral agency with self-transforming spirit, is, in contrast, deep, strong, ever-maturing, and rational,... by her character and deeds she reduces suffering and promotes friendliness, compassion, joy, and peace. In contrast with Western virtues tradition, the Buddhist *paramitas* viewpoint tends, in matters of self and community, to be biocentric and ecological. First, Buddhism does not begin with the premise of the substantial, separable, and distinctive self of Aristotelian and Christian thought. In Buddhism, the idea of the atomistic, self-empowering monad-godling of Western individualism is well known, but understood as a delusion born of ignorant desires and fears, resulting in a wish-fantasy for domination. Compared to Western concepts, the self-concept of Buddhism is processional, relational, and "fuzzy."

While the moral saint as individualized hero, above and apart from others, is not unknown in Buddhism, the open, relational nature of selfhood stresses the solidarity of those who act virtuously with those for whom they act or, better, with whom they practice the perfecting goods of generosity, patience, and so forth. For Buddhist thought, the self is fundamentally incomplete, evolving, and interpenetratively co-dependent with others. Since we are imbedded in mutual dependent community, training in the *paramitas*, moral and otherwise, is necessarily training with others and for others. Because of this solidarity and because *paramitas* practice nurtures body, speech, and the mind-heart, the Buddhist believes her moral efforts flow necessarily into the community on many levels, materially, verbally, and mentally, in a subtle, looping reciprocity.

Second, Buddhist tradition differs from the Western in defining membership in the moral community, the "considered others" to whom *paramitas*-defined practices are to be extended. In the dominant traditions of Western culture, at least since Aristotle, the community of character and virtue has clearly been the human community. The politics in which an individual's ethics and virtue find their completion is a human politics - almost always an anthropocentric, urban politics. The Buddhist community of virtue is biocentric, far more inclusive of animals and other sentient beings as objects of moral consideration (in the practice of the six *paramitas*, for example, giving aid to animals) than Western virtues tradition.

Because of this biocentric orientation, Buddhist moral practices must include specific training and self-cultivation in our relations with nature, as well as human society, extending *dana, "sîla, ksanti,* and so on to non-human sentient beings and to the biosphere itself as a community of communities. Given the exurban settings of Buddhist monasteries and universities, and other factors, Buddhist ethics did not elaborate itself often into urban, class-oriented political theory, a theory of revolutionary change, or a theory legitimizing divine rule... although Buddhist thinkers did propose all three. The community scale imaged by the samgha was smaller and more nurturing of personal development perhaps that of a village set within nature.

Perhaps this goes to explain partially why even urban Buddhists have tended to re-create or simulate in the grounds of their city temples a contrasting, natural refuge, for people, animals, fish, birds, and even insects. A Japanese tea ceremony garden and hut in the middle of Tokyo express this microtopic, exurban focus most eloquently and ironically. Like the Aristotelian virtues tradition, Buddhist ethics tends to be ahistorical, in that it regards human life as having an important and profound constancy in its nature and goal, persistent amidst the general flow and struggles of actual personal and historical forces. That constancy for the Buddhist lies not in a substantial or eternal self, but in our common, almost irrefragable experience of suffering and in our inherent capacity to work toward an awakened, moral virtuosity, in wisdom and fellow-feeling.

With respect to the question of historicity, one think that, in comparison with the Christian virtues tradition, Buddhist ethics did not develop so extensive a quasi-historical hagiography, a "sense of narrative," concerning the lives of the virtuous and their exemplars, the saints. The Jataka Tales, while we classify them as "animal" fables, may be similar in appearance to a "Lives of the Saints." But we should probably resist calling them "narrative" because they display a narrow range of the Buddhist reality picture, and we should hesitate to call them unqualifiedly Buddhist, because the stories are from a pre-Buddhist tradition. This comparative absence of emphasis on individual "drama," which may be more of degree than type, applies even to the most obvious Buddhist saint, the Buddha, whose "story" does not serve for Buddhists the whole range of functions that we find centered in the Gospels, in Roman Catholic hagiography or in Muslim *hadith* tradition.

On another theme of contemporary virtues theory, begin by acknowledging without apology that Buddhism makes moral claims that are universalistic. Buddhists have imagined utopian times and settings for the virtuous, the perfected, the awakened... and projected a utopic future when "all beings are awakened." But, like all ethical traditions centered on virtues, Christian, Muslim, Confucian, or Aristotelian, the Buddhist *paramita* tradition looks to the establishment of particular and appropriately designed communities to optimize favorable conditions for self-cultivation and happiness in the good life. Virtue ethics traditions, often focused in small groups engaged in voluntary training, tend to spend little time on the ethical strategies necessary in non-voluntary, pluralistic, very large, or coercive societies.

Consequently and not surprisingly, they tend to lack a viable social ethic in modern terms that is a policy-generating set of principles that can be institutionalized on a mass scale, while protecting individual rights-claims with coercive means. So, while espousing the general tenets and principles of a universal ethics, Buddhist ethics tends, in practice, to define and effectuate *paramita*-cultivation in community-specific terms. At the mind-and-heart level, the broad intention "to help others" may be similar across many communities, but at the levels of linguistic and physical practice, the *paramitas* have a local aspect, and in that sense display a modest "historical" quality.

For example, while the virtue of giving, *dana-paramita*, may show local nuances of expression in almsgiving rites, these local forms are practiced with recognition of their universal applicability in their intention, but not in their formal, material, local features. A tolerant awareness of distinctions between inner and outer aspects of Buddhist practices may result in much less zealous enforcement of verbal, symbolic, and physical conformity in moral (and contemplative) practices in Buddhist contexts. The resulting diversity, flexibility, and tolerance sustain the Buddhist tradition, at the risk of appearing very soft and highly "contextual" in social ethics and politics. Nevertheless, one does find conformity in the moral forms and practices within Buddhist voluntary communities, of which the *Sangha* is the classical exemplar.

Conformity is in keeping not only with the needs of any community for the standardization and predictability of behaviors that enhance trust and efficiency. Shared forms are especially necessary and appropriate to a community guided by virtue ethics. The Buddhist's cultivation of the *paramitas* requires a community designed to respond to awakened virtue practices with specific structures of support and correction. Each Buddhist community has a distinctive shape and style, governed primarily by a common goal, the awakened virtue of each member-in-community. This perfectionist aim is universalized and idealized by extending it to encompass the awakening of "all sentient beings." But, on-the-ground, the community's purpose is realized in the details... of distinctive forms of etiquette, and in the characters of exemplary individuals; in shared schedules, and a common submission to rules; in rituals of giving and receiving, and procedures for correcting and expelling delinquent members.

These are communities where one learns and practices what it quite precisely means, mentally and physically, morally and psychologically, to act as an "awakened virtue being." That is, one learns to act, to perform, to talk, walk, sit, sort things out, and take out the garbage like a Buddha. It should be obvious by now that learning to act like a Buddha means something other than becoming spontaneous, inventive, and free of Victorian inhibitions.

The practice of awakened virtue in Buddhist communities requires diligent learning of the forms in and through which one can perform like an awakened virtue being. In the moral sphere, these practices require repeated experiences in learning how to give, to listen patiently, and to call up courage in overcoming fear and desire, to observe non-violence in the way one walks, to steady the mind and heart, to make friends with the seasons, and so on. In the meditative sphere, similar forms of practice are observed, submitted to, tasted, repeated, tested, and perfected, in cultivation of the contemplative virtues.

Finally, the Buddhist community, like any virtue-oriented community, is defined in the characters of its persons, as well as in their stories and the forms of their practices. Its continuation and success depend necessarily upon the degree to which community members become successful practitioners of the community's full repertoire of virtues. Thus, Buddhism will flower in the West only when Western Buddhists take up a fully balanced Buddhist way of life, by cultivating both the moral and the contemplative *paramitas* in proper balance. "Awakened virtue" is the balanced platform upon which to practice the ultimate, transformative, Nirvanic virtues constituting the flowering of the spiritual life of Buddhists.

IMPLICATIONS FOR BUDDHIST ETHICS IN THE WEST

If we accept the propositions that Buddhist ethics is ineluctably and essentially an "ethics of virtue" and, second, that the Buddhist life is necessarily at every stage integrative of moral and spiritual practices, several implications emerge for Buddhism as it grows in the West. Some of these implications are corrective of recent Western Buddhist troubles, while others may indicate real limits to Buddhism's success in and impact on the West. Soon, with the passing away of the pioneering, older generations of Western Buddhists, I hope we will see Buddhism in the West turning from its role as a raft carrying Westerners away from the eroding shores of Victorian-or Judaeo-Christian-or technological-or imperialist-or patriarchal culture. While the function of Buddhism as a means of liberation from suffering and oppression is a central one, it is not the only one.

The other function of Buddhism is to carry the suffering to the other shore, to awakened virtue, to becoming a Buddha in Buddha fields where Buddhas flourish. This means working to construct and preserve relationships and communities, as much as cultivating oneself. And this means the renewal of a *paramitas*-approach in Buddhist thought and life. One corrective consequence of renewing the *paramitas* in Buddhist lives and communities will be the denial of authority to imbalanced Buddhist teachers by the communities that support them. Too many Buddhist teachers in the West in the 1980's have demonstrated that they cannot balance well the moral and the spiritual. However, a virtues-oriented ethic has limitations in meeting problems caused by the vices of individuals in the practicing community.

This is because a virtue ethic focuses on the person-as-agent developing over time, in a learning process often of trial and error. This long-term focus devalues the moral significance of particular acts; even transvaluing them into "teachable moments," while often overlooking the consequences of flawed or vicious acts for others and the community. A particular moral failure is excused as "out-of-character." The result is a greater tolerance of isolated acts of harming others, for example, unless the acts constitute an intolerable "pattern" of vice that forces community or individual reaction... perhaps too late. Every virtue ethics guides us to the good life by means of models of "the good person." The model may be a living person or a narrative character (i.e., the Buddha, Vimalakîrti, Vessantara, Queen "Srîmala, etc.).

A focus on character tends to obscure or override the role of general principles and rules as guides to decision-making and mutual regulation. But rules, however flawed, sometimes have a place. For example, a rule-orientation is preferable in some circumstances and relationships to counter teacher-disciple abuses and distortions. Traditionally, Buddhism depends heavily on its teachers and on the belief that profound qualities of an awakened teacher can be passed directly, through "mind-to-mind" transmission, to her students. Of course, teachers are capable of transmitting the forms of the *paramitas*, moral and contemplative, through imitation, familiarization, direct instruction, and, I will grant, a kind of psychic "osmosis."

But, far more difficult to transmit to one's students and friends are the all-important balance and integration of the *paramitas* in a given person, because they are partly contingent on the individuality of the novice's personality. It is wrong to believe that this balance can be given to the student, rather than earned by self-effort in the corrective view of a vital community. Buddhist tradition poses to each Buddhist a momentous question: "Who is Buddha?" How do we know that someone is advanced in the practices of "awakened virtue"? That she's a "good person"? The answer is critical, for it is these people one turns to for instruction, advice, example, confidence, and even faith.

A *paramitas*-oriented approach carries us some distance to the answer, because of its dual focus on character and communally validated moral practices. Consequently, the living meaning of awakened virtue is less dependent on the character of single persons upon whom a community focuses, and more dependent on several persons and the community (the samgha-community) in its evolving solidarity. Viewing the practicing community as Buddha, as itself a virtue-oriented awakening being, reduces personality cults and deepens community resources. The *paramitas* emphasis I am advocating will tend to develop protective standards of a more public nature, to test those who seek to join or lead communities. But a Buddhist virtues approach requires shoring up with useful ethical strategies developed in the West both to assess particular acts and to generate moral rules.

The Western Buddhist milieu may also require a heuristic recovery of the Vinaya tradition of Buddhist monastic regulation. The Vinaya may have strayed into the trap of legalistic casuistry, but it did define and set procedures for adjudicating particular acts of monks that could not be tolerated, that had to result in suspension or expulsion. Western Buddhist communities are only now beginning to face up to this kind of decision-making, for which a virtues-orientation is sometimes inadequate.

Having said all this, act-evaluations and rule-adjudications must be secondary instruments in Buddhist ethics; necessary as they may be in particular moments of particular communities. Essentially, Buddhist ethics is centered in and on "character in community." This focus needs to be kept, for upon it depends the future development of a Buddhist ethics more aimed at relationships than principles, more interested in mutual support than a defense of rights, more empathic than rational, more compassionate than just. Ethical strategies focusing on rational rules and judgments of particular outward acts are the essential feature of groups so large that they constitute a society of strangers, threatened by the Hobbesian shadows of competition and governed by laws of contract, restraint, coercion, property, and command.

Laws are secondary to virtue in a Buddhist setting (and in this I agree with Western Buddhists who resist "code" or rule-oriented moralizing as a dominant approach to self- or community-discipline). Nevertheless, while secondary, they are not dispensable. The primary focus on persons, character, and virtuous practices in Buddhist ethics cannot be sustained without community, places where we know each other well enough to call each other into the intimacies of an ethics of intention and practice, as in a family. This means that Buddhist communities must ever be small, small enough that people intimately know each other and the other sentient beings sharing their life and death. I propose that they can be too small, in that a group of four or six can hardly challenge and support the full range of self-cultivation practices necessary to awakened virtue.

The problem of size for many Buddhists in the West lies at the "too small" end of the spectrum. But that's better than to be at the "too large" end. One cannot identify a practicing community that has become too large (say, more than 200 active members), unless one looks at the large metropolitan communities in San Francisco and Los Angeles, which are arguably too large, too complex, and too absorbed in the entropic tasks of organization maintenance of buildings, mortgages, and so on. We know from reading Aristotle and MacIntyre that an ethics focused in virtue does not picture the way to the good life in abstract or individual or universal terms.

The paths of virtue are marked by lived practices special to each community. Virtue-oriented groups and communities, if we are to believe MacIntyre and Hauerwas, depend more on their traditional "narrative" reality- frames, their memories and stories of good persons practicing the good life, than on their laws or universal principles. But, we also know that Western Buddhists today live in a post-Nietzschean world, where the "stories" are many and "memory" is tattered. It is not at all clear to many Western people that their chosen or inherited stories invoke human reality in a coherent and compelling way. In the postmodern West, the Buddha's story or the life of awakened virtue can be told and tested only in small, marginalized zones appropriately distanced from the dominant power and value structures.

The criteria of testing are two: 1) the plausibility of the story of a person who, through specific practices in a certain kind of community, "awakened, by and through virtuous practices, in wisdom and compassion;" and 2) the evident goodness in the people and communities now engaged in practices of the Dharma. These people are the Buddha. Their story is the Buddha's story. Acceptance of the virtues approach in ethics presents specific challenges and advantages to Buddhist thinkers and other scholars.

For example, we need to develop a more historical scholarship of the *paramitas* dimension in Buddhism. But, hopefully, we can also help people in today's Buddhist communities to think through the tensions among the *paramitas*, the problems of priorities, the meanings of practicing in lay life, and a host of other on-the-ground issues. We need to help Western Buddhists distinguish among therapeutic, aesthetic, moral, economic, political, and spiritual practices and choices. What is the optimum balance of attention and consideration between self and others? What is Buddhist friendship? Does it include mosquitoes? How and why do Buddhists fail morally after years of practice? How does a virtues orientation link up with social justice issues and the development of a Buddhist social ethics?

Far more moral and ethical questions buzz in Western Buddhists' lives, awaiting creative, practical inquiry by philosophers, new generation Buddhologists, and others. It needs a fuller development, in order to carry Buddhist morality into an inevitable, serious and mutually constructive dialogue with Western philosophers and theologians. The most constructive future of Buddhism in the West rests on its manifestation in the characters of people, not in eloquent prose, fundraising efforts, temple-building, or incomplete life modeling. Hopefully, a new generation will increasingly take the path of balancing samadhi-exercise with *paramitas*-practices.

Put simply, the future depends on a few good women and men who reveal a balanced, integrative life-of "awakened virtue" practices, in families, jobs, and communities. It is through good lives that the Buddha's Dharma can fully flower in the West, transforming our sufferings and awakening in us, each and all, that which is best, inch by inch, moment by moment, breath by breath. As a child, Siddhartha the Buddha was troubled by some of the same thoughts that children today have. They wonder about birth and death.

They wonder why they get sick and why grandfather died. They wonder why their wishes do not come true. Children also wonder about happiness and the beauty in nature. Because the Buddha knew what was in the hearts of children and human kind, he taught everyone how to live a happy and peaceful life. Buddhism is not learning about strange beliefs from faraway lands. It is about looking at and thinking about our own lives. It shows us how to understand ourselves and how to cope with our daily problems.

THE LIFE OF THE BUDDHA

LIFE IN THE PALACE

Buddhism is one of the major religions in the world. It began around 2,500 years ago in India when Siddhartha Gautama discovered how to bring happiness into the world. He was born around 566 BC, in the small kingdom of Kapilavastu. His father was King Suddhodana and his mother was Queen Maya. Soon after Prince Siddhartha was born, the wise men predicted that he would become a Buddha. When the king heard this, he was deeply disturbed, for he wanted his son to become a mighty ruler. He told Queen Maya, "I will make life in the palace so pleasant that our son will never want to leave."

At the age of sixteen, Prince Siddhartha married a beautiful princess, Yasodhara. The king built them three palaces, one for each season, and lavished them with luxuries. They passed their days in enjoyment and never thought about life outside the palace.

THE FOUR SIGHTS

Soon Siddhartha became disillusioned with the palace life and wanted to see the outside world. He made four trips outside the palace and saw four things that changed his life. On the first three trips, he saw sickness, old age and death. He asked himself, "How can I enjoy a life of pleasure when there is so much suffering in the world?" On his fourth trip, he saw a wandering monk who had given up everything he owned to seek an end to suffering. "I shall be like him." Siddhartha thought.

RENUNCIATION

Leaving his kingdom and loved ones behind, Siddhartha became a wandering monk. He cut off his hair to show that he had renounced the worldly lifestyle and called himself Gautama. He wore ragged robes and wandered from place to place. In his search for truth, he studied with the wisest teachers of his day. None of them knew how to end suffering, so he continued the search on his own. For six years he practiced severe asceticism thinking this would lead him to enlightenment. He sat in meditation and ate only roots, leaves and fruit. At times he ate nothing. He could endure more hardships than anyone else, but this did not take him anywhere. He thought, "Neither my life of luxury in the palace nor my life as an ascetic in the forest is the way to freedom. Overdoing things can not lead to happiness. "He began to eat nourishing food again and regained his strength.

ENLIGHTENMENT

On a full-moon day in May, he sat under the Bodhi tree in deep meditation and said. "I will not leave this spot until I find an end to suffering." During the night, he was visited by Mara, the evil one, who tried to tempt him away from his virtuous path. First he sent his beautiful daughters to lure Gautama into pleasure. Next he sent bolts of lightning, wind and heavy rain. Last he sent his demonic armies with weapons and flaming rocks. One by one, Gautama met the armies and defeated them with his virtue. As the struggle ended, he realized the cause of suffering and how to remove it. He had gained the most supreme wisdom and understood things as they truly are. He became the Buddha, 'The Awakened One'. From then on, he was called Shakyamuni Buddha.

THE BUDDHA TEACHES

After his enlightenment, he went to the Deer Park near the holy city of Benares and shared his new understanding with five holy men. They understood immediately and became his disciples. This marked the beginning of the Buddhist community. For the next forty-five years, the Buddha and his disciples went from place to place in India spreading the Dharma, his teachings. Their compassion knew no bounds; they helped everyone along the way, beggars, kings and slave girls. At night, they would sleep where they were; when hungry they would ask for a little food.

Whenever the Buddha went, he won the hearts of the people because he dealt with their true feelings. He advised them not to accept his words on blind faith, but to decide for themselves whether his teachings are right or wrong, then follow them. He encouraged everyone to have compassion for each other and develop their own virtue, "You should do your own work, for I can teach only the way." He never became angry or impatient or spoke harshly to anyone, not even to those who opposed him. He always taught in such a way that everyone could understand. Each person thought the Buddha was speaking especially for him. The Buddha told his followers to help each other on the Way. Following is a story of the Buddha living as an example to his disciples.

Once the Buddha and Ananda visited a monastery where a monk was suffering from a contagious disease where poor man lay in a mess with no one looking after him. The Buddha himself washed the sick monk and placed him on a new bed. Afterwards, he admonished the other monks. "Monks, you have neither mother nor father to look after you. If you do not look after each other, who will look after you? Whoever serves the sick and suffering, serves me?"

THE LAST YEARS

Shakyamuni Buddha passed away around 486 BC at the age of eighty. Although he has left the world, the spirit of his kindness and compassion remains. The Buddha realized that that he was not the first to become a Buddha. "There have been many Buddhas before me and will be many Buddhas in the future," The Buddha recalled to his disciples. "All living beings have the Buddha nature and can become Buddhas." For this reason, he taught the way to Buddhahood. The two main goals of Buddhism are getting to know ourselves and learning the Buddha's teachings.

To know who we are, we need to understand that we have two natures. One is called our ordinary nature, which is made up of unpleasant feelings such as fear, anger, and jealousy. The other is our true nature, the part of us that is pure, wise, and perfect. In Buddhism, it is called the Buddha nature. The only difference between us and the Buddha is that we have not awakened to our true nature.

BASIC TEACHINGS OF THE BUDDHA

One day, the Buddha sat down in the shade of a tree and noticed how beautiful the countryside was. Flowers were blooming and trees were putting on bright new leaves, but among all this beauty, he saw much unhappiness. A farmer beat his ox in the field. A bird pecked at an earthworm, and then an eagle swooped down on the bird. Deeply troubled, he asked, "Why does the farmer beat his ox? Why must one creature eat another to live?" During his enlightenment, the Buddha found the answer to these questions. He discovered three great truths. He explained these truths in a simple way so that everyone could understand them.

Nothing is Lost in the Universe

The first truth is that nothing is lost in the universe. Matter turns into energy, energy turns into matter. A dead leaf turns into soil. A seed sprouts and becomes a new plant. Old solar systems disintegrate and turn into cosmic rays. We are born of our parents; our children are born of us.

We are the same as plants, as trees, as other people, as the rain that falls. We consist of that which is around us; we are the same as everything. If we destroy something around us, we destroy ourselves. If we cheat another, we cheat ourselves. Understanding this truth, the Buddha and his disciples never killed any animal.

Everything Changes

The second universal truth of the Buddha is that everything is continuously changing. Life is like a river flowing on and on, ever-changing. Sometimes it flows slowly and sometimes swiftly. It is smooth and gentle in some places, but later on snags and rocks crop up out of nowhere. As soon as we think we are safe, something unexpected happens. Once dinosaurs, mammoths, and saber-toothed tigers roamed this earth and they all died out, yet this was not the end of life and other life forms like smaller mammals appeared and eventually humans, too. Now we can even see the Earth from space and understand the changes that have taken place on this planet. Our ideas about life also change. People once believed that the world was flat, but now we know that it is round.

Law of Cause and Effect

The third universal truth explained by the Buddha is that there is a continuous change due to the law of cause and effect. This is the same law of cause and effect found in every modern science textbook. In this way, science and Buddhism are alike. The law of cause and effect is known as karma. Nothing ever happens to us unless we deserve it. We receive exactly what we earn, whether it is good or bad. We are the way we are now due to the things we have done in the past. Our thoughts and actions determine the kind of life we can have. If we do good things, in the future good things will happen to us. If we do bad things, in the future bad things will happen to us. Every moment we create new karma by what we say, do, and think. If we understand this, we do not need to fear karma. It becomes our friend. It teaches us to create a bright future.

The Buddha said,

"The kind of seed sown

will produce that kind of fruit.

Those who do good will reap good results.

Those who do evil will reap evil results.

If you carefully plant a good seed,

You will joyfully gather good fruit."- *Dhammapada*

THE FOUR NOBLE TRUTHS

Once there was a woman named Kisagotami, whose first-born son died. She was so stricken with grief that she roamed the streets carrying the dead body and asking for help to bring her son back to life. A kind and wise man took her to the Buddha. The Buddha told her, "Fetch me a handful of mustard seeds and I will bring your child back to life." Joyfully Kisagotami started off to get them. Then the Buddha added, "But the seeds must come from a family that has not known death."

Kisagotami went from door to door in the whole village asking for the mustard seeds, but everyone said, "Oh, there have been many deaths here", "I lost my father", I lost my sister". She could not find a single household that had not been visited by death. Finally Kisagotami returned to the Buddha and said, "There is death in every family. Everyone dies. Now I understand your teaching." The Buddha said, "No one can escape death and unhappiness. If people expect only happiness in life, they will be disappointed." Things are not always the way we want them to be, but we can learn to understand them. When we get sick, we go to a doctor and ask:

- What's wrong with me?
- Why am I sick?
- What will cure me?
- What do I have to do get well?

The Buddha is like a good doctor. First a good doctor diagnoses the illness. Next he finds out what has caused it. Then he decides what the cure is. Finally he prescribes the medicine or gives the treatment that will make the patient well again.

The Four Noble Truths:

- There is Suffering- Suffering is common to all.
- Cause of Suffering -We are the cause of our suffering.
- End of Suffering- Stop doing what causes suffering.
- Path to end Suffering- Everyone can be enlightened.

1. *Suffering: Everyone suffers from this thing*

Birth- When we are born, we cry.

Sickness- When we are sick, we are miserable.

Old age- When old, we will have ache and pains and find it hard to get around.

Death- None of us wants to die. We feel deep sorrow when someone dies.

Other things we suffer from are:

- Being with those we dislike,

- Being apart from those we love,
- Not getting what we want,
- All kinds of problems and disappointments those are unavoidable.

The Buddha did not deny that there is happiness in life, but he pointed out it does not last forever. Eventually everyone meets with some kind of suffering. He said:

"There is happiness in life,

happiness in friendship,

happiness of a family,

happiness in a healthy body and mind,

but when one loses them, there is suffering." - *Dhammapada*

2. *The cause of suffering*

The Buddha explained that people live in a sea of suffering because of ignorance and greed. They are ignorant of the law of karma and are greedy for the wrong kind of pleasures. They do things that are harmful to their bodies and peace of mind, so they can not be satisfied or enjoy life. For example, once children have had a taste of candy, they want more. When they can't have it, they get upset. Even if children get all the candy they want, they soon get tired of it and want something else. Although, they get a stomach-ache from eating too much candy, they still want more. The things people want most cause them the most suffering. Of course, there are basic things that all people should have, like adequate food, shelter, and clothing. Everyone deserves a good home, loving parents, and good friends. They should enjoy life and cherish their possessions without becoming greedy.

3. *The end of suffering*

To end suffering, one must cut off greed and ignorance. This means changing one's views and living in a more natural and peaceful way. It is like blowing out a candle. The flame of suffering is put out for good. Buddhists call the state in which all suffering is ended Nirvana. Nirvana is an everlasting state of great joy and peace. The Buddha said, "The extinction of desire is Nirvana." This is the ultimate goal in Buddhism. Everyone can realize it with the help of the Buddha's teachings. It can be experienced in this very life.

4. *The path to the end of suffering*

The path to end suffering is known as the Noble Eightfold Path. It is also known as the Middle Way.

THE NOBLE EIGHTFOLD PATH

When the Buddha gave his first sermon in the Deer Park, he began the 'Turning of the Dharma Wheel'. He chose the beautiful symbol of the wheel with its eight spokes to represent the Noble Eightfold Path. The Buddha's teaching goes round and round like a great wheel that never stops, leading to the central point of the wheel, the only point which is fixed, Nirvana. The eight spokes on the wheel represent the eight parts of the Noble Eightfold Path. Just as every spoke is needed for the wheel to keep turning, we need to follow each step of the path.

1. Right View- The right way to think about life is to see the world through the eyes of the Buddha- with wisdom and compassion.
2. Right Thought- We are what we think. Clear and kind thoughts build good, strong characters.
3. Right Speech- By speaking kind and helpful words, we are respected and trusted by everyone.
4. Right Conduct- No matter what we say, others know us from the way we behave. Before we criticize others, we should first see what we do ourselves.
5. Right Livelihood- This means choosing a job that does not hurt others. The Buddha said, "Do not earn your living by harming others. Do not seek happiness by making others unhappy."
6. Right Effort- A worthwhile life means doing our best at all times and having good will toward others. This also means not wasting effort on things that harm us and others.

7. Right Mindfulness- This means being aware of our thoughts, words, and deeds.
8. Right Concentration- Focus on one thought or objects at a time. By doing this, we can be quiet and attain true peace of mind.

Following the Noble Eightfold Path can be compared to cultivating a garden, but in Buddhism one cultivates one's wisdom. The mind is the ground and thoughts are seeds. Deeds are ways one cares for the garden. Our faults are weeds. Pulling them out is like weeding a garden. The harvest is real and lasting happiness.

FOLLOWING THE BUDDHA'S TEACHINGS

The Buddha spoke the Four Noble Truths and many other teachings, but at the heart they all stress the same thing. An ancient story explains this well. Once a very old king went to see an old hermit who lived in a bird's nest in the top of a tree, "What is the most important Buddhist teaching?" The hermit answered, "Do no evil, do only good. Purify your heart." The king had expected to hear a very long explanation. He protested, "But even a five-year old child can understand that!" "Yes," replied the wise sage, "but even an 80-year-old man cannot do it."

THE TRIPLE JEWEL

The Buddha knew it would be difficult for people to follow his teachings on their own, so he established the Three Refuges for them to rely on. If a person wants to become Buddhists take refuge in and rely on the Buddha, the Dharma, and the *Sangha*. These are known as the Triple Jewel. The *Sangha* are the monks and nuns. They live in monasteries and carry on the Buddha's teaching. The word *Sangha* means 'harmonious community'. The Buddha, the Dharma, and the *Sangha* together possess qualities that are precious like jewels and can lead one to enlightenment.

A refuge is a place to go for safety and protection, like a shelter in a storm. Taking refuge does not mean running away from life. It means living life in a fuller, truer way. Taking refuge is also like a man traveling for the first time to a distant city. He will need a guide to show him which path to follow and some traveling companions to help him along the way.

- The Buddha is the guide.
- The Dharma is the path.
- The Sangha are the teachers or companions along the way.

There is a special ceremony for taking refuge with the Triple Jewel. With a sincere mind, one recites the following verse in front of an ordained monk or nun.

I go to the Buddha for refuge.

I go to the Dharma for refuge.

I go to the *Sangha* for refuge.

For a Buddhist, taking refuge is the first step on the path to enlightenment. Even if enlightenment is not achieved in this life, one has a better chance to become enlightened in a future life. One who takes the precepts is called a lay person.

THE FIVE PRECEPTS

All religions have some basic rules that define what good conduct is and what kind of conduct should be avoided. In Buddhism, the most important rules are the Five Precepts. These have been passed down from the Buddha himself.

The Buddha said, "Life is dear to all beings. They have the right to live the same as we do." We should respect all life and not kill anything. Killing ants and mosquitoes is also breaking this precept. We should have an attitude of loving-kindness towards all beings, wishing them to be happy and free from harm. Taking care of the earth, its rivers and air is included. One way that many Buddhists follow this precept is by being vegetarian.

No Stealing

If we steal from another, we steal from ourselves. Instead, we should learn to give and take care of things that belong to our family, to the school, or to the public.

No sexual Misconduct

Proper conduct shows respect for oneself and others. Our bodies are gifts from our parents, so we should protect them from harm. Young people should especially keep their natures pure and develop their virtue. It is up to them to make the world a better place to live. In happy families, the husband and wife both respect each other.

No Lying

Being honest brings peace into the world. When there is a misunderstanding, the best thing is to talk it over. This precept includes no gossip, no back-biting, no harsh words and no idle speech.

No Intoxicants

The fifth precept is based on keeping a clear mind and a healthy body. One day, when the Buddha was speaking the Dharma for the assembly, a young drunkard staggered into the room. He tripped over some monks who were sitting on the floor and started cursing loudly. His breath reeked of alcohol and filled the air with a sickening stench. Mumbling to himself, he reeled out the door. Everyone was astonished at his rude behavior, but the Buddha remained calm. "Great assembly!" he spoke, "Take a look at this man! He will certainly lose his wealth and good name. His body will grow weak and sickly. Day and night, he will quarrel with his family and friends until they abandon him. The worst thing is that he will lose his wisdom and become stupid." Little by little, one can learn to follow these precepts. If one sometimes forgets them, one can start all over again. Following the precepts is a lifetime job. If one kills or hurts someone's feelings by mistake, that is breaking the precepts, but it was not done on purpose.

THE WHEEL OF LIFE

Buddhists do not believe that death is the end of life. When one dies, one's consciousness leaves and enters one of the six paths of rebirth.

- Heavenly Beings
- Humans
- Asuras are beings who have many good things in life, but still like to fight. They appear in the heavens or on earth as people or animals.
- Hungry ghosts are beings who suffer from constant hunger.
- Hell-beings

These are the six states on the wheel of life. At the top are the heavens, where everyone is happy. Below are the hells where the suffering is unbearable. Beings can rise or fall from one path to another. If one does good deeds, one will be born into the paths of gods, humans, or asuras. If one does evil deeds, one will be born into the paths of animals, hungry ghosts, or hell-beings. From one life to the next one can suddenly change from an human to an animal or from a ghost to a hell-being, according to the things one has done.

The wheel of life and death is kept turning by the three poisons of greed, hatred, and stupidity. By cutting off the three poisons, we can escape the wheel and become enlightened. There are four stages of enlightenment.

- Buddhas- perfect in enlightenment.
- *Bodhisattvas*- enlighten themselves as well as others.
- *Pratyekabuddhas*- hermits who retreat from the world to enlighten themselves.
- *Arhats*- enlighten themselves.

THE BUDDHIST COMMUNITY

In Asia, it is considered the highest honor if a member of one's family leaves the home life. Westerners, however, may be shocked at the idea of anyone leaving their family to become a monk or nun. They may think this is selfish and turning ones back on the world. In fact, monks and nuns are not selfish at all. They dedicate themselves to helping others. They don't wish to own a lot of things, or to have money or power. They give these things up to gain something far more valuable-spiritual freedom. By living a pure simple life with others on the same path, they are able to lessen their greed, hatred, and ignorance. Although monks and nuns live in a monastery, they do not entirely give up their families. They are allowed to visit and take care of them when they are ill.

LIFE IN A MONASTERY

A day in a temple begins early for monks and nuns. Long before daybreak, they attend morning ceremony and chant praises to the Buddha. The ceremonies lift one's spirit and bring about harmony. Although the *Sangha* lead simple lives, they have many responsibilities to fulfill. Everyone works diligently and is content with his or her duties. During the day, some monks and nuns go about teaching in schools or speaking the Buddha's teachings. Others may revise and translate Buddhist Sutras and books, make Buddha images, take care of the temple and gardens, prepare for ceremonies, give advice to laypeople, and care for the elders and those who are sick. The day ends with a final evening ceremony.

In the daily life of work and religious practice, the monks and nuns conduct them-selves properly and are highly respected. By leading a pure, simple life, they gain extraorinary insight into the nature of things. Although their life is hard and rigorous, the results are worth it. It also keeps them healthy and energetic. The laity, who lives in the temple or visits, follows the same schedule as the *Sangha* and works along with them.

THE SHAVEN HEAD, ROBE AND OFFERING BOWL

Ideally, monks and nuns own only a few things, such as robes and an offering bowl. While most people spend lots of time and money on their hair, Buddhist monks and nuns shave their heads. They are no longer concerned with outward beauty, but with developing their spiritual lives. The shaven head is a reminder that the monks and nuns have renounced the home life and are a part of the *Sangha*. Offering food to monks and nuns is a part of Buddhism. In Asia, it is not unusual to see monks walking towards the villages early in the morning carrying their offering bowls. They do not beg for food, but accept whatever is offered. This practice not only helps the monks and nuns to be humble, but gives laypeople an opportunity to give. In some countries laypeople go to the monastery to make offerings.

The robes of monks and nuns are simple and made from cotton or linen. Their color varies according to different countries.

For instance, yellow robes are mostly worn in Thailand, while black robes are worn in Japan. In China and Korea, gray and brown robes are worn for work, while more elaborate robes are used for ceremonies. Dark red robes are worn in Tibet. Robes and offering bowls are very important to monks and nuns. The Buddha said, "Just as a bird takes its wings with it wherever it flies, so the monk takes his robes and bowl with him wherever he goes."

THE IMPORTANCE OF THE LAITY IN BUDDHISM

The laity is very important in Buddhism, for they are the supporting members of the Buddhist community. They build the temples and monasteries and give offerings of food, robes, bedding, and medicine to the monks and nuns. This enables the *Sangha* to carry on the Buddha's work. In this way the *Sangha* and laity benefit each other and together keep the Dharma alive. In Buddhism, it is also important to support the poor and needy. Giving to support religious people, however, is considered a very meritorious deed. The Buddha not only encouraged giving to Buddhists, but to any spiritual person who is sincere.

The Buddha taught his disciples to be tolerant of other religions. For example, when one lights a candle from the flame of another candle, the flame of the first candle does not lose its light. Instead, the two lights glow more brightly together. It is the same with the great religions of the world. Whether one is a member of the *Sangha* or a lay person, the ideal is to practice Buddhism for the sake of all.

DIFFERENT KINDS OF BUDDHISM

TWO SCHOOLS OF BUDDHISM

In the centuries following the Buddha's lifetime, his followers faithfully preserved his teachings and spread them to many countries in Asia. Today, there are two main schools of Buddhism: Theravada and Mahayana. Theravada means 'the teaching of the Elders'. Theravada monks follow the practices that have been passed down by the senior monks from the Buddha's time, such as living in the forests and meditating. The goal in Theravada Buddhism is to become an Arhat, a person who is free of suffering. Theravada is practiced mainly in southern Asian countries such as Sri Lanka, Thailand and Myanmar (Burma).

Mahayana stresses following the Buddha's example of going out into the world and doing good. Mahayana means 'Great Vehicle'. The goal in Mahayana Buddhism is to follow the *Bodhisattva* Path. A *Bodhisattva* is one who enlightens oneself as well as others. In Mahayana Buddhism, there are many Buddhas and *Bodhisattva*s. It mainly spread to northern Asian countries like China, Tibet, Korea, Vietnam and Japan. Recently, both Theravada and Mahayana Buddhism have been introduced into the West.

VISITING BUDDHIST TEMPLES

In this unit, we will pretend to visit different Buddhist temples. When visiting a temple, we should dress modestly and follow the rules and customs of the temple. Buddhists pay their respects to the Triple Jewel by facing the altar and bowing when entering the temple. Visitors may join in the worship rituals or just watch quietly. In Buddhism, the monks and nuns are treated with great respect. They sit or stand in front of everyone else and take their food first. When we talk to them, we should put our palms together and speak politely.

THERAVADA BUDDHISM

Our first visit is to a Theravada Buddhist monastery in the forest in Thailand where only the monks live. We sit in the quietness of a small bamboo temple built on stilts, surrounded by the sounds of chirping birds and rustling trees. A young monk who is our guide explains to us. "The monks live alone in huts called 'kutis'. They are built on stilts to keep the animals and insects out. There they practice sitting and walking meditation, which is very important for their spiritual life. In front of each hut is a path for walking meditation. The monks sweep them clean to keep from stepping on insects and killing them."

The guide continues, "Early in the morning and in the evening, the monks meet together for meditation and recitation. After the ceremonies called pujas, they study the Dharma. Before entering the temple they wash their feet with water carried up to the monastery from a stream below. It is traditional for the monks and nuns to live in the forest as part of their early training. The older ones, however, are not required to do so. Some monks and nuns may live all their lives in the forest, while others live in the temples in towns and cities.

Someone asks, "Living in the jungle, aren't you afraid of tigers?" The monk answers, "Sometimes, when the monks are walking in the jungle, they sense tigers following them. But since they hold the precept of no killing, they're not afraid and the tigers know they will not be harmed."

TIBETAN BUDDHISM

Next we will visit a Tibetan temple. A young Tibetan boy named Lobsang is our guide. He smiles as he talks, "Our temple is very colorful. It is decorated with many kinds of Buddha images and wall hangings called *thankas.* On the altars are beautiful lamps and incense holders. Big prayer wheels are set into the walls of the temple. *Mantras,* written on strips of rice paper, are placed inside the wheels. They are symbolic phrases with deep spiritual meanings. We recite them over and over as we turn the prayer wheels. There are also hand-held prayer wheels that people whirl as they walk about.

"To us Tibetans, Buddhism is a happy religion. My favorite days are the festivals. People in masks and costumes act out dramas about the life of the Buddha. Bright, new prayer flags are hung on these days. They blow in the wind along the hillsides and remind us to live in harmony with nature. Now that your visit is over, may you go with the spirit of the Buddha?"

JAPANESE BUDDHISM

At a Japanese temple, we are met by Taro. She will tell us about her Sunday school: "We chant 'Namo Amida Butsu' to show our gratitude to Amida Buddha, the Buddha of Infinite Light. We believe that by reciting his name we will have a good life and be reborn in his Western Pure Land. You can see a statue of Amida in the front of the hall. On the altar you can see other beautiful things, but the most important is the offering of rice cakes.

"I will tell you why. Rice is very important to Asian people. If you were to ask a young Japanese boy or girl, 'What did you eat today?' He or she would probably say, 'Rice'" When we see rice offered, it reminds us to offer our best to the Buddha. In Sunday school, we sit in meditation on cushions called zafus. Japanese meditation is called Zen.

CHINESE BUDDHISM

Today we are visiting a Chinese-American monastery in California. It is called the City of Ten Thousand Buddhas. There are over ten thousand small Buddha statues inside the main worship hall. Our guide is a young novice named Gwo Cheng from mainland China. She came to the United States when she was 10 years old and became a novice at age 11. Gwo Cheng: "The City of Ten Thousand Buddhas is a Buddhist community where people from all over the world come to study Buddhism. The City has its own schools, but you do not have to be a Buddhist to attend our schools or to live here.

"A day at the temple begins at 4:00 a.m. with the morning ceremony. After that we bow, sit in meditation, and recite Sutras. These ceremonies lift everyone's spirits and help us live together in harmony. We do our ceremonies in both English and Chinese.

There are many ceremonies throughout the day. We finish off the day with an evening ceremony and a Dharma talk. "Everyone goes to work or school at 8:00 in the morning. In our school, we learn the way of truth and goodness We also learn both Chinese and English. We young novices attend school and are in training to become nuns. We can become fully ordained nuns when we are twenty-one, so we have time to make up our minds. We are not expected to do everything the nuns do, but we do our best. At first it was difficult to get up so early and to sit in meditation, but now we are used to it. It's a healthy life!

"After school, we help with the temple duties and do other chores. I really like gardening and planting. Many people ask me if the novices ever have any fun. We do! We are very good friends and enjoy studying together. We go on walks and picnics and sing Buddhist songs. The nuns are always thinking of fun things for us to do. We also like to see our families who live here and visit with us."

BUDDHIST SCRIPTURES, SYMBOLS AND FESTIVALS

BUDDHIST SCRIPTURES

The Dharma reveals the Buddha's understanding of life. The Buddha instructed countless people, but he, himself, wrote nothing down, just as Jesus wrote anything down. They both lived a complete life. His disciples remembered his talks and recited them regularly. These talks were collected into books called Sutras. There are many Sutras, so Buddhism does not have just a single holy book, like the Christian Bible or the Koran of Islam. The first Sutras were written on palm leaves in Pali and Sanskrit, ancient Indian languages. They have been gathered together in a collection called the Tripitaka, which means 'three baskets'. It is divided into three parts.

- Sutra Pitaka-Sutras and their explanations
- Vinaya Pitaka-Rules for monks and nuns
- Abhidharma Pitaka-The psychology and philosophy of the Buddha's teachings

Buddhists treat Sutras with great respect and place them on the highest shelves in the most respected areas.

BUDDHIST SYMBOLS

Buddhist symbols have special meanings that remind us of the Buddha's teachings. The main room or building is called a shrine or a Buddha Hall. In the front of this room, there is an altar. There are many beautiful things on the altar. Here are some of them.

- Images of the Buddha
- Traditional offerings
- Dharma instruments

Some people believe that Buddhists worship idols, but this is not true. Buddhists bow or make offerings of flowers and incense in reverence to the Buddha, not to the image. When they do so they reflect on the virtues of the Buddha and are inspired to become like him. Buddha images are not necessary, but they are helpful. The most important thing is to follow the Buddha's teachings. There are many different kinds of Buddha and *Bodhisattva* images that show different qualities. For example, a statue of the Buddha with his hand resting gently in his lap reminds us to develop peace within ourselves. A statue with the Buddha's right hand touching the ground shows determination.

Traditional Offerings

Traditional offerings are to show respect to the Buddha.

- Flowers- are offered as reminders of how quickly things change
- Light from lamps or candles- symbolizes wisdom
- Incense- reminds one to be peaceful
- Water- represents purity
- Food- reminds us to give our best to the Buddhas.

Dharma Instruments

The instruments used in ceremonies and meditation are called Dharma instruments. Each instrument has a specific use. For instance, the wooden fish is hit to keep rhythm

- Bells- gives signals in ceremonies and meditation
- Drums-announces ceremonies and keeps rhythm
- Gongs- announces ceremonies and activities
- Wooden fish-keeps rhythm while chanting

Lotus Flower

The lotus flower represents enlightenment described in the poem.

The lotus has its roots in the mud,

Grows up through the deep water,

And rises to the surface.

It blooms into perfect beauty and purity in the sunlight.

It is like the mind unfolding to perfect joy and wisdom.

The Bodhi Tree

The Bodhi Tree is a pipal tree, a kind of fig tree found in India. After the Buddha attained enlightenment under this tree, it became known as the Bodhi Tree, the *Tree of Enlightenment*. It is located in Bodhgaya, where people visit to pay their respects to the Buddha. Although the parent tree is no longer alive, its grandchildren are still there.

The Buddhist Flag

As the Buddha sat beneath the Bodhi Tree after his enlightenment, six rays of light came out from his body and spread for miles around. The colors were yellow, blue, white, red, orange and a mixture of all the colors. The Buddhist flag was designed after these colors.

Stupas and Pagodas

Stupas and *pagodas* are monuments where the relics of the Buddha and high monks and nuns are kept so that people can show their respects. These relics are jewels that remain after cremation.

BUDDHIST FESTIVALS

Buddhists have many festivals throughout the year. These festivals celebrate events in the lives of Buddhas, *Bodhisattvas* and famous teachers. During these occasions people can also take refuge and precepts, or leave the home life to become monks and nuns.

Buddha Day

For the Buddhist community, the most important event of the year is the celebration of the Birth of the Buddha, his Enlightenment and Nirvana. It falls on the full-moon day in May. On this day, Buddhists take part in the ceremonial bathing of the Buddha. They pour ladles of water scented with flowers over a statue of the baby Siddhartha. This symbolizes purifying one's thoughts and actions. The temples are elaborately decorated with flowers and banners; the altars are laden with offerings; vegetarian meals are provided for all; and captive animals, such as birds and turtles are set free. This is a very joyous day for everyone.

Dharma Day

Asalha Puja, known as 'Dharma Day', is celebrated during full-moon in July. This holiday commemorates the first sermon of the Buddha to the five monks in the Deer Park at Benares.

Sangha Day

Sangha Day or Kathina Day is usually held in October. In the Theravada tradition, monks and nuns go on a three-month retreat during the rainy season. After the retreat, the laity offers robes and other necessities to them. This day symbolizes the close relationship between the *Sangha* and laity.

Ullambana

The observance of Ullambana is based on the story of Maudgalyayana, a disciple of the Buddha. When Maudgalyayana's mother died, he wanted to know where she was reborn. Using his spiritual powers, he traveled into the hells and found her suffering miserably from hunger. He brought her a bowl of food, but when she tried to swallow it, the food turned into hot coals. The distressed Maudgalyayana asked the Buddha, "Why is my mother suffering in the hells?"

The Buddha replied, "In her life as a human, she was stingy and greedy. This is her retribution." He advised, "Make offerings to the *Sangha*. The merit and virtue from this act will release your mother and others from the hells." As a result of Maudgalyana's offering, his mother and thousands of others were released from their unhappy state. After this, making offerings to release departed relatives and others from the hells became popular in Mahayana countries. Usually, it takes place in September.

BUDDHISM IN THE EAST

Buddhism was first introduced into Sri Lanka from India in the 3rd century BC by Mahinda, the son of King Asoka. There it achieved great popularity and is still flourishing today. In the early centuries AD, Buddhism was introduced taken to Southeast Asia by merchants and missionaries. The great monuments like Borobudur in Indonesia and Angkor Thom in Cambodia are evidence of the splendor of Buddhism in these regions. In the 1st century AD, Buddhism reached China where many Sutras were translated into classical Chinese. In the 4th century AD, Buddhism found its way to Korea and on into Japan.

BUDDHISM IN THE WEST

Even before the 17th century, people in the West heard of the Buddha and his teachings from early travelers such as Marco Polo and Christian missionaries. By the early 20th century, many Europeans had traveled to the East to study Buddhism. Some of them became monks and inspired Buddhism in the West. In the 19th century, Chinese and Japanese immigrants brought many different traditions of Buddhism to America. Today, there are numerous Buddhist centers spread across Europe and North and South America.

JATAKA TALES AND OTHER BUDDHIST STORIES

The Buddha was a great storyteller and often told stories to get his message across. Stories were also told about the Buddha by his followers both to explain and understand the Dharma. These stories have been passed down to the present day and the most popular ones are the Jataka tales, a collection of hundreds of tales about the Buddha's past lives. They show the kind of life one should lead to become a Buddha one day. In many of these stories, the Buddha appears as an animal to teach the value of qualities such as kindness, compassion, and giving.

The Monkey King and the Mangoes

Once upon a time, the Buddha came into the world as a Monkey King and ruled over 80,000 monkeys. He was very tall and strong and had wisdom like the sun. In his kingdom on the banks of the Ganges River, there was a mango tree as big as the moon. The 80,000 monkeys jumped from branch to branch chattering and eating the lovely fruit that was big and sweet and delicious. Sometimes a ripe mango fell into the river. One day, the Monkey King strolled downstream and came upon a river palace where a human king lived. "Soon danger will come if the mangoes float downstream," he told the monkeys. "Pick all the mangoes and flowers on the trees and take them deep into the forest."

But one mango, hidden by a bird's nest, was left unseen by the 80,000 monkeys. When it was large and ripe, it fell into the river and floated downstream where the human king was bathing. The human king, who was very curious, tasted the beautiful mango. "This is delicious!' he exclaimed."I must have more. Servants, find all the mangoes and bring them to me at once!"

Deep in the forest, the servants found hundreds of mango trees. In the trees were the 80,000 monkeys. When the human king heard about the monkeys, he was very angry, "The monkeys are eating my mangoes. Kill them all!" he ordered his archers. "Very well," said the archers and chased the monkeys to the edge of the forest where they came to a deep cliff. There was no way for the monkeys to escape. Shivering with fright, they ran to the Monkey King asked, "What shall we do?"

"Don't be afraid. I will save you," said their king. Quickly, he stretched his huge body as far as possible and made a bridge over the cliff to a bamboo grove on the other side. "Come monkeys, run across my back to the bamboo grove," he called. And so the 80,000 monkeys escaped. The human king watched all that happened. He was amazed, "This Monkey King has risked his life to save his whole troop! And all I'm doing is being selfish. I have learned a great lesson." Then he called to his archers, "Put down your bows. It isn't right to kill this King of Monkeys." Forgetting about the mangoes, the human king went back to his palace by the river and ruled kindly and wisely for the rest of his life.

The Deer King

Long ago in a forgotten forest, lived a deer named Banyan. He was golden like the sun and his horns glistened like silver. His body was as large as a colt and his eyes sparkled like jewels-alight with wisdom. He was a King of Deer and watched over a herd of 500 deer. Not far away, another herd of deer was watched over by another golden deer named Branch. In the tall grass and shadows of the deep forest, the two herds lived in peace.

One day, the King of Benares was out on a hunt and spied the beautiful green forest where the deer lived. "What a perfect hunting ground!" he declared and into the forests he dashed with his thousands of hunters and came upon the two herds of deer. Without a moment's hesitation, he notched an arrow in his bow. Suddenly he spotted the two golden deer. Never had he seen such beautiful creatures! "From this day on," he commanded, "No one is to harm or kill these golden deer." Thereafter, he came to the forest everyday and killed more deer than was needed for his dinner table. As the weeks went by, many deer were wounded and died in great pain.

Finally Banyan Deer called the two herds together, "Friends, we know there is no escape from death, but this needless killing can be prevented. Let the deer take turns going to the chopping block, one day from my herd and the next day from Branch's herd." All the deer agreed. Each day the deer whose turn it was went to the chopping block on the edge of the forest and laid its head upon the block. One day, the turn fell to a pregnant doe from Branch's herd. She went to Branch Deer and begged, "Grant that I be passed over until after my fawn is born. Then I will gladly take my turn." Branch Deer replied, "It is your turn. You must go."

In despair, the poor doe went to Banyan Deer and explained her plight. He gently said, "Go rest in peace. I will put your turn upon another." The deer king went and laid his golden head upon the chopping block. A deep silence fell in the forest. When the king of Benares came and saw the golden deer ready for sacrifice, his heart skipped a beat, "You are the leader of the herd," he exclaimed, "You should be the last to die!" Banyan Deer explained how he had come to save the life of the doe. A tear rolled down the cheek of the king. "Golden Deer King," he exclaimed. "Among men and beasts, I have not seen one with such compassion. Arise! I spare both your life and hers.

"So we will be safe. But what shall the rest of the deer do?" "Their lives I shall also spare." "So the deer will be safe, but what will the other four-footed animals do?" "From now on they too will be safe." "And what of the birds?" "I will spare their lives." "And the fish in the water" "The fish shall be spared- all creatures of the land, sea, and sky will be free." Having saved the lives of all creatures, the golden deer raised his head from the chopping block and returned to the forest.

The Wounded Swan

One day when Prince Siddhartha and his cousin Devadatta were walking in the woods, they saw a swan. Quickly, Devadatta drew his bow and shot the swan down. Siddhartha rushed to the wounded swan and pulled out the arrow. He held the bird in his arms and caressed it. Devadatta angrily shouted at Prince Siddhartha, "Give me the swan. I shot it. It belongs to me!"

"I shall never give it to you, you will only kill it!" said the prince firmly. "Let's ask the ministers of the court and let them decide." The ministers all had different views. Some said, "The swan should be given to Devadatta." Others said, "It should go to Prince Siddhartha." One wise minister stood up and said, "A life belongs to one who saves it, not to one who will destroy it. The swan goes to the prince." Prince Siddhartha took care of the swan until it could fly again. Then he turned it loose so it could live freely with its own kind.

Aniruddha and the Golden Rabbit

Once there was a poor farmer who offered his only bowl of rice to a holy man who was even poorer than he. This meant he would have nothing to eat that day. He went back to his work and forgot all about having given his rice away. Suddenly a rabbit hopped alongside the farmer and jumped on his back. The surprised farmer tried to brush it off. He tried to shake it off, he tried to knock it off, but the rabbit would not bulge. He ran home to his wife, crying, "Get this rabbit off my back!" By this time the rabbit had turned into solid gold! The wife flipped the rabbit into the air. It hit the floor with a "Crackkk!" One of its golden legs broke off and another one magically grew in its place. From that day on, whenever the farmer and his wife needed money, they would break off a piece of the golden rabbit. And from that life onward, Aniruddha was never poor. This was his reward for giving.

CONCENTRATION ON THE BREATH

A very simple way of meditating is concentrating on your breath. The breath is like a bridge between your body and mind. When you concentrate on your breath for a while, your body becomes relaxed and your mind becomes peaceful.

- Sit in a comfortable position with your back straight.
- Place your hands in your lap with the left hand on the bottom.
- Keep your eyes half-closed or closed.

- Concentrate on the tip of your nose. Notice your breath going in and out.

Lotus Posture

Full lotus is the best sitting posture. Begin by sitting in half-lotus, then work your way up to full lotus.

- Full-lotus- Sit on the edge of a cushion. Place your left ankle on your right thigh. Then lift your right ankle onto your left thigh.
- Half-lotus- Lift your left ankle onto your right thigh.

2

From Monastic Ethics to Modern Society

There are two temptations to be resisted when approaching Buddhist moral theory. The first is to assimilate Buddhist ethics to some system of Western ethics, usually either some form of Utilitarianism or some form of virtue ethics. The second is to portray Buddhist ethical thought as constituting some grand system resembling those that populate Western metaethics. The first temptation, of course, can be avoided simply by avoiding the second. In Buddhist philosophical and religious literature we find many texts that address moral topics, and a great deal of attention devoted to accounts of virtuous and vicious actions, virtuous and vicious states of character and of virtuous and vicious lives.

However, we find very little direct attention to the articulation of sets of principles that determine which actions, states of character or motives are virtuous or vicious, and no articulation of sets of obligations or rights. This is not because Buddhist moral theorists were and are not sufficiently sophisticated to think about moral principles or about the structure of ethical life, and certainly not because Buddhist theorists think that ethics is not important enough to do systematically. It is instead because from a Buddhist perspective there are simply too many dimensions of moral life and moral assessment to admit a clean moral theory. Buddhist ethical thought has instead been concerned with understanding how the actions of sentient beings are located and locate those beings within the web of dependent origination, or *pratitya-sammutpada.*

This web is complex, and there is a lot to be said. And so Buddhists have had a lot to say. But the web is also untidy, and so what Buddhists have had to say resists easy systematization. There is one last temptation to resist, and that is to see the various Buddhist philosophical and religious traditions as constituting a homogenous whole. An enormous variety of positions have been defended within the Buddhist world on just about every philosophical position, and ethics is no exception. Here I will confine my remarks to one strand of Buddhist moral thought, that beginning with the articulation of the four noble truths at Sarnath and running through the work of Nagarjuna in his *Ratnavali,* Candrakirti in *Madhyamakavatara,* and Santideva in *Bodhicaryavatara.*

In particular, I will be ignoring a rich lode of moral literature comprised by the *Jataka* tales and the vast corpus of Buddhist morality tales that populate Buddhist literature that offer a range of moral examples, ideals, and cases for consideration. I hope that the observations I offer regarding this narrow path through Indian Buddhist moral thought will serve to show that Buddhist moral thought represents a reasonable alternative way of thinking about our moral life, one that can engage Western moral theory in profitable dialogue. I believe that each tradition of ethical thought has a great deal to learn from the other, and that learning begins with attention to what each has to say on its own terms.

Thinking about the good from a Buddhist perspective begins from the first principle of Buddhist metaphysics—the fact of thoroughgoing interdependence. Every event and every phenomenon is causally and constitutively dependent upon countless other events and phenomena and in turn is part of the causal ancestries and constitutive bases of countless other phenomena. Moral reflection on action must take all of these dimensions of dependence into account. To focus merely on motivation, or on character, or on the action itself, or on its consequences for others, would be to ignore much that is important. Interdependence is relevant when thinking about identity and interest as well. Many Western moral theorists begin by taking a kind of ontological and axiological individualism for granted in several respects.

First, agency is taken to reside in individual actors, with an attendant focus on responsibility as a central area of moral concern. Second, interest is taken to be fond of an individual matter, and even when the self is consciously deconstructed, as it is by Parfit, interest is taken to attach to individual stages of selves. Third, and consequent on these, a conflict between egoistic and altruistic interests and motivations is regarded as at least prima facie rational, if not morally defensible or ultimately rational. Buddhist accounts of identity reflect the commitment to interdependence.

The boundary between self and other are regarded as at best conventional and relatively insignificant, and at worst deeply illusory. Agency is not taken as a primary moral category, at least if taken to indicate a unique point of origin of action in an individual self, and so moral responsibility is not foregrounded in moral reflection. Interest is hence also seen as a shared phenomenon and egoism as fundamentally and obviously irrational. We will work out the ramifications of these views as we proceed. Nagarjuna argues persuasively that to understand dependent origination is to understand the four noble truths. The truth of suffering sets the problem that Buddhism sets out to solve.

The universe is pervaded by suffering and the causes of suffering. The Buddha did not set out to prove this at Sarnath. He took it as a datum, one that is obvious to anyone on serious reflection, though one that escapes most of us most of the time precisely because of our evasion of serious reflection in order not to face this fact. The Buddha also assumed that suffering is a bad thing. If one disagrees with this assessment, moral discourse has on basis. There is no problem to be solved. If you just love headaches, don't bother taking aspirin. If you don't, you might consider how to obtain relief.

The Buddha then argued that suffering does not just happen. It arises as a consequence of actions conditioned by attachment and aversion, each of which in turn is engendered by confusion regarding the nature of reality. This triune root of suffering is represented in the familiar Buddhist representation of the Wheel of Life with the pig, snake and rooster at the hub, the six realms of transmigration (or aspects of the phenomenology of suffering as we might understand them less cosmologically) turning around them, structured by the twelve links of dependent origination (a detailed psychology of perception and action), all of which is depicted as resting in the jaws of death, the great fear of which propels so much of our maladaptive psychology and moral failure.

Attention to the second noble truth allows us to begin to see how very different Buddhist moral thought is from most Western moral thought: the three roots of suffering are each regarded as moral defilements, and are not seen as especially heterogeneous in character. None of them is seen is especially problematic in most Western moral theory, and indeed each of the first two- attachment and aversion- is valourised in at least some contexts in some systems, particularly that of Aristotle. The third, confusion, is rarely seen in the West as a moral matter, unless it is because one has a duty to be clear about things. But this is far from the issue in Buddhist moral theory. Buddhism is about solving a problem; the problem is suffering; the three root vices are vices because they engender the problem.

The moral theory here is not meant to articulate a set of imperatives, or to establish a calculus of utility through which to assess actions, nor to assign responsibility, praise or blame, but rather to solve a problem. The problem is that the world is pervaded by unwanted suffering. The diagnosis of the cause of the problem sets the agenda for its solution. The third truth articulated at Sarnath is that, because suffering depends upon confusion, attraction and aversion, it can be eliminated by eliminating these causes.

And the fourth, which starts getting the ethics spelled out in a more determinate form, presents the path to that solution. The eightfold path is central to an articulation of the moral domain as it is seen in Buddhist theory, and careful attention to reveals additional respects in which Buddhists develop ethics in a different way than do Western moral theorists. The eightfold path comprises correct view, correct intention, correct speech, correct propriety, correct livelihood, correct effort, correct mindfulness and correct meditation.

While many, following the traditional Tibetan classification of three trainings, focus specifically on correct speech, action and livelihood as the specifically ethical content of the path, this is in fact too narrow, and misses the role of the path in Buddhist practice and in the overall moral framework through which Buddhism recommends engagement with the world. The eightfold path identifies not a set of rights or duties, nor a set of virtues, but a set of areas of concern or of dimensions of conduct.

The path indicates the complexity of human moral life and the complexity of the sources of suffering. To lead a life conducive to the solution of the problem of suffering is to pay close heed to these many dimensions of conduct. Our *views* matter morally. It is not simply an epistemic fault to think that material goods guarantee happiness, that narrow self-interest is the most rational motivation, that torture is a reasonable instrument of national policy or that women are incapable of rational thought. Such views are morally problematic.

To hold such views is not to commit a morally neutral cognitive error, like thinking that Florida is south of Hawai'i. It is to be involved in a way of taking up with the world that is at the very root of the suffering we all wish to alleviate. It is not only what we do that matters, but what we intend. Intention grounds action, and even when it misfires, it matters to who we are and to what we become what we intend to do.

The eightfold path, which represents the earliest foundation of Buddhist ethical thought, must always be thought of as a path, and not as a set of prescriptions. That is, it comprises a set of areas of concern, domains of life on which to reflect, respects in which one can improve one's life, and in sum, a way of moving cognitively, behaviorally and affectively from a state in which one is bound by and causative of suffering to one in which one is immune from suffering and in which one's thought, speech and action tends to alleviate it.

The eightfold path may be represented as broadly consequentialist, but it is certainly not utilitarian, and it is consequentialist only in a thin sense—that is, what makes it a path worth following is that things work out better to the extent that we follow it. By following this path, by attending to these areas of concern in which our actions and thought determine the quality of life for ourselves and others, we achieve greater individual perfection, facilitate that achievement for those around us, and reduce suffering.

There is no boundary drawn here that circumscribes the ethical dimensions of life; there is no distinction between the obligatory, the permissible and the forbidden; there is no distinction drawn between the moral and the prudential; the public and the private; the self-regarding and the other-regarding. Instead, there is a broad indication of the complexity of the solution to the problem of suffering.

ACTION THEORY AND KARMA

The term "karma" plays a central role in any Buddhist moral discussion. It is a term of great semantic complexity and must be handled with care, particularly given its intrusion into English with a new range of central meanings. Most centrally, "karma" means action. Derivatively, it means the consequences of action. Given the Buddhist commitment to the universality of dependent origination, all action arises from the karmic consequences of past actions, and all action has karmic consequences. Karma is not a cosmic bank account on this view, but rather the natural causal sequellae of actions.

Karma accrues to any action, simply in virtue of interdependence, and karmic consequences include those for oneself and for others, as well as both individual and collective karma. Buddhist action theory approaches human action and hence ethics in a way slightly divergent from that found in any Western action theory, and it is impossible to understand moral assessment without attention to action theory.

Buddhist philosophers distinguish in any action the intention, the act itself (whether mental, purely verbal, or non-verbally physical as well) and the completion or the final state of affairs resulting directly from the action itself. If I intend to give ten dollars to Care, hand over the ten dollars to a Care worker, who then uses it to bribe a policeman, beneficial karma accrues from the intention, beneficial karma from the act, but non beneficial karma from the completion. If I intend to steal your medicine, but instead pocket the poison that had been placed on your bedstand by your malicious nurse, thereby saving your life, negative karma accrues from the intention, but positive karma from the act and from the completion, and so forth. It is important to see that karma isn't additive or subtractive.

There is no calculus of utility or of merit points here. The fact that something I do is beneficial does not cancel the fact that something else I do is harmful. It just means that I have done something good and something harmful. I have generated both kinds of consequences, not achieved some neutral state. No amount of restitution I pay for destroying the garden you worked so hard to cultivate takes away the damage I have done. It only provides you with some benefit as well. Truth and reconciliation commissions do indeed reveal the truth and promote reconcilisation, and that is good. But to pretend that they thereby erase the horrific consequences of the deeds they reveal for those who are reconciled is naïve.

Note as well that the relevant kinds of karma include the impact on my character and that of others, such as the tendency to reinforce or to undermine generosity or malice and the degree to which the action promotes general well-being. There is hence attention both to virtue and to consequence here and attention to the character of and consequences for anyone affected by the action. The fundamental facts relevant to moral assessment are causal interdependence and the moral equivalence of all moral agents and patients. Buddhist moral assessment and reasoning hence explicitly takes into account a number of dimensions of action. We cannot in this framework ask whether a particular action is good or evil simpliciter, nor can we ask what our obligations or permissions are.

Instead we ask about the states of character reflected by and consequent to our intentions, our words, our motor acts, and their consequences. We ask about the pleasure and pain produced, and about how actions reflect and enhance or ignore and undermine our universal responsibility. In sum, we ask how these actions are relevant to solving our collective problem—the omnipresence of suffering. The fact that a terrible outcome ensues from a good intention does not make the outcome morally acceptable; nor does a good outcome somehow cancel malicious intent. Each component of action has its consequences and reflects morally relevant features of its genesis.

Attention to this approach to moral assessment and reasoning reveals that in this framework there is no morally significant distinction between self-regarding and other-regarding actions. Nor is there any distinction between moral and prudential motivations. Motivations that appear to be immoral but prudential are, on deeper analysis, simply confused. Nor is there any limit to the domain of the ethical. Karma is ubiquitous; interdependence is endless. Responsibility, as HH the Dalai Lama constantly reminds, can only be universal.

VIRTUE, CONSEQUENCE AND OBLIGATION

We can now see that Buddhist moral theory is neither purely consequentialist nor purely areteic nor purely deontological. Elements of each kind of evaluation are present, but there is no overarching concern for a unified form of moral assessment. And none of these is thematized as the focus of moral assessment. Rather, as I emphasized at the outset, the concern of Buddhist reflection on ethics is the solution of a fundamental, pervasive problem, the problem of suffering. The problem is complex, its roots are complex, and so its solution can be expected to be complex.

Suffering is both caused and constituted by fundamental states of character, including pre-eminently egocentric attraction, egocentric aversion and confusion regarding the nature of reality. Hence the cultivation of virtues that undermine these vices is morally desirable. Suffering is perpetuated by our intentions, acts and their consequences. Hence attention to all of these is necessary for its eradication. Our own happiness and suffering are intimately bound up with that of others. Hence we are responsible for other and obligated to take their interests into account. This is not to say that Buddhist ethics is simply an amalgamation of Aristotle, Mill and Kant into an incoherent jumble.

Instead it represents a distinct moral framework addressed to problem-solving that takes action not to issue from a free will bound by laws, but from a dependently originated, conditioned continuum of causally interdependent psychophysical processes. It takes the relevant consequences of action not to be pleasure and pain conceived of as introspectible experiences of persons, but to be states of sentient continua of genuine suffering, that which conduces to suffering, genuine liberation, or that which conduces to genuine liberation, whether or not those are desired or detested, or experienced as desirable or detestable by the sentient beings imputed on the basis of those continua.

When we put this complex account of the moral status and dimensions of evaluation of action together with the tripartite theory of action and the tripartite distinction between kinds of action, we see that there is little sense in taking the action-centered component of Buddhist moral theory to be either a species of deontological or a species of consequential ethics as these appear in the tradition of Western ethics, although there are genuine kinships to each. The relevant categories of assessment, and the relevant considerations in deliberation are unified by distinct overarching vision of the complexity of ethical life, by a distinct overarching vision of the purpose of moral reflection and of moral cultivation and by a distinct overarching vision of the nature of agency and of the nature of life. If we fail to attend to this framework we see a patchwork. When we attend to the framework, we see a unitary, alternative way of taking up with ethics. Finally, Buddhist moral theory takes the relevant virtues to be cultivated to be those that conduce to the alleviation of suffering. The adumbration of those virtues begins in the Pali literature, but it is addressed most completely in the Mahayana tradition, as developed in texts such as Santideva's *Bodhicaryavatara* and Candrakirti's *Madhyamakavatara*. We now turn to an examination of Buddhist moral psychology as developed in this tradition.

THE BODHISATTVA PATH AND BUDDHIST MORAL PSYCHOLOGY

As I have been emphasizing, Buddhist ethics is directed at solving the problem of suffering in the context of the nexus of dependent origination. Careful attention to the nature of suffering and its causes in this context reveals that the causes and effects of any one sentient being's suffering include the states of indefinitely many other sentient beings, and that there is nothing special about the suffering of any particular sentient being that gives it pride of place in moral consideration. Together these drive one to a universal concern for the enlightened welfare of all sentient beings and to the cultivation of states of character that reflect this awareness and commitment. Let us take these points in turn, and then consider the relevant range of virtues as adumbrated in Buddhist moral psychology.

First, it is an important fact about human beings in particular, but more generally about any beings with sufficient sentience to have moral standing that their cognitive, affective and motivational states are linked inextricably with those of indefinitely many others in a vast causal nexus. For present purposes, let us focus on the case of those social animals we know as *Homo sapiens*. Our happiness, suffering amd moral progress depends at all times on the actions and attitudes of others, as well as on their welfare. If others cooperate and support our projects and our development, success is far more likely; if their attitudes are hostile, happiness and progress are difficult to obtain.

If we know of others' weal or woe, we are either motivated to celebrate of to regret. Celebration of others' welfare benefits both ourselves and others; *Schaudenfreude* is not only detrimental to those around us but ultimately, through undermining the relations that sustain us, to ourselves as well. Similarly, our own actions, mental, verbal and physical have endless ramifications both for our own affective and moral well-being and for that of those around us. These are natural facts and to ignore them is to ignore the nature of action and its relevance to our moral, psychological and social lives.

Confusion regarding the nature of reality in the moral realm manifests itself most directly in the grasping of oneself and of that which most immediately pertains to one as having special importance and justifiable motivational force. In the Buddhist literature this is referred to as the two-fold self-grasping involving the grasping of 'I' and "being-mine," and issues directly in the moral duality of self and other. Such a duality leads to the distinction between prudential and moral concern, self-regarding and other-regarding acts and between those to whom one owes special regard and those to whom one does not, all taken by Buddhist philosophers to be spurious, and in general to a view of the world as comprising me, et al., a view not rationally sustainable once one sees that it is equally available, and so equally unjustifiable, for any moral subject.

It is for this reason, at bottom, that confusion is a root moral delusion, and not simply an epistemological problem. In the Mahayana, moral attention is focused on the cultivation of a set of perfections, or virtues, including those of generosity, patience, propriety, attention, meditation and wisdom. Once again, this list might seem odd to the Western ethicist, in virtue of the inclusion of such *prima facie* non-moral virtues as those of attention, meditation and wisdom on the same list as generosity, patience and propriety. Once again, though, attention to the focus of Buddhist ethics on solving the problem of suffering, and attention to the role of inattention, failure to develop the insights and traits of character cultivated in meditation, and ignorance as causes of and maintainers of suffering should dispel this sense of oddness.

It is also important to recognize that while one signal conceptual innovation in the Mahayana movement is the overlay of this distinctively aretaic conception of moral development on the framework of the eightfold path with its delineation of areas of concern, and on the account of the nature of action and karma familiar from earlier Buddhism, this is not an abandonment of the more basic framework, but an enrichment and a refocus. The eightfold path remains a central guide to the domains in which the perfections figure and the perfections are manifested in the propensity to perform cognitive, verbal and physical actions of the kind assessable in the familiar framework of Buddhist action theory.

The framework of the perfections hence only represents an approach to morality more focused on states of character than on their manifestations as the fundamental goals of moral practice. The most important innovation in Mahayana moral theory, however, is not the framework of the perfections but the installation of compassion as the central moral value and the model of the *bodhisattva*'s compassionate engagement with the world as the moral ideal. The compassion at issue is not a passive emotional response, and not a mere desire. That is sloppy sympathy, and benefits nobody.

Instead it is a genuine commitment manifested in thought, speech and physical action to act for the welfare of all sentient beings. It is in this most sophisticated flowering of Buddhist ethics, with the anticipations of such moral theorists as Hume and Schopenhauer that Buddhist moral theory makes its closest contact with Western ethics. Compassion in this tradition is founded upon the insight that suffering is bad, per se, regardless of whose it is. To fail to take another's suffering seriously as a motivation for action is itself a form of suffering and is irrational.

This is a deep insight, and one over which we should not pass too quickly: the *bodhisattva* path is motivated in part by the realization that not to experience the suffering of others as one's own and not to take the welfare of others as one's own is to suffer even more deeply from a profound existential alienation born of a failure to appreciate one's own situation as a member of an interdependent community. Our joys are social joys; our sorrows are social sorrows; our identity is a social identity; the bounds of our society are indefinite.

We both suffer and rejoice together in the recognition of our bonds to one another, or we languish in self-imposed solitary confinement, afflicted both by the cell we construct, and by the ignorance that motivates its construction. Compassion, grounded in the awareness of our joint participation in global life, hence is the wellspring of the motivation for the development of all perfections, and the most reliable motivation for morally decent actions. Compassion is also, on this view, the direct result of a genuine appreciation of the emptiness and interdependence of all sentient beings.

Once on sees one as non substantial and existing only in interdependence, and once one see that the happiness and suffering of all sentient beings is entirely causally conditioned, the only rational attitude one can adapt to others is a compassionate one. Compassion requires one to develop upaya, or skillful means, in order to realize one's objectives. Compassionate intention is only genuine if it involves a commitment to action and to the successful completion of action, enabled by the skills requisite for that action.

A desire to eradicate world hunger is not genuinely compassionate in this sense if it leads nowhere. But moving to eradicate world hunger requires that one know how to act, if only to know to which organizations to donate, let alone to help others to grow or distribute food. It is in the domain of upaya that Buddhist and Western ethics converge in practice and it is in this domain that each can learn from the other. Often the best way to ensure that minimal human needs are met, for instance, is to establish rights to basic goods, and to enshrine those rights in collective moral and political practice.

Often the best way to ensure that human dignity is respected is to enshrine values that treat persons as individual bearers of value. Often the best way to ensure plenty is to develop social welfare policies. And often the best way to develop flourishing citizens is to articulate a theory of virtue. Western moral theorists have been good at this. Liberal democratic theory and a framework of human rights has been a very effective device for the reduction of suffering, though hardly perfect or unproblematic. So has utilitarian social welfare theory. And virtue theories have been useful in moral education.

These Western articulations of the right, the good and the decent provide a great deal of specific help in the pursuit of the *bodhisattva* path. On the other hand, Buddhist moral theory provides a larger context in which to set these moral programs, and one perhaps more consonant with a plausible metaphysics of personhood and action, and with the genuine complexity of our moral lives. To the extent that that world is characterized by omnipresent suffering, and to the extent that that is a real problem, perhaps the fundamental problem for a morally concerned being, Buddhist moral theory may provide the best way to conceptualize that problem *in toto.* But Buddhist moral theory and Western moral theory can meet profitably when we ask how to solve that problem in concrete human circumstances, and it is in these concrete human circumstances that we must solve it.

Venerable Sheng-Yen, in the Prologue to *Buddhist Ethics and Modern Society*, says "The precepts (Vinaya) form the basis of Buddhist ethics." He goes on to say that "Buddhist lay members need obey only 5, or at the most 8, Buddhist novices must obey 10, while adult monks and nuns have to obey anywhere from 250 to more than 300." Although Sheng-Yen is wrong in not distinguishing the basis of ethical conduct for the laity as separate from the monastic code of the Vinaya, a traditional association in East Asian Buddhism where the terms *sila* and Vinaya are compounded, his mistake is rather commonly made even the Indian tradition where the terms are indeed separate and never compounded.

Akira Hirakawa has offered considerable insight on the need to separate the traditional compound *sila*/Vinaya into its component parts for a proper understanding of each term, but it is rather ordinary and regular, I think, for scholars to associate Vinaya *rather* than *sila* with ethics.

It is critical for our study to understand *why* the distinction between these terms is so important, and precisely *how* the distinction impacts on our original topic. The technical term Vinaya, derived from the Sanskrit prefix *vi* + "*nî*, is often rendered as (some variant of) training, education, discipline, or control. John Holt, utilizing another etymologically valid approach suggests, "Vinaya, the reified noun form of the verb *vi* + "*nî* therefore leads us to the general meaning of 'that which separates,' or 'that which removes.'" Holt goes on:

Our translation of the term Vinaya *begs* the question: what is being removed? To answer that question in the simplest terms, that which is being removed are wrong states of mind, the conditions of grasping, desire and ignorance which stem from the delusion that we have a "self" that can be satiated. The discipline of the Vinaya *pitaka* represents a systematic assault on the idea of "ego-consciousness."

Charles Wei-hsun Fu, utilizing Hirakawa's etymological analysis which captures the essence of both meanings cited above, comes to the same conclusion: "Vinaya *referred* to the established norms of the *Sangha* that all members were expected to observe to maintain the monastic order and insure its continuation." In other words, the Vinaya *was* as much concerned with the *parisuddhi* or complete purity of the community, individually and organizationally, as it was with the specifics of ethical conduct. Under no circumstances should we presume that ethical concerns were superseded in the Vinaya, but rather were included in a series of tiered concerns that focused on institutional, but not exclusively ethical conduct.

Sila, more difficult etymologically than Vinaya, is probably derived from the verb "*sil* and generally translated as virtue, moral conduct, morality, or some similar variant (although Buddhaghosa in the *Visuddhimagga* traces it to a different verb root, associated with "cooling" and Vasubandhu in the *Abhidharmakosa* suggests it derives from the verb "si, which he too associates with cooling). As such, it is a highly ethical term, almost exclusively applied to the individual, and referenced to his or her self-discipline. Additionally, one finds such references continually in the literature. Unlike the Vinaya, which is externally enforced, *sila* refers to the internally enforced ethical framework by which the monk or nun structures his or her life.

Taken in this light, we can see that *sila* is an incredibly rich concept for understanding individual ethical conduct. Thus, as Fu points out, with respect to *sila* and Vinaya:

Hirakawa's analysis of the two words seems to have enormous significance for Buddhist ethics. Our present inquiry into the essential meaning of Buddhist ethics and morality, to address the task of its constructive modernization, demands that we give serious consideration to the means for maintaining a balance between autonomy (*sila*) [sic], expressing the inner spirit of Dharma, and the heteronomous norms or precepts (Vinaya) of the Buddhist order.

Although the *Sutravibhanga* and its paracanonical precursor, the *Pratimoksa* (that portion of the Vinaya *Pitaka* devoted to precepts for the individual monks and nuns), contain many rules reflective of significant ethical awareness and concern, is it appropriate to identify the *Sutravibhanga* as an exclusively ethical document? If we could establish that the canonical Vinaya *texts*, of which the *Sutravibhanga* is a critical part, have their basis in the precepts of *sila*, then such an argument might be well taken. In this regard, one of the pioneers of comparative *Pratimoksa* study, W. Pachow, argues for precisely that position in asserting that the Buddhist disciplinary code was little more than an embellishment of the traditional, widely known, and quite early, *pañcasila* or five ethical precepts.

Pachow says, It would not be unreasonable to say that the code of discipline of the *Sangha* is but an enlarged edition of the *Pañcasila* which have been adopted by the Buddhists and the Jains from the Brahmanical ascetics. And under various circumstances, they have developed subsidiary rules in order to meet various requirements on various occasions. Thus appears to us to be the line of development through which the growth of these rules could be explained.

He then attempts to identify a clear developmental relationship between the individual precepts of the *pañcasila* and the lesser, secondary rules of the *Pratimoksa*. Pachow's interesting approach is cited by most scholars researching the problem. Holt, for example, says, "If this hypothesis were absolutely sound, we could somehow relate all of the disciplinary rules in some way to the four *parajikas* or to the *pañcasila*. Unfortunately, we are not able to do this." Using the Pali text as the benchmark, 139 of the 227 *Patimokkha rules* can be explained. Nonetheless, 88 rules cannot be reconciled! Undaunted, Pachow simply creates new categories to accomodate them.

The problem is further exacerbated by the fact that the *pañcasila* largely mirror the rules for Brahmanical ascetics and Jain monks. Holt summarizes well:

Thus, if we are to argue that the fundamental basis of Buddhist discipline consists of the primary concerns of *sila*, we would have to admit that the basis of Buddhist discipline is not exclusively Buddhist, nor *sramanic*, not even monastic for that matter: not a very satisfying finding.

In the beginning of his important chapter on "Aspects of *Sîla*" in *The Nature of Buddhist Ethics*, Thus, it becomes necessary to question whether it is possible for the textual material on *sila* to be functional in a transtemporal and transcultural fashion? Damien Keown clearly identifies the impact of the above argument: "Overall, there seems to be no reason to assume that the Vinaya is either derived from a simpler set of moral principles or founded upon a single underlying principle or rationale." The remarks of Holt and Keown mirror what I said rather directly in 1980: the "*Pratimoksa* is not just monastic 'glue' holding the *Sangha* together, but the common ground on which the internally enforced life of *sila* is manifested externally in the community."

More recently, and aggressively, Lambert Schmithausen has made the same point. He notes, "The Vinaya *is* not concerned, primarily, with morality proper but rather with the internal harmony and external reputation of the Order." He goes on to say, "One of the main purposes of the *Patimokkha* (though some of its prohibitions do also refer to morality proper) is no doubt, besides internal harmony, the correct and decorous behaviour of the Order and its members in society." If Upali's recitation of the first council of Rajagaha has as much to do with communal administration and conduct as it does with individual moral behavior, and if the canonical Vinaya *Pitaka*, even in the *Sutravibhanga*, devotes more than one-third of its regulations to matters that could at best be referred to as *etiquette*, where, if anywhere in the Buddhist canon, can we find a fuller exegesis of *sila*, acknowledged to be a more comprehensive, apt, and better descriptive term for Buddhist ethical concerns than Vinaya ?

Further, although the commentarial tradition associated with the Vinaya *presents* an immense literature in Pali, replete with *tîkas, sub-tîkas*, and the like, it remains somewhat limited in scope with regard to more modern issues. If we acknowledge that the most general and consistent treatment of ethics in Buddhism is revealed by its expositions on *sila*, then it also becomes critical for an accurate understanding of Buddhist ethics to ask the question clearly put by Winston King in 1964: "What is the relation of ethics to the total structure of Buddhist doctrine and practice, particularly with regard to the definition of moral values, their metaphysical status if any, and the nature of ultimate sanctions."

The traditional way of expressing King's question considers the relationship between the three aspects of the eightfold path, *sila*, *samadhi*, and *prajña*, and their connection to *nirvana*. Damien Keown reviews several longstanding notions on how these soteriological elements relate. Keown first cites the most common view that *sila* leads to *samadhi* which leads to *prajña*, and that *prajña* is identified with *nirvana*. In this context, the ethical concerns expressed by *sila* are at best subsidiary to the others, and are generally thought to be transcended with the attainment of *nirvana*. Secondly, it may be argued that ethical enterprise may facilitate enlightenment, and following the attainment of *nirvana*, once again become operative. Thirdly, ethics and knowledge (i.e., *prajña*) may both be present in the attainment of the final goal.

About his review Keown concludes:

> The three possibilities outlined above represent very different visions of the role of ethics in the Buddhist soteriological programme. In the first two cases, which I have bracketed together, ethics is extrinsic to *nibbana*, dispensable, and subsidiary to *pañña*. In the third it is intrinsic to *nibbana*, essential, and equal in value to *pañña*.

Although the prevailing viewpoint in Buddhist scholarship has tended toward a utilitarian conclusion on the issue of *sila*, especially with regard to Theravada studies, and despite the contrariness of Mahayana-based testimony, an ever-increasing volume of new scholarship has rejected the so-called "transcendency thesis," in favor of a more valued role for those practices collected under the categorical term *sila*. In so doing, it becomes possible to consider those principles categorized as *sila* collectively, as a synthetic reflection of *both nikaya* Buddhism and Mahayana, and perhaps to at least reconsider, and at most dispel, such notions as *sila* representing a purely mundane goal, largely considered as the highest pursuit for the laity, and practiced by monks and nuns only as a preparation for *samadhi*.

If we summarize the relationship between *sila*, *samadhi*, and *prajña*, it becomes possible to delineate a clear and precise connection:

> The fact that the Eightfold Path begins with *sîla* does not mean that morality is only a preliminary stage. The Eightfold Path begins with *sîla* but ends with *sîla* and *pañña*. *Sîla* is the starting point since human nature is so constituted that moral discipline (*sîla*) facilitates intellectual discipline (*pañña*). Until correct attitudes, habits, and dispositions have been inculcated

it is easy to fall prey to speculative views and opinions of all kinds. This does not mean that there is a direct line leading through *sîla* to *paññ*a, or that morality is merely a means of limbering up for the intellectual athlete. No: morality is taken up first but constantly cultivated alongside insight until the two fuses in the transformation of the entire personality in the existential realisation of selflessness.

Finally, the author of the above quotation integrates the role of *samadhi* in the progression as well. He says, "In the scheme of the Eightfold Path, *samadhi* stands between *sîla* and *paññ*a and supplements them both. It is a powerful technique for the acceleration of ethical and intellectual developments towards their perfection in *nibbana*." Having established the efficacy of *sila* rather than Vinaya *as* the primary and most essential category of inquiry for matters pertinent to the ethical tradition in Buddhism, and having established *sila* as critical throughout the Buddhist path to enlightenment and after its attainment, we can now proceed to an examination of the *Sutra*, and to a lesser extent, *Abhidharma* literature fundamental to the *sila* tradition.

The clearest and most detailed exposition of *sîla* in the Pali Canon can be found in the first thirteen suttas of the *Dîgha Nikaya*, a section collectively referred to as the *Sîlakkhandhavagga.* The first, and perhaps most important of these thirteen texts cited above, is the *Brahmajala-sutta* or the "Discourse on Brahma's Net." The preliminary, critical portion of this text is divided into three sections termed, respectively, the short (*cu7a*), medium (*majjhima*), and long (*maha*) divisions. These three sections occur in each of the thirteen suttas of the *Sîlakkhandhavagga!* Thomas W. Rhys Davids, in the notes to his translation of these sections of the *Dîgha Nikaya*, refers to them as the "*Sîla Vagga*," and says that "the tract itself must almost certainly have existed as a separate work before the time when the discourses, in each of which it recurs, were first put together."

The short tract (as Rhys Davids calls the division) contains 26 items of moral conduct, the medium tract 10, and the long tract 7, and while *each* tract is important for understanding the developing notion of Buddhist morality, it is the *short tract* that is most critical. Compared to the various codes of precepts that have become the standard of proper Buddhist conduct, namely, the (in Pali) *pañcasîla* (five precepts), *atthangasîla* (eight precepts), *dasasîla* (ten precepts), *dasakusalakammapatha* (ten good paths of action), and *Patimokkha* (formal monastic disciplinary code), one can correlate four of the five *pañcasîla* to the short tract, seven of the eight *atthangasîla*, nine of the ten *dasasîla*, seven of the ten *dasakusalakammapatha*, and, as we have seen above, 139 of the 227 offenses of the *Patimokkha*.

This close correspondence is important because "....the conduct of the ideal *samana* as defined in the Short Tract becomes the foundation of Buddhist ethics." Although the *Brahmajala-sutta* is possibly the clearest exposition of all the discourses in the *Sîla Vagga*, a number of other texts are also especially important for understanding *sîla* in a contextual framework consistent with Buddhist soteriology. The *Samaññaphala-sutta* or "Discourse on the Fruits of the Religious Life," for example, links the practice of *sîla* to meditative attainment, destruction of the imperfections known as *asavas* (usually translated as "outflows" or "cankers"), and the achievement of arhanthood.

The famous eightfold path, with its division into *sîla*, *samadhi*, and *pañña*, is mentioned in the *Mahali-sutta* ("Discourse to Mahali") and the *Kassapasîhanada-sutta* ("Discourse on the Lion's Roar to Kassapa"). Nor should we conclude that ethicality is not emphasized in the other parts of the canon, as the *Mangala-sutta* of the *Khuddaka Nikaya*, *Metta-sutta* of the *Suttanipata*, and *Sigalovada-sutta* of the *Dîgha Nikaya* are among the most important Theravada texts on this subject. It would also be incorrect to presume *sila* as topically important only in the *sutras.* It is also of much interest to *Abhidharma* and later commentarial authors as well. Nowhere is this more plainly visible than the Theravadin *Abhidhamma*, the first text of which (i.e., the *Dhammasanganî)* classifies mental elements around a markedly ethical base.

According to G.S.P. Misra, to *Puggalapaññatti* as well "deals with the task of the classification of human types in which ethical consideration, among others, is the most dominant principle." Anuruddha's *Abhidhammattha-sangaha* offers a list of 14 immoral and 19 moral mental constituents (*cetasikas*). Additionally, ethical concerns abound in the appropriate sections of Buddhaghosa's *Visuddhimagga* and virtually throughout the *Milindapañha*. In the Sarvastivadin tradition too, 28 of the 46 *caittas* have clear ethical import: 10 positive mental constituents known as *kusala-mahabhumika-dharmas* and 18 negative mental constituents (composed of 6 *klesas* or defilements, 2 *akusala-mahabhumika-dharmas* or universally bad elements, and 10 *upaklesas* or secondary defilements).

The ethical considerations in Vasubandhu's *Abhidharmakosa* are simply too numerous to cite. What it boils down to is this: "The *Abhidharma* posits two classes of mental forces which produce either defilement or purification of the mind."

How do the above present a consistent, harmonious picture for the early Buddhist? In the *Kassapasîhanada-sutta*, Buddha says, of his own ethical attainment:

Now there are some recluses and Brahmans, Kassapa, who laid emphasis on conduct. They speak, in various ways, in praise of morality. But so far as regards the really noble, the highest conduct, I am aware of no one who is equal to me, much less superior. And it is I who has gone the furthest therein; that is, in the highest conduct (of the Path).

Of course the Pali word utilized to indicate "highest conduct" is *adhisîla*. The implication of Buddha's statement is clear enough: Buddha's attainment was unquestionably motivated by compassion and fueled by moral development of the highest order, but also that *the attainment of Buddhahood (or, for that matter, arhantship) does not preclude ethical propriety.* No doubt the cultivation of meditational attainment, as we indicated earlier, bridges the proverbial gap between *sîla* and *pañña*, and not only does this suggest that meditational experience has serious impact on the moral life, but also that "*Sîla* is a central feature of the conduct of the enlightened...."

Keown notes that "the *Arahat* certainly has not gone beyond *kusala*, and *kusala* is the term which *par excellence* denotes ethical goodness." Ethical goodness, as manifested by Buddha or *any* serious practitioner, is a reflection of his sympathy (*anukampa*) for all sentient beings and manifested by cultivation of the four *Brahmaviharas* or "Divine Abodes," as Aronson has amply demonstrated.

If the above paragraph demonstrates that Buddhist ethical development takes its inspiration from Buddha's personal example, it is not unreasonable to conclude about the Buddha, as Lal Mani Joshi does, that:

> His love of solitude and silence was matched only by his universal compassion towards the suffering creatures. Hînayana seems to have laid emphasis on the former while Mahayana on the latter aspect of the Buddha's personality and ideal.

Such an approach leads Joshi and others to identify the ethical approach of the Buddhist *nikayas* as narrower and more limited in scope than Mahayana. About Mahayana, Joshi remarks, "Its aim is higher, its outlook broader, and its aspiration more sublime than that of Hînayana." One should not read Joshi's evaluation too aggressively, or as a rejection of the earlier understanding of *sila*, but rather as what Keown aptly calls a "paradigm shift." This paradigm shift is of course reflected by the Mahayana emphasis on the *bodhisattva* ideal.

Nalinaksha Dutt, in his still important *Aspects of Mahayana Buddhism and Its Relation to Hînayana*, notes that the Chinese pilgrim I-ching "who was chiefly interested in the Vinaya, remarks that the Mahayanists had no Vinaya *of* their own and that theirs was the same as that of the Hînayanists." Dutt, however, goes on to list a large number of Mahayana *sutras* that deal with ethical issues, including the *Bodhisattvacaryanirdesa*, *Bodhisattva-Pratimoksa-sutra*, *Bhiksu Vinaya*, *Akasagarbha-sutra*, *Upalipariprccha-sutra*, *Ugradattapariprccha-sutra*, *Ratnamegha-*

sutra, and *Ratnarasi-sutra*. Of these, the *Bodhisattva-Pratimoksa-sutra* and the *Upalipariprccha-sutra* are clearly the best known. The former was edited by Dutt and published in *Indian Historical Quarterly*, 7 (1931), but to my knowledge, has never been translated into English. It is a *sutra* only in name, comprised primarily of fragments taken from the *Upalipariprccha-sutra* and the *Bodhisattvabhumi*.

Nonetheless, it is not a code of monastic rules for *bodhisattvas*, as its name implies, but rather a general ethical guide for both lay and monastic *bodhisattvas*. The *Upalipariprccha-sutra* has benefitted from the fine scholarly translation of Pierre Python.

There is little doubt that at least three major texts form the basis of Mahayana ethics: the (1) (Mahayana) *Brahmajala-sutra*, an apocryphal Chinese work (2) *siksasamuccaya* of santideva, and (3) *Bodhicaryavatara* of santideva. The *siiksasamuccaya* was of sufficient importance to prompt Joshi to state, "The fundamental principle of Mahayana morality is expressed in the first verse of the *siksasamuccaya*: 'When to myself as to my fellow-beings, fear and pain are hateful, what justification is there that I protect my own self and not others?'"

Structurally, the text is organized into three parts, beginning with twenty-seven *karikas* outlining the ethical ideal of the *bodhisattva*. A second part offers an extensive commentary on these verses, with the third part offering a huge compendium of supporting quotations from additional Buddhist texts. Taken collectively, its three parts form a comprehensive statement on *bodhisattva* ethics. The *Bodhicaryavatara* is possibly the best known Mahayana text associated with the conduct of the *bodhisattva*. This does not mean to say that the *sila-paramita* is omitted; Verse 11 mentions it by name. Specifically ethical concerns are also considered, known as "*Papa-desana*" or "Confession of Evil." Overall, an incredible breadth and scope of ethical issues are considered.

Curiously, it is not from these famous Mahayana ethical texts alone that we find the key which unlocks the major emphasis of *bodhisattva* conduct. Two further texts are critically important here: the *Mahayanasamgraha* and the *Bodhisattvabhumi*, and it is on the basis of their evidence that many authors, Buddhist and otherwise, have advanced the theory of the superiority of Mahayana ethics over that of *nikaya* Buddhism. In fact, the tenth or "ethical" chapter of the *Bodhisattvabhumi* was the focus of a complete translation and study by Mark Tatz.

Keown, in *The Nature of Buddhist Ethics*, provides an extremely careful exposition of the argument. The *Mahayanasamgraha* suggests that Mahayana morality is superior to Hînayana in four ways: (1) in its classifications (*prabheda-visesa*), (2) in its common and separate rules, (3) in breadth (*vaipulya-visesa*), and (4) in depth (*gambhîrya-visesa*).

The first category is the most important of the four since it supports the other three, and is itself composed of three sections: (a) morality as temperance (*samvara-sila*), (b) morality as the pursuit of good (*kusala-dharma-samgrahaka-sila*), and (c) morality as altruism (*sattva-artha-kriya-sila*). The threefold categorization of morality as temperance, the pursuit of good, and altruism is further developed by the *Bodhisattvabhumi*, concluding that it is the element of altruism that enables Mahayana morality to surpass its *nikaya* Buddhist counterpart.

The extreme importance of the issue of altruism in asserting the superiority of Mahayana ethics has not gone unnoticed by modern Theravadins. Walpola Rahula, for example, says, The *bhikkhu* is not a selfish, cowardly individual thinking only of his happiness and salvation, unmindful of whatever happens to the rest of humanity. A true *bhikkhu* is an altruistic, heroic person who considers others' happiness more than his own. He, like the *Bodhisattva* Sumedha, will renounce his own *nirvana* for the sake of others. Buddhism is built upon service to others.

Other Theravadin authors echo Rahula's sentiment. Regarding the specific conduct of *bodhisattvas*, the *Bodhisattvabhumi* postulates a code having fifty-two rules, of which only the first four are categorized (as *parajayika-sthaniya-dharma*) and a number of which allow the violation of (some of) the ten good paths of action. The second category explores the differentiation between serious and minor offenses, emphasizing that while both *bodhisattvas* and *sravakas* are enjoined to observe all the major rules of conduct, *bodhisttvas* may breach minor matters of deportment while *sravakas* may not. Of course the circumstances under which a *bodhisattva* may engage in this kind of behavior are also stated. The third category is essentially a summary. Finally, the fourth category is the most innovative, focusing on the notion of skill-in-means (*upaya-kaualya*) in relation to Mahayana ethics.

In the fourth chapter of the *Bodhicaryavatara*, one reads "The son of the Conqueror, having grasped the Thought of Enlightenment firmly, must make every effort, constantly and alertly, not to transgress the discipline (*siksa*)." "Thus enlightened, one ought to be constantly active for the sake of others. Even that which generally is forbidden is allowed to the one who understands the work of compassion." How can these two conflicting views appear in the same text, and in such close proximity?

The answer lies in a proper understanding of *upaya-kausalya* and its role in Mahayana ethics: it is a theme that permeates santideva's writings. Throughout the *siksasamauccaya* on "Purification from Sin" (*Papasodhanam*), citations abound, especially from the *Upalipariprccha-sutra* and the *Upayakausalya-sutra*, in which ethical trangressions are allowed and sanctioned in the name of skill-in-means.

Keown concludes from all these examples "that the freedom allowed to a *bodhisattva* is enormous and a wide spectrum of activities are permitted to him, even to the extent of taking life." He goes on, however, to say:

When actions of these kinds are performed there are usually two provisos which must be satisfied: (a) that the prohibited action will conduce to the greater good of those beings directly affected by it; and (b) that the action is performed on the basis of perfect knowledge (*prajña*) or perfect compassion (*karuna*).

The relationship between *sila* and *prajña* in Mahayana is thus parallel to that noted above with respect to *nikaya*

Buddhism in which it was remarked that "the two fuse in the transformation of the entire personality in the existential realisation of selflessness". What seems not to be parallel is that the *nikaya* Buddhist adept is at no time allowed to breach the practice of proper morality while the Mahayana *bodhisattva* may, under certain circumstances invariably linked to altruistic activities and based on *karuna*, *upaya-kausalya*, and *prajña*, transcend conventional morality. G.S.P. Misra, for example, notices that, "In the *Bodhisattvabhumi* we find an enumeration of the circumstances under which a *Bodhisattva* may justifiably commit transgressions of the moral precepts; the governing factor, however, is always compassion and a desire to save others from sinful acts."

The above passages notwithstanding, parallel references can be also found emphasizing a strict observance of the precepts for *bodhisattvas*. As a result, we find ourselves confused over the apparent incongruency in the textual accounts of Mahayana ethical conduct, and wondering just how breaches of conventional ethical behavior are sanctioned. The solution emerges from the postulation of two uniquely different types of *upaya-kausalya*.

About the first, which he categorizes as normative ethics and calls *upaya*, Keown says:

Upaya does not enjoin laxity in moral practice but rather the greater recognition of the needs and interests of others. One's moral practice is now for the benefit of oneself and others by means of example. Through its emphasis on *karuna* the Mahayana gave full recognition to the value of ethical perfection, making it explicit that ethics and insight were of equal importance for a *bodhisattva*.

The second type of *upaya* has nothing to do with normative ethics or ordinary individuals. It is the province of those who have already perfected ethics and insight. Thus:

... It is the *upaya* of *bodhisattvas* of the seventh stage (*upaya-kausalya-bhumi*) and beyond, whose powers and perfections are supernatural. *Upaya* is depicted as an activity of the Buddhas and Great *Bodhisattvas (Bodhisattva-Mahasattvas)* and it is only they who have the knowledge and power to use it. It is by virtue of *upaya* that *bodhisattvas* transgress the precepts from motives of compassion and are said to do no wrong.

There can be little doubt that *upaya* is *not* the model by which ordinary beings perfect themselves but rather the pragmatic moral outcome of the attainment of the seventh stage of the *bodhisattva* path. *Upaya* is the social expression of a genuine understanding of the notion of emptiness (*sunyata*) in which no precepts can even be theorized. It is emphasized throughout the Mahayana literature on emptiness, but nowhere as eloquently as in the discourse between Vimalakîrti and Upali of the *Vimalakîrtinirdesa-sutra*:

Reverend Upali, all things are without production, destruction, and duration, like magical illusions, clouds, and lightning; all things are evanescent, not remaining even for an instant; all things are like dreams, hallucinations, and unreal visions; all things are like the reflection of the moon in water and like a mirror-image; they are born of mental construction. Those who know this are called the true upholders of the discipline, and those disciplined in that way are indeed well disciplined.

As such, it represents the far extreme of the ethical continuum, a Buddhist situation ethics established not simply on love, as in Fletcher's system, but on the highest and most profound manifestation of compassion. Having concluded in the above pages that *sila* is operative throughout the individual's progress on the *nikaya* Buddhist path, even after the attainment of *prajña*, and that the same claim can be made for Mahayana, enhanced by the altruistic utilization of *upaya* up to the attainment of the seventh *bodhisattva* stage, after which *upaya* becomes operative, albeit in rather antinomian fashion, it now becomes important to address the issue of whether textually based Buddhist ethics can be truly current; whether an ethical tradition solidly grounded on the textual heritage can serve as the foundational basis for a socially engaged Buddhism, effective in addressing the complex concerns cited in the growing literature on the subject. The relative vitality of Buddhist ethics in today's world is a concern that cannot be minimized. Indeed, Kôshô Mizutani, in the *Prologue* to *Buddhist Ethics and Modern Society* asserts, "I submit that a study of Buddhism that emphasizes its ethical aspects will be the most important task facing Buddhists in the twenty-first century." Studies abound stressing the difficulties of living effectively in a postmodern society that is becoming increasingly pluralistic and secular.

This dilemma is further exacerbated for Buddhists in that "Buddhists today face the question not only of how to relate to other religions, but also how to relate to other forms of Buddhism from different traditions." In 1987, Rick Fields delivered a paper on "The Future of American Buddhism" to a conference entitled "Buddhism and Christianity: Toward the Human Future," held at the Graduate Theological Union in Berkeley, California.

Although case specific to the American Buddhist situation, Fields concluded his presentation with a sketch of eight features that he felt would be critical in the on-going development of American Buddhism. All eight points were directly or indirectly related to issues of Buddhist ethics, prompting Fields to comment: "The *Bodhisattva* notions of direct involvement in the world will tend to overshadow tendencies towards renunciation and withdrawal. Buddhist ethics, as reflected in the precepts, the paramitas, and the *Bodhisattva* vow, will be applied to the specific problems of day-to-day living in contemporary urban North America."

It is difficult to consider Fields' words, and those of similar, like-minded individuals such as the contributors to works in the genre of *The Path of Compassion* edited by Fred Eppsteiner without feeling much sympathy for the predicament facing Buddhists in Asia and America as they try to confront ethical dilemmas directly. Consequently, when we read articles by Sulak Sivaraksa, Thich Nhat Hanh, Jack Kornfield, Joanna Macy and others we must commend them for the depth of their sincerity and commitment, the expanse of the timely issues they confront, and wonder why there is rarely a footnote, hardly a textual reference in their writings which might provide additional and persuasive authority to their arguments.

In an exciting article, drawing heavily on the work of recent biblical scholarship, Harold Coward points out that:

> The relationship between a religious community and its scripture is complex, reciprocal and usually central to the normative self-definition of a religion. The awareness of this relationship is the result of postmodern approaches that no longer see scriptures as museum pieces for historical critical analysis, but recognize them to be the products of human perception and interaction-both in their own time and in today's study by scholars.

The problem of precisely how ethical guidelines can be appropriately reinterpreted in the context of changing times and cultures was confronted early on in Buddhist religious history. By including only the presumed words of Buddha, referred to as *Buddhavacana*, within a closed canon, *nikaya* Buddhism in general and Theravada in particular made a clear statement about the relationship of community and scripture in the early tradition. Mahayana chose the opposite approach. As Coward points out: "Rather than closing off the canon as the *Theravada* school had done, *Mahayana* maintained an open approach and added to the 'remembered words' of Ananda new *sutras* such as the *Prajñaparamita Sutras* and the *Lotus Sutra*."

This openness allowed Buddhists the occasion to utilize Buddha's own approach in transmitting the substance of his teaching if not his exact words. Robinson and Johnson point this out clearly in *The Buddhist Religion*: "Both strictness in preserving the essential kernel and liberty to expand, vary, and embellish the expression characterize Buddhist attitudes through the ages toward not only texts but also art, ritual, discipline, and doctrine. The perennial difficulty lies in distinguishing the kernel from its embodiment."

The openness in creating new scripture emphasized by Mahayana, and the utilization of an on-going commentarial tradition, as fostered by earlier Buddhism, conjointly provide the potential for a profoundly *current* Buddhist ethics that is also *textually grounded.* Such an approach is solidly in keeping with the program outlined by Charles Wei-hsun Fu (in a slightly different context). Fu says, "The Buddhist view of ethics and morality must be presented in the context of open discussion in a free and democratic forum." To be successful, it requires that:

> A philosophical reinterpetation of the Middle Way of *paramartha-satya/samvrti-satya* must be undertaken so that the original gap between these two can be firmly bridged, thereby accomplishing the task of constructive modernization of Buddhist ethics and morality. On the theoretical level, a new ethical theory based on the Middle Way of *paramartha-satya/ samvrti-satya* can meet the challenge of modern times.

When I wrote *American Buddhism,* I suggested that much of the future of Buddhism in the 1970s, or for that matter, in longer term perspective, would be dependent on the changing face of American religious life in general. This is especially important in examining Buddhism's situation with regard to everyday life. By the late 1970s, America was in the throes of severe social anomie, largely fueled by the vast ethical uncertainty that gripped the cultural and religious landscape. At that time, I maintained that Buddhism's traditional view of Vinaya and *sila,* monastic and individual guidelines for everyday, institutional and ethical conduct was grossly ineffective and needed serious commentary and reform. I believe that significant reform is now taking place in American Buddhist communities.

Needless to say, in this short context, I cannot pursue the many, varied ways Theravada, Mahayana, and Vajrayana Buddhist groups in America are specifically engaging the ancient tradition in a new dialogue that elevates precepts beyond a facile understanding merely as *siksa,* as rigid regulations. Such an exposition would require an elucidation of new approaches to the literature so as to provide a result that is truly transtemporal and transcultural. In his earlier mentioned 1987 paper Fields also commented Buddhism's future in America was intimately tied up with its ability to develop a Vinaya *for* lay people, its concern for promoting a just and compassionate society, and its regard for identifying an ethical pattern for women.

Fields is by no means the first to say this, but he is absolutely correct in his assertion.

In the three decades that I have been writing about Buddhism in America, I have consistently argued that since the vast majority of Buddhists in this country were members of the laity, for Buddhism to be truly American, it would need to address the dilemma of tailoring the major emphasis of Buddhist practice to lie rather than monastic life. Initially, the suggestion was rather widely and aggressively attacked by what seemed to me like most of the Buddhists groups in America. The substance of the critique presumed that I ignored the monastic *Sangha*, the very basis and foundation of Buddhist community life.

Of course I did nothing of the kind. I simply acknowledged what Buddhists in Asia have recognized for more than two millennia. Most practitioners, for an enormous variety of entirely valid reasons, cannot make the full and complete commitment to the rigorous practice associated with monastic life.

That doesn't mean we should ignore the monastic tradition, or exclude it from American Buddhist life, but rather that we provide the context for all Buddhists in America to practice in a fashion appropriate to their choice of approach. In so doing, we would simply be following, and perhaps adapting, an Asian Buddhist model predicated on the notion that there have always been more members of the laity than members of the monastic tradition, but that both endeavors needed to be affirmed and endorsed for the successful development of Buddhist religious life. Such an approach has not always been clear in the popular literature.

In Spring 1992, the *Tricycle* editorial observed that "Just now, ours is not predominantly a Buddhism of removed monasticism. It is out of robes, in the streets, in institutions, workplaces, and homes." The editorial closed with this remark: "While Buddhist history is steeped in monasticism, our own democratic traditions compel us to share the burden of social problems." For some Buddhists in this country, monastic and otherwise, the above comments may be perceived as highly inflammatory, possibly even reflective of a rejection of the entire monastic vocation. To be sure, American Buddhism might redefine somewhat the nature of the symbiosis between the two main component groups of the Buddhist *Sangha*, but neither enterprise would ever be disparaged by the other.

In Don Morreale's 1988 volume *Buddhist America*, Jack Kornfield called the same process *integration*, and along with democratization and feminism, considered it one of three major themes in North American Buddhism. So, within a decade, many writers, mostly identified with non-ethnic American Buddhism, had begun to echo my own sentiment. No one, however, has made the argument so eloquently, and with such awareness of the complexity of the task, as Rita Gross, in her extremely important book *Buddhism After Patriarchy*. Gross recognizes that what she refers to as "monasticism after patriarchy," while understanding that new and vital archetypes must replace Buddhism's current "very weak models for meaningful lay life," must forge new monastic paradigms that are androgynous and free of prejudice or discrimination.

The movement to a truly post-patriarchal monastic tradition is at least as threatening to traditional Buddhism in Asia as to the conflict between the "Two Buddhism's" in America, and of course Gross argues persuasively for an androgynous lay Buddhism as well. Additionally, Gross identifies, addresses, and validates the emphasis of those Buddhists who are trying to work out an intermediary lifestyle that incorporates both monastic and lay features into serious, rigorous Buddhist practice. Associated with the struggle to redefine community life in American Buddhism, accommodating both ethnic and largely non-ethnic groups, is a new emphasis on active expressions of compassion as perhaps the major component of a revitalized Buddhist ethics that has been called "socially engaged Buddhism."

In an interesting book titled *Inner Peace, World Peace*, edited by Kenneth Kraft, the editor provides an interesting survey chapter in which he chronicles many of the activities collected under the above rubric, such as the founding of the Buddhist Peace Fellowship in 1978, Thich Nhat Hanh's many significant endeavors in North America, the Dalai Lama's efforts, and, most importantly, the growing body of literature that has accompanied the effort. Kraft shows how socially engaged Buddhism in America has utilized well-known methods of social action in this culture: voter mobilization, letter writing campaigns, volunteer charity work, tax resistance, product boycotts, and so forth. What is most puzzling here is that one of the major foci of socially engaged Buddhists in the West consists of providing aid and support to ethnic Buddhist groups, both here and in Asia, while, with few exceptions, ethnic Buddhists in America seem not to be especially active in the movement.

A creative commentary on Buddhism's attempt to renew its commitment to generating and practicing a revitalized, value-oriented ethical life is the development of Thich Nhat Hanh's "Order of Interbeing," the successor to Vietnam's Tiep Hien Order. It tries to provide a creative (even experimental) individual and collective methodology for the application of Buddhist principles to today's world. The major thrust of the group is to practice the traditional five vows of the laity, in conjunction with fourteen additional precepts that amplify and augment the values underlying the original five. Moreover, Nhat Hanh has struck a careful balance between meditational training and political activism, emphasizing each activity as mutually influencing.

In so doing, both ethnic and non-ethnic American Buddhist groups are provided with an agenda for activism that benefits all Buddhists. Despite its clever use of what Fields calls "cross-cultural borrowing" and genuine potential for an honorable rather than politically correct multiculturalism in American Buddhism, this approach has not been uniformly accepted. One of the most fruitful approaches to understanding the attitudinal differences between ethnic and non-ethnic American Buddhists can be extracted from Kenneth Kraft's work in *Inner Peace, World Peace.* He suggests that Buddhists in Asian and Third World countries are often engaged in serious struggle for political and cultural survival.

He notes that "Those involved in such conflicts typically have little interest in the theoretical implications of nonviolence or the latest innovations in spiritual/activist practice." Most Western Buddhists have never shared that tragic experience; it's a form of suffering they've never experienced. Yet their teachers have. Chögyam Trungpa's Born in Tibet remains a chilling testament to the fallout of a world filled with suffering. Thich Thien-an's work with Vietnamese refugees both before and after the fall of Saigon documents how suffering sometimes fosters what one writer called "the exigencies of a major transplantation of human beings to a totally new environment."

Many years ago, in the "Introduction" to my edited 1992 volume *Buddhist Ethics: A Cross-Cultural Approach,* I suggested that Buddhists could look to the synthesis of two traditional ethical frameworks in fulfilling the suggestions noted by Fields: (1) the four *brahmaviharas* or "Divine Abodes," consisting of love (*maitrî*), compassion (*karuna*), sympathetic joy (*mudita*), and equanimity (*upeksa*), and (2) the six *paramitas* or "perfections," of giving (*dana*), morality (*sila*), patience (*ksanti*), vigor (*vîrya*), meditation (*samadhi*), and wisdom (*prajña*). Although the *brahmaviharas* are more generally applied to Theravada thought, and the *paramitas* to Mahayana thought, they might be reinterpreted conjointly through an entirely new commentarial literature in reconfiguring a modern American Buddhist ethics.

In so doing, American Buddhism will arrive at a wisdom that is grounded in equanimity, understanding properly that, "...although fully liberated beings have abandoned all the negative emotions of attachment, hatred, and delusion, they have not destroyed *all* emotion and feeling. They have the ability to develop a whole range of rich and satisfying emotions and are encouraged in scripture to do so." Consequently, a powerful new ethical tool is developed that stands outside of time and culture.

Not to beg the original question, the above more than argues for the composition of new commentarial literature focusing on those significant texts mentioned earlier and including especially, the: 13 suttas identified as the "short tract" (*Sîlakkhandhavagga*) of the *Dîgha Nikaya, Mangala-sutta, Metta-sutta, Sigalaovada-sutta, Dhammasanganî Puggalapañnatti, Abhidhammattha-sangaha, Visuddhimagga,* and *Milindapañha* of the Theravadin tradition. Mahayana texts worthy of new consideration would also include those with the richest heritage of ethical underpinnings, for example, the: *Brahmajala-sutra, siksasamuccaya, Bodhicaryavatara, Mahayanasamgraha, Bodhisattvabhumi, Bodhisattva-Pratimoksa-sutra, and Upalipariprccha-sutra.* Certainly this does not mean to say that there are no other texts of ethical import for Buddhism, but simply that the ones cited above represent the most fertile, reasonable place from which to begin a new and revitalized textual tradition. The process would be a high expression of what Coward calls "the reciprocal relationship between text and tradition in Buddhism," a profound demonstration that Buddhist ethics can indeed be meaningfully current and textually supported.

3

Buddhism and Human Rights

Here we consider what it means to characterize certain rights as human rights, and pursue further the discussion initiated in the preceding section as to whether Western notions of human rights are compatible with Buddhism. The point has already been made that what are today called human rights were originally spoken of as "natural" rights, in other words, rights which flow from human nature. In the seventeenth century philosophers and statesmen began to define these rights and enshrine them in early constitutions such as the Fundamental Orders of Connecticut as early as 1639.

Documents of this kind inspired the publication of other declarations, charters and manifestos in a tradition which has continued into modern times. As an example of a modern charter of human rights we may take The Universal Declaration of Human Rights proclaimed by the General Assembly of the United Nations in December 1948. Since its promulgation this thirty- article code has been used as a model for many subsequent human rights charters. What is the Buddhist position with respect to declarations of this kind? It may be useful to begin by asking whether Buddhism would endorse the Universal Declaration of Human Rights.

The repeated calls by the Dalai Lama for respect for human rights give some reason to think that it would. The signing of the *Global Ethic* by many Buddhists also suggests that Buddhism has no reservations about subscribing to charters or manifestos which seek to secure universal human rights. Moreover, there seems to be nothing in any of the thirty articles to which Buddhism would take exception. Perera's commentary on each of the thirty articles of the Universal Declaration shows them to be in harmony with early Buddhist teachings both in letter and in spirit. In his *Foreword* to the commentary Ananda Gurugeí writes:

> Professor Perera demonstrates that every single Article of the Universal Declaration of Human Rights- even the labour rights to fair wages, leisure and welfare- has been adumbrated, cogently upheld and meaningfully incorporated in an overall view of life and society by the Buddha.

But how are these rights to be justified with reference to Buddhist teachings? In asking this question I am not seeking justification by reference to textual passages which seem to support the rights claimed. There are many passages in the Pali Canon, as Perera has ably demonstrated, which support the view that early Buddhist teachings were in harmony with the spirit of the Declaration. The justification required at this point has more to do with the philosophical presuppositions underlying these passages and the overall Buddhist vision of individual and social good.

The various declarations on human rights themselves rarely offer a justification for the rights they proclaim. MacIntyre observes dryly how "In the United Nations declaration on human rights of 1949 [*sic*] what has since become the normal UN practice of not giving good reasons for any assertion whatsoever is followed with great rigor." A gesture towards justification is sometimes made in recital clauses by reference to the "inherent dignity... of all members of the human family" or some similar form of words. The *Global Ethic*, which provides a fuller statement than most, echoes the Universal Declaration in its call for "the full realization of the intrinsic dignity of the human person".

It states: "We make a commitment to respect life and dignity, individuality and diversity, so that every person is treated humanely." This is amplified as follows:

This means that every human being without distinction of age, sex, race, skin, color, physical or mental ability, language, religion, political view, or national or social origin possesses an inalienable and untouchable dignity. And everyone, the individual as well as the state, is therefore obliged to honor this dignity and protect it.

Elsewhere, as part of his dialogue with world religions, Kung makes a constructive suggestion on this point that students of Buddhism might do well to pay heed to:

Should not Buddhist thinkers, as they critically assess their own and alien traditions, make a more direct effort to establish anthropology centered on human dignity (which the Buddha himself deeply respected)? Buddhists are fully aware that man can be adequately understood only as conditioned in every way, as a relational being within the totality of life and the cosmos. But should they not reflect more earnestly, especially in an ethical vein, on the problems of the unique, inviolable, noninterchangeable human self, with its roots in the past and its future destiny?

It is by no means apparent, however, how human dignity is to be grounded in Buddhist doctrine. The very words "human dignity" sounds alien in a Buddhist context as talk of rights. One looks in vain to the "The Four Noble Truths" for any explicit reference to human dignity, and doctrines such as no-self and impermanence may even be thought to undermine it. If human dignity is the basis of human rights Buddhism would seem to be in some difficulty when it comes to providing a justification for them. The theistic religions, on the other hand, seem much better equipped to provide an account of human dignity. Christians, Muslims and Jews typically refer to the ultimate source of human dignity as divine.

Article one (paragraph 1700) of the most recent *Catechism of the Catholic Church*, for instance, states: "The dignity of the human person is rooted in his creation in the image and likeness of God." Buddhism, clearly, would not wish to make such a claim. Kung notes how leading Buddhists at the

Parliament of the World's Religions felt called upon to protest at calls for "a unity of religions under God," and at references to "God the Almighty" and "God the Creator" in invocations during the proceedings. He suggests, however, that these differences are reconcilable since the Buddhist concepts of "Nirvana, Shunyata and Dharmakaya... fulfil analogous functions to the concept of God" and can be regarded by Christians as "parallel terms for the Absolute."

It may or may not be the case that Mahayana schools recognize a transcendent reality which resembles the Christian concept of God as the Absolute, and there are those better qualified than myself to address such a question. Here I will make only three brief points regarding the problems which arise in regarding these things as the source of human dignity. The first is that since these concepts are understood differently by the main Mahayana schools they are unlikely to provide the common ground which is required as a foundation for human rights.

The second is that it is difficult to see how any of these things can be the source of human dignity in the way that God can, since no school of Buddhism believes that human beings are created by them. The third point is that even if some metaphysical ground of the above kind can be identified in Mahayana Buddhism it still leaves the problem of how human dignity is to be grounded where Theravada Buddhism is concerned. For the Theravada, Nirvana is not a transcendent Absolute, nor do the concepts of "Shunyata and Dharmakaya" have anything like the meaning or significance they attain later. No grounding for human rights can be truly satisfactory, I would suggest, unless it unambiguously forms part of the core teachings of classical Buddhism as a whole.

One suggestion as to how human rights can be grounded in Buddhist doctrine has been made by Kenneth Inada. In a discussion of "The Buddhist Perspective on Human Rights," Inada suggests "there is an intimate and vital relationship of the Buddhist norm or *Dhamma* with that of human rights." He explains the relationship as follows:

Human rights is indeed an important issue, but the Buddhist position is that it is ancillary to the larger or more basic issue of human nature. It can be asserted that the Buddhist sees the concept of human rights as a legal extension of human nature. It is crystallization, indeed formalization, of the mutual respect and concern of all persons, stemming from human nature. Thus, human nature is the ultimate source, the basis from which all other attributes or characteristics are to be delineated. They all have their respective *raison d'etre* in it. They are reflections and even byproducts of it. The reason for assigning human nature the basic position is very simple. It is to give human relations a firm grounding in the truly existential nature of things: that is, the concrete and dynamic relational nature of persons in contact with each other, that which [*sic*] avoids being caught up in rhetorical or legalistic tangles.

Few would disagree with the proposition that human rights are grounded in human nature. Towards the end of the extract, however, Inada seems to move away from his initial suggestion that human nature is the "ultimate source" of human rights towards the view that the ultimate ground is the "dynamic relational nature of persons in contact with each other." In other words, it is in the interrelatedness of persons rather than in the persons themselves that the justification for human rights is to be found. This is confirmed a little later:

Consequently, the Buddhist concern is focused on the experiential process of each individual, a process technically knows as relational origination (*paticca-samuppada*). It is the great doctrine of Buddhism, perhaps the greatest doctrine expounded by the historical Buddha. It means that, in any life-process, the arising of an experiential event is a total, relational affair.

How is the link between dependent-origination and human rights to be forged? The argument reaches its conclusion in the following passage:

Like a storm which consumes everything in its wake, an experience in terms of relational origination involves everything within its purview. Hence, the involvement of elements and, in our case, human beings as entities should not be in terms of mere relationship but rather a creative relationship which originates from the individual locus of existence. In other words, each individual is responsible for the actualization of an "extensive concern" for everything that lies in his or her path of experience. So, we may say that the sum total of the "extensive concerns" can be referred to as a mutually constituted existential realm, and it thereby becomes a fact that there will be mutual respect of fellow beings. It is on this basis that we can speak of the rights of individuals. These rights are actually extensions of human qualities such as security, liberty, and life.

In simple language, the argument seems to be as follows. Human beings, like everything else, are part of the relational process described in the doctrine of dependent-origination; since no-one exists independently we should look out for one another; looking out for one another means respecting each other's rights; examples of the rights we should respect are security, liberty and life.

Although I have described this as an "argument" it is little more than a series of assertions. Working backwards, it is difficult to know what sense to give the concluding sentence: "These rights are actually extensions of human qualities such as security, liberty and life." It is unclear what is meant by "human qualities" here. In what sense is security a "human quality" (perhaps a "need")? Why is life described as a "quality" of a human being? Even granted that these things are "human qualities," what does it mean to say that rights are extensions of "human qualities"? In the first extract quoted above, Inada suggests that "the Buddhist sees the concept of human rights as a legal extension of human nature." What is left unexplained, however, is how human nature (or "human qualities") becomes legal rights.

Do all "human qualities" extend into rights or only some? If so, which and why? Finally, if "human qualities" are what give rise to rights, why invoke the doctrine of dependent-origination? The derivation of human rights from the doctrine of dependent-origination is a conjuring trick. From the premise that we live in "a mutually constituted existential realm" (we all live together) it has "thereby become a fact" that there will be "mutual respect of fellow beings." In the twinkling of an eye, values have appeared from facts like a rabbit out of a hat. However, the fact that human beings live in relationship with one another is not a moral argument about how they ought to behave. By itself it offers no reason why a person should not routinely abuse the rights of others. Inada's suggestion that human rights can be grounded in the doctrine of dependent- origination turns out to be little more than a recommendation that people should be nice to one another on the ground that we are "all in this together."

The approach adopted by Perera is rather different. Perera's main concern is to demonstrate that the articles of the Universal Declaration are adumbrated in early Buddhist teachings, rather than explore their philosophical foundations. He acknowledges that "Buddhism credits the human personality with a dignity and moral responsibility" but does not explain fully whence this arises or how it provides a foundation for human rights. In a number of places he suggests certain possibilities regarding the source of human dignity, not all of which seem to be compatible. At one point he defines "the ethical assumption on which the Buddhist concept of human rights is founded" as the "fundamental consideration that all life has a desire to safeguard itself and to make itself comfortable and happy."

Basing rights on desires, however, is problematic. One reason is that certain people, for example those who seek to end their lives through suicide, seem to lack the desire in question. Nor is difficult to conceive of a justification for human rights abuses along the lines that the victims "no longer cared what happened to them." If they themselves had no interest in their future, whose rights would have, been violated? A deeper problem is that the mere existence of desires establishes nothing from a moral point of view. Desires are many and varied and can be met in manifold ways. Moral questions arise both at the level of whether a desire should be met and how it should be met. The identification of a desire may be a starting point for moral reflection, but it is certainly not its end.

On the preceding page Perera suggests an alternative foundation for human rights, one which links it to human dignity. He writes: "Buddhism posits, as Jean Jaques Rousseau did much later, that the essence of human dignity lies in the assumption of man's responsibility for his own governance." No Buddhist sources are cited in support of this claim, and I believe it is unlikely that Buddhism would wish to link human dignity quite so closely to politics. Perhaps if this suggestion were developed a little further it would make reference to underlying human capacities such as reason and autonomy which enable men to constitute themselves into orderly societies, and then point to these as the underlying source of human dignity.

While political institutions may be produced through the exercise of distinctively human capacities, however, it is unlikely that Buddhism would locate "the essence of human dignity" in their creation. According to the *Aggannasutta*, the evolution of political societies is the consequence of depravity and decline, which makes them a dubious testament to human dignity. Where then, should the foundations for a Buddhist doctrine of human rights be sought?

The proper ground for a doctrine of human rights, I suggest, lies elsewhere than in the doctrine of dependent-origination, as suggested by Inada, or in either the desire for self- preservation or the acceptance of responsibility for self-government, as proposed by Perera. Perera, in fact, comes closest to what in my view is the true source of human rights in Buddhism in his commentary on Article 1. In discussing the first sentence of the Article ("All human beings are born free and equal in dignity and rights") he comments that "Buddhahood itself is within the reach of all human beings... and if all could attain Buddhahood what greater equality in dignity and rights can there be?" To focus attention upon the goal, I believe, is more promising than any of the other approaches considered thus far. Perera seems to grasp its significance in a remark towards the end of his commentary on Article 1. He writes:

> It is from the point of view of its goal that Buddhism evaluates all action. Hence Buddhist thought is in accord with this and other Articles in the Universal Declaration of Human Rights to the extent to which they facilitate the advancement of human beings towards the Buddhist goal.

I believe the above statement provides the key to understanding human rights from a Buddhist perspective. What is missing in Perera's commentary, however, is the explicit linkage between the goal and human dignity, and it is this which I will now try to establish. What I will suggest in general is that the source of human dignity should be sought not in the analysis of the human condition provided by the first and second noble truths (the area where Buddhist scholarship has myopically focused its attention) but in the evaluation of human good provided by the third and fourth. Human rights cannot be derived from any factual non-evaluative analysis of human nature, whether in terms of its psycho-physical constitution (the five "aggregates" which lack a self), its biological nature (needs, urges, drives), or the deep structure of interdependency (*paticca-samupada*).

Instead, the most promising approach will be one which locates human rights and dignity within a comprehensive account of human goodness, and which sees basic rights and freedoms as integrally related to human flourishing and self-realization. This is because the source of human dignity in Buddhism lies nowhere else than in the literally infinite capacity of human nature for participation in goodness. The connection between human rights and human good can be illustrated by asking what the various declarations on human rights see to secure.

Documents which speak of human rights commonly announce a list of specific rights and freedoms and proclaim them to be inviolable. The rights proclaimed by the Universal

Declaration include the right to life, liberty, security of person, equality before the law, privacy, marriage and protection of family life, social security, participation in government, work, protection against unemployment, rest and leisure, a minimum standard of living, and enjoyment of the arts. The exercise of these rights is subject only to such general limitations as are necessary to secure due recognition and respect for the rights and freedoms of others and the requirements of morality, public order and general welfare (Article 29.2).

Otherwise, the rights are expressed in categorical forms such as "Everyone has..." and "No-one shall..." For example, Article 3: "Everyone has the right to life, liberty and security of person." And Article 4: "No one shall be held in slavery or servitude; slavery and the slave trade shall be prohibited in all their forms." The document thus understands the rights it proclaims as both "universal" and exceptionless. Using the terminology introduced earlier it can be seen that some of these rights are claim rights while others are liberty rights. Article 2 confirms this when it speaks of an entitlement to both the "rights and freedoms set forth in this Declaration."

What do these rights and freedoms amount to? It might be said that they map the parameters of human "good-in-community." In other words, these rights and freedoms are what is required if human beings are to lead fulfilled lives in society. Article 29.1 recognizes this when it observes "Everyone has duties to the community in which alone the free and full development of his personality is possible." In the absence of human rights the scope for human development and fulfillment through social interaction is drastically reduced. The rights specified define and facilitate aspects of human fulfillment. The right to life is clearly fundamental since it is the condition for the enjoyment of all other rights and freedoms.

The right to "liberty and security of person" (Article 3) is also basic to any understanding of human good. Without these minimum conditions the scope and opportunity for human fulfillment would be intolerably restricted. The same would apply in the case of slavery (Article 4), torture (Article 5), and the denial of rights before the law (Article 6). It can also be seen that many of the detailed rights identified are actually derived from more fundamental ones. Article 3, for example, "No one shall be held in slavery," is clearly implied in Article 2, "Everyone has the right to... liberty." It might thus be said that many of the thirty articles articulate the practical implications of a relatively small number of fundamental rights and freedoms which are the basis of the common good.

It may be noted that the Universal Declaration itself and modern charters like it do not offer a comprehensive vision of human good. This is not intended as a criticism, for the purpose of such charters is to secure only what might be termed the "minimum conditions" for human flourishing in a pluralistic milieu. The task of articulating a comprehensive vision of what is ultimately valuable in human life and how it is to be attained falls to the competing theories of human good found in religions, philosophies and ideologies. Buddhism provides one view of human nature and its fulfillment, Christianity another, secular philosophies a third.

To pursue any of these different paths, however, requires the substructure known as "human rights," a complex of fundamental rights and liberties which are the preconditions for the realization of the particular opportunities made available by the competing ideologies. If the aim of human rights declarations is understood in the way outlined above then human rights is fundamentally a moral issue. Where there is no right to life, liberty and security of person, and where torture is routine, the opportunities for the realization of human good are greatly reduced. Freedom of religion (Article 18), for example, is vital to the Buddhist vision of individual and social good, and the consequences of the loss of these rights are all too obvious in Tibet. Human rights is thus an area in which religions have a legitimate and vital stake, and there is every reason why it would be proper for Buddhism both to endorse the Universal Declaration and call upon others to respect and implement it.

If religions have a legitimate stake in human rights, we might expect to find many of the rights and liberties spelled out in human rights charters present in either an express or implied form in their moral teachings. These typically include commandments or precepts forbidding killing, stealing, adultery, and lying, as do the first four of the Five Precepts. These evils are prohibited because it is immediately apparent that they are antithetical to human flourishing-in-community. The rationale for these prohibitions, I suggest, coincides to a large extent with that of the various human rights manifestos.

These manifestos, indeed, may be regarded as a translation of religious precepts into the language of rights. The process of casuistry can be seen at work in both. Just as a limited number of moral precepts can be expanded to meet the needs of different social situations (many of the extensive Vinaya rules, for example, have their source in a handful of moral precepts), so the many articles in human rights charters are extrapolated from a comparatively small number of basic rights and freedoms.

It must be admitted there are grounds for skepticism towards the parallel which has just been suggested since it cannot be denied that the Buddhist precepts look and sound very different from contemporary declarations on human rights. The Buddhist precepts make no reference to "rights" at all, and are couched instead in the form of undertakings. Let us examine what these undertakings involve. On the basis of our earlier analysis it would seem that "taking the precepts" in Buddhism is actually the formal acknowledgment of a subsisting duty, a duty which arises from Dharma. The person who takes the precepts is saying in effect "I hereby recognize my Dharmic duty not to do x, y, and z."

Since duties have their correlative in rights, however, rights must also be implicit in the good the precepts seek to promote. We saw earlier that rights provide a way of talking about what is just and unjust from a special angle. We noted further that a person who has right has a benefit, a benefit which can be described as either a claim or a liberty. In the context of the precepts, then, the right-holder is the one who suffers from the breach of Dharmic duty when the precepts are broken. In the case of the first precept this would be the person who was unjustly killed. The right the victim has may therefore be defined as a negative claim-right upon the aggressor, namely the right not to be killed. In simple terms we might say that the victim has a right to life which the aggressor has a duty to respect.

That the translation between precepts and rights is accurate, and that the agreement between the two formulations is more than superficial or accidental, is supported by the authenticity with which the Dalai Lama was able to affirm the *Global Ethic*. Kuschel comments as follows:

Something else seems decisive to me: authenticity and humanity. The reason why the Dalai Lama's speech was so convincing, and indeed seized people's hearts, so that it was often interrupted by spontaneous applause, was that this man simply wanted to be an 'authentic Buddhist'. His plea for mutual respect, dialogue and collaboration, for understanding between peoples and respect for creation, was not an adaptation to Christian or Western values, but came from the depths of his own Buddhist spirituality.

Further evidence of the linkage between the Buddhist precepts and social justice is found in the Theravada tradition. Writing on the theme of "Justice in Buddhism" Vajiragnana states:

Man is responsible for society. It is he who makes it good or bad through his own actions. Buddhism, therefore, advocates a five-fold disciplinary code for man's training in order to maintain justice in society... These five... precepts are extremely important fundamental principles for promoting and perpetuating human welfare, peace and justice.

I suggest, then, that the apparent differences between the moral teachings of Buddhism and human rights charters are one of form rather than substance. Human rights can be extrapolated from Buddhist moral teachings in the manner described above using the logic of moral relationships to illumine what is due under Dharma. A direct translation of the first four precepts yields a right to life, a right not to have one's property stolen, a right to fidelity in marriage, and a right not to be lied to. Many other human rights, such as the rights to liberty and security can either be deduced from or are extant within the general corpus of Buddhist moral teachings. A right not to be held in slavery, for example, is implicit in the canonical prohibition on trade in living beings.

These rights are the extrapolation of what is due under Dharma; they have not been "imported" into Buddhism but were implicitly present. If modern conceptions of human rights and Buddhist moral teachings are related in the way I have suggested, certain conclusions follow for our understanding of the Buddhist precepts. If there are universal and exceptionless rights, as human rights charters affirm, there must be universal and exceptionless duties. If human rights such as a "right to life" (by which I understand a right not to have one's life taken unjustly) are exceptionless, there must also be an exceptionless duty to abstain from unjustly depriving a human being of life. The First Precept in Buddhism, therefore, should be understood as an exceptionless duty or moral absolute.

Is this reverse translation, from absolute human rights to absolute moral duties, supported by textual sources? There is every reason to think that it is. Such an understanding of the precept is clearly evident in classical Buddhism, which tirelessly reiterates the principle of the sanctity of life found in the pan- Indian teachings on non-harming (*ahisa*), and which gives no reason to suppose that its moral precepts are to be understood as anything other than exceptionless norms. If, on the other hand, it is thought that the precepts are *not* to be understood as moral absolutes, then it is difficult to see what justification there can be for Buddhists to hold that there are universal and exceptionless human rights. It would be inconsistent to affirm the latter but deny the former.

The above account of human rights in Buddhism has been given entirely within the context of an understanding of human good which has its apex in nirvana-in-this-life. Reference to the transcendent dimension of human good and its ground has been avoided for several reasons. The first is that no reference need be made to transcendent realities in order to ground human rights. That this is so can be seen from the absence of any reference to such realities in contemporary human rights charters, and the fact that many atheists are vigorous defenders of human rights.

Where Buddhism is concerned, the vision of human good set out in the third and fourth noble truths provides the necessary basis for a doctrine of human rights. Human rights turn out in essence to be what justice requires if human good is to be fulfilled. The second reason for avoiding reference to transcendent realities is that my aim has been to suggest a basis for human rights acceptable to classical Buddhism as a whole. Since all schools of Buddhism affirm the third and fourth noble truths and the vision of human good they proclaim, the required common ground for a pan-Buddhist doctrine of human rights is present.

The above should not be read as a denial that there can be a transcendent ground for human rights in Buddhism. Because the transcendent dimension of human good is left obscure in Buddhist teachings, however, the transcendent ground for human rights is also obscure. In terms of the account given here, the transcendent ground for human rights would be post-mortem nirvana, not in the sense of an absolute reality (as suggested by Kung) but as the universalization of human good on a transcendent plane. The twin axes of human good are knowledge (*prajna*) and moral concern (*karuna*) and on the graph defined by these axes can be plotted the soteriological coordinates of any individual.

Through participation in these twin categories of good, human nature progressively transcends its limitations and becomes saturated with nirvanic goodness. Eventually, in post-mortem nirvaa.na, this goodness attains a magnitude which can no longer be charted. If a transcendent ground for human rights is desired, this is where it should be sought. To sum up: it is legitimate to speak of both rights and human rights in

Buddhism. Modern doctrines of human rights are in harmony with the moral values of classical Buddhism in that they are an explication of what is "due" under Dharma.

The modern idea of human rights has a distinctive cultural origin, but its underlying preoccupation with human good makes it at bottom a moral issue in which Buddhism and other religions have a legitimate stake. The *Global Ethic* endorses the view that the principles it sets forth on human rights are neither new nor "Western" when it states: "We affirm that a common set of core values is found in the teachings of the religions, and that these form the basis of a global ethic." A final thought. Above I have spoken only of human rights, and in the context of Buddhism this perspective may be unduly narrow in that it seems to preclude the universe of sentient non-human beings from any entitlement to rights.

Buddhists may feel, therefore, that it is less prejudicial in discussions of this kind to revert to the older terminology of "natural" rights. Whether or not animals have rights, and whether these are the same rights as human beings, is a matter which requires separate discussion. If human rights flow from human nature, as suggested, it may be that rights of different kinds flow from natures of different kinds.

Such would seem to be the understanding of classical Buddhism. On 10 May 1998 Buddhists all over the world celebrate Visakha-puja (Vesakh). It is the most important day of observance for Buddhists, the day we commemorate the Lord Buddha's Birth, Awakening, and Parinibbana. On this day Buddhists remind themselves of their undertaking to follow Buddha's path towards Enlightenment. The International Network of Engaged Buddhists (INEB) would like to take the opportunity of this holy day to invite everyone to work towards a culture and global implementation of Non-violence and Human Rights.

BUDDHISM AND HUMAN RIGHTS

Notions of rights derive from ethical principles. There is a clear convergence between Buddhist ethics and modern discussions on human rights, particularly in the common focus on responsibility and indivisibility/interdependence. The non-dual understanding of Buddhism gives rise to an ethics of inter-responsibility, or *Bodhicitta* - what His Holiness the Dalai Lama calls Universal Responsibility. In the Theravada we speak of Samma-sankappa or Right Thought, which leads to Bodhi, the Awakened Mind. This principle is expressed in everyday terms by the teaching of loving-kindness, non-violence, compassion, and particular responsibilities. For monks and nuns these are set down in the rule or Vinaya; for lay people in the Sigalovada Sutta and for rulers in the Dasaraja *Dhamma*.

All human beings, according to Buddhism, are equal, and each has the potential to realize the truth by his or her own will and endeavour, and can help others to realize it. Buddhist concepts recognize the inherent dignity and the equal and inalienable rights of all human beings. The teaching of the Buddha holds that all human beings are endowed with reason and conscience. It recommends a Universal spirit of brotherhood and sisterhood. Buddhist theory holds that the "three poisons" of hatred, greed and delusion are at the root of violence in the world, and that the solution is for us to see so deeply into these factors that we are no longer dominated by them.

In the early, organic, societies the Buddha was addressing, these specific responsibilities were assumed to be adequate guidelines for human behaviour, with no need to identify the corresponding rights. In modern, fragmented societies, however, where the fulfillment of responsibilities cannot be guaranteed by the immediate community, these guidelines or skillful means (*upaya*) have been supplemented by corresponding rights. These are specified and protected by States and International Organisations. In large part these bodies derive their legitimacy from their promotion and protection of human rights. A State which does not guarantee the enjoyment of human rights by its people loses its claim to legitimacy.

Buddhism is widely regarded as the most tolerant of all religious traditions. However, Buddhist countries like Sri Lanka, Burma, and Cambodia have seen some of the highest levels of religious and ethnic intolerance in the world, with Buddhists among the main perpetrators. In other places it is Buddhists who are persecuted by the State, which fears the influence of Buddhism on the people. In Burma, Tibet and Vietnam, for instance, thousands of Buddhists (especially monks and nuns) have been persecuted, with well-documented instances of torture and executions. In Tibet most of the country's monasteries have been demolished. The depiction of rights as simply a Western invention fails to understand the relationship of rights to responsibilities and ethical norms.

The central values of all societies are very much the same. All ethical systems encourage people to respect each other, and discourage killing, violence and so on. Rights are skillful means designed to assist the implementation of these ethics. Human Rights discourse has moved on during the past 50 years and has expanded and enriched the somewhat individualistic principles set out in the 'Universal Declaration of Human Rights' which was adopted and proclaimed by the General Assembly of the United Nations on 10 December 1948.

The dialectic of universalism and cultural relativism, for instance, is an immensely creative process as well as a cause for countless conflicts. The work since 1982 on the rights of indigenous peoples - group rights - is another important development. The cultural, social and political development of a nation is a dynamic process. The orientation of the process should not only be based in our own roots and traditions, but must also be shaped by innovative new ideas. Cultural diversity is a factor that enriches the modern approach to human rights, rather than hindering the universal respect for and observance of human rights.

BUDDHIST COMMITMENT TO HUMAN RIGTHS

As H.H. the Dalai Lama stressed: "I truly believe that individuals can make a difference in society. Since periods of great change such as the present one come so rarely in human history, it is up to each of us to make the best use of our time to help create a happier world".

In this spirit:

1. We call on all Buddhists to look into themselves, their institutions and teachings, in order to renew Buddhism as a way of peace and non-violence, not only in individual, but also in collective practice and theory. Buddhists must adopt an active approach to reducing suffering. This can be done by working for the active implementation of peace and human rights, including economic, social and cultural rights. The activities related to the 50th anniversary of the Universal Declaration of Human Rights offer an excellent opportunity to renew and expand our efforts in this field.
2. We request all Buddhists to show solidarity with those who are persecuted by their governments and to stand up for their human rights.
3. We urge all Governments, especially in Burma, Viêt Nam and the Peoples Republic of China, to stop immediately the severe human rights violations against Buddhists and others and to ensure that human rights become a reality in their countries.
4. We invite all Buddhist communities and organizations to include human rights education in their programs and to distribute information and educational materials.
5. We encourage Buddhist leaders to give importance to the human rights issues in their communities and countries.
6. We support the appeal of H.H. the Dalai Lama and other Nobel Peace Prize laureates that the UN should declare the years 2000-2010 the "Decade for a Culture of Non-Violence".

"It is important for those of us who love freedom to realize that love of freedom alone is not enough; that freedom may well depend on our capacity to realize a multiplicity of conflicting values simultaneously, in a socio-economic and political setting that makes this possible, and that the singleminded pursuit of a single value, or a single goal, is the greatest enemy of freedom This struggle (for freedom) requires from... the single individuals who are not only willing to stand up for their own rights, but also for those of their neighbors, a great deal of courage and tenacity, but above all the intelligence in knowing how to wage the struggle for freedom without destroying it in the process... " - Soedjatmoko, "Development and Freedom" Ishizaka Memorial Lectures, 1979.

The ideal of human rights, like that of democracy and many other sociopolitical nomenclatures, has now become a beleaguered concept. It is subject to conflicting interpretations and practices that have brought about confrontations around the world. The phenomenon is one of those human ironies that seem to be much taken for granted and, worse still, with resignation. It has become even an acceptable rule of thumb for one-individual, class, or nation-to preach human rights and yet act against human rights and this out of strong but rigid and sectarian sense of self-righteousness on all sides. Underlying such contradictions in human behaviour are worldwide conflicting ideologies and class and national interests.

Their threat to human life and dignity cannot be overemphasized. It looms large in the forms of economic and political rivalries and oppressions, militarism and armaments, all of which put humanity as a whole in jeopardy. The world today is indeed at a most critical crossroad. Soedjatmoko's words quoted above should very well serve as an ominous warning to all those-earnestly-perhaps too earnestly-concerned with the issues of human rights. They are articulated at a time that is in great need of a hard rethinking, which is already long overdue, on the concept of human rights itself. The issues and contradictions cannot be settled by a mere compiling of lists, however comprehensive, of human rights, such as illustrated in the Universal Declaration of Human Rights, the International Covenants of Economic and Social Cultural Rights, and of Civil and political Rights.

While all these may be said to have been motivated by well-meaning efforts to accommodate those specific issues and problems that did empirically arise, they seem to be lacking, in some kind of a holistic worldview that needs to be investigated.. In the face of hard reality of today's power politics, within and among nations, it would of course take a long, long time indeed for the major conflicts of views and interests to possibly come to terms with one another. But before that comes about at all and prior to any meaningful social and institutional innovations, there must be a starting point, that is to say, a fresh look at the moral and spiritual basis of the principle and practice of human rights.

Perhaps it is no mere coincidence that serious doubts have now been raised, both in the East and the West, as to the validity of the liberal conception of human rights. C.G. Weeramantry, former Supreme Court judge of Sri Lanka, is one notable example, who touching on the problem of "the inappropriateness of Western concepts," sees the issue of inequality most relevant to the Third World's real needs and problems, and thus stresses the need to "seek a view of equality which means more than the perpetuation of inequality-a view of equality more substantial than one which means the equal right to remain unequal."

This incidentally, only reminds one of what John Strachey some time ago observed in Capitalism, the historical moving force of liberalism, "innate tendency to extreme and ever growing inequality.'' Also Fauad Ajami of Princeton University, while questioning the impartiality or "completeness" of the concept of liberalism, strongly and significantly, points to the dire need for "the politics of love and compassion" as against the conventional but now discredited politics of "realism". Taken together with Soedjatmoko's line of approach to the problem of development and freedom, all this really strikes one with a deep sense of relief and intellectual uplift.

It certainly is not just an exercise in futility to think and act in terms of "the politics of love and compassion", and "the intelligence in knowing how to wage the struggle for freedom without destroying it in the process". By the standard of today's politics of realism so-called, one can imagine how revolutionary it would be if ever love, compassion, and intelligence come to serve as a guide to social and political behaviour and action. But this is the crux of the whole matter. The sad truth is that human mind is not always filled with love, compassion, and intelligence. Whether one likes it or not, the mind always has priority over the matter in the sense that all human behaviour and action are basically derived from it, as the Buddha is so fully aware in His moral precept: "Cease to do evil; Learn to do Good, Cleanse your own heart; This is the teaching of the Buddhas."

And this is because:

"All that we are is the result of what we have thought: it is founded on our thoughts and made up of our thoughts. If a man speaks or acts with and evil thought, suffering follows him as a wheel follows the hoof of the beast that draws the cart "... If a man speaks or acts with a good thought, happiness follows him like a shadow that never leaves him."

So also with the concept and practice of human rights, which is no less susceptible to do good or to do evil according to the states of mind on the part of particular individuals, classes, and nations. And, as with the human heart, the concept of human rights no less needs to be cleansed of all the parochialism and sectarian prejudices so as to be able to cease to do evil and to learn to do good - the most basic problem with which Buddhism is concerned.

Contrary to what the title of this chapter might suggest, there is no need at all to search for a place of human rights in the Buddhist tradition. Freedom is indeed the essence of Buddhism, as will be seen. Neither is Buddhism to be presented here as another alternative ism or supplement to the current schools of thought-Liberalism, Socialism, and even Fascism in one form or another-all engaged in the crude struggle in the name of democracy and human rights. To do so would merely add fuel to the conflicts and contradictions already vastly harmful to the cause of human rights.

But amidst the uncompromising ideologies and forces, Buddhism could serve positive purposes as conceptual synthesis drawing upon all the positive values of both libertarian and egalitarian traditions, with moral and spiritual contribution of its own. This, in Christmas Humphreys' view, "is no weak compromise, but a sweet reasonableness which avoids fanaticism and laziness with equal care, and marches onward without that haste which brings its own reaction, but without ceasing." In this sense, too, Buddhism is to be presented not so much in terms of religious doctrine, but rather as a science of living whereby one can learn to live one's life with objective understanding and the intelligence in knowing.

ON SOCIAL PURPOSE AND PROGRESS

However, since Buddhism, even as a science of living tends more often than not to be popularly prescribed and practiced with the sole concern for one's own salvation or Nirvana, a preliminary explanation seems to be well in order here by way of trying to examine and fathom the social and cultural meaning of Buddhism. This is necessary for one to get a true perspective on Buddhist thought. It goes without saying of course that this writer can claim to be no authority on this great religion. Systematic and elaborate treatment of specific points must be referred to scholarly sources elsewhere.

As a student of social and political affairs, the author ventures the task, through somewhat rudimentary readings and reflection on the subject mainly out of a growing concern for today's practical problems, especially those problems associated with social change. Change, whether one likes it or not, is part and parcel of our life. Life itself breeds suffering and therefore problems the critical point is whether change could be made for better or for worse, for more or less suffering. Historically, religion could play a very crucial role in this respect. Christianity notably demonstrated its positive and innovative power in the great reformation movement. If we are to believe in social progress, to be later touched upon, as the criterion of human evolution leading towards a better society and better life with freedom and justice.

Buddhism, to this writer's mind, truly points the way. Setting out as a social reform movement, it has its own dynamic attitude towards life and great innovative potential. On the other hand, Buddhism, as an institution, could also be vulnerable, again like Christianity in the middle Ages, to a relapse into a mere dogma incapable of living up to the new challenge, that is, the crisis of change. There will then be a danger in that it would tend to serve the status quo and the powers that be, instead of humankind which is the central purpose of Buddhism. Then, again, there will be further danger in that it could even degenerate into becoming a coercive and oppressive instrument, instead of promoting the Path towards human liberation which is the ultimate goal of Buddhism. If such is the case, Buddhism, like any other religion, would need its own transformation to be of true service to mankind.

Many will no doubt frown upon this sort of concern. But the observation, to be sure, is in full agreement with a good Buddhist's own norm of non-neglect of mindfulness, and seems not too far off the mark in view of the actual situation nowadays. Such a gap between ideal and practice, if left unbridgeable, cannot but help bring about disintegrative effects on social and human life. Furthermore, we are living in a world of rapid technological change and increasingly complex social and economic relations. In this new environmental context, it is essential to develop a more positive social orientation of Buddhism and translate this into practice. We have been taught enough about how to behave ourselves morally, There is of course no denying the fact that morally right acts and conduct are desirable and beneficial.

On closer examination, however, there is a vast difference between doing morally good things from an individual and personal standpoint, and from a social perspective. The two are to an extent interacting. But if, as has been observed, in the course or historical development, Theravada Buddhism under which many including this writer are living, has become too oriented towards individuals' personal definition of man's ideal rather than socio-cultural preference as stressed in Mahayana, then one needs to rise above the past and superficial division in order to search out the essence and the true purpose. In any case, fortunately, the distinction here is more apparent than real.

In truth, concern for social and ethical value is fundamental throughout the Buddha's teaching, as Phra Srivisudhimolee (presently Phra Rajavoramunee) asserts: "Buddha-*Dhamma* (The Buddha's Teaching) looks into man's inner life in relation to the external, i.e., social, value as well, and takes these twin values as interrelated, inseparable and being in such harmony as to be one and the same." (Phra Srivisudhimolee, Buddha Dharma) (translated from the Thai)

Finally in the field of social studies such as human rights and perhaps many others, one can also find in the Buddhist system of thought a most objective and relevant conceptual framework that, regrettably, tends to be overlooked. It starts from a plain and simple premise as a pragmatic approach close to everyday problems and presents an intellectual outlook that could serve as an empirical basis for rational inquiries. In the words of another leading Buddhist scholar:

"Man has been the central problem of Buddhist philosophy. Metaphysical speculation concerning problems not related to human activities and the attainment of Enlightenment-such as whether the world is infinite or finite, whether the soul and the body are identical or different from each other or whether a perfect person exists after his death-is discouraged. Admitting the transitoriness of everything, the Buddha did not want to assume the existence of any metaphysical substance. This attitude was logically derived from his fundamental standpoint. The Buddha reduced things, substances and souls, to forces, movements, functions, and processes, and adopted a dynamic conception of reality. Life is nothing but a series of manifestations of generation and extinction. It is a stream of becoming and change."

Religion has come into existence as a result of the human struggle to solve the basic problem of life that is, suffering. "If there were no birth, decay and death," the Buddha says, "the Enlightened One would not have arisen in the world and his teachings would not have spread abroad." He also proclaims again and again that a Buddha arises in the world for the good and happiness of the many, out of compassion for the world, for the benefit, for the advantage and for the happiness of gods and men. This is the same with the preaching of the Dharma, the lastingness of his Dispensation and the solidarity of the *Sangha*. Thus, just as the worth of medicine lies in the cure of the disease, so the value of religion is ascertained by its efficacy in the alleviation and elimination of human suffering.

Broadly speaking, when a religion helps people to live together in peace and helps the individual to be at peace with him, it can be said to have fulfilled its functions. However, that is still a vague picture of religious functioning. The picture will become clearer only when we look deeper to see what outlook the religion has on man and suffering and how it functions to relieve or get rid of that suffering. All men are born equal, but only in some respects. In many other respects, no man is born equal to any other man. Man's mistreatment of, or wrong attitude towards, this equality and inequality has given rise to all kinds of problems, from the social to the spiritual ones.

According to Buddhism, all men are equal in that they are all subject to the same law of nature. All are subject to birth, old age and death. The law of Karma is binding on everyone. Everyone reaps what he sows and the world keeps going on after the Karma activities contributed to by everyone. Man is the best of trainable or educable beings. He has the potentiality of self-perfection by which a life of freedom and happiness can be realized. In order to attain this perfection, man has to develop himself physically, morally, psycho-spiritually and intellectually. Right development of oneself leads naturally and by necessity to self-perfection. This is the law of the Dharma of which the law of Karma in turn forms a part and wherefrom the latter is derived. By this law, it entails that every individual should be let free, if not provided with the opportunity, to develop himself so that his potentiality can unfold itself and work its way towards perfection.

Ideally, all conditions, both social and natural, should be made favourable to and all kinds of help should be provided for the self-development of every individual. As Buddhism fundamentally believes in this potentiality of man and sets the perfection of freedom, and happiness as the goal to be achieved by every individual, freedom of self-development and the encouragement of opportunities for it have become a foundation of the Buddhist ethics. This is to say, in other words; that every individual has the right to self-development. Hence, the Buddha's repeated teachings on the refutation of the caste system of the Hindus, and his stress on the equality of men of all classes before the law of Karma and, ultimately, under the law of the Dharma. The Buddha's standpoint is that good life is open to everyone and the highest truth is the common treasure claimable by everybody; there can be no restriction because of castes or classes. Moreover, he teaches the goal of freedom that is to be reached by means of freedom and a happy means that leads to a happy end.

If the right to self-development is denied or restricted, it is right to struggle for it. If help and favourable conditions are not provided for it, it is good to make exertion towards the encouragement of the same. However, there are some words of caution. That every human being has the right to self-development and, thus to freedom and happiness is an imperative of the ethics which is based on the law of the Dharma. This law enjoins, as it were, that let a man sincerely do what is right and the process will work out of itself a corresponding result. This means that one should act out of wholesome motivation. If he is to struggle, he should do it for the sake of the Dharma, that is, for the good and for the righteous, out of love and compassion, not for personal gains or from any selfish motives, not out of greed or hatred.

Only in this way can man attain to his righteous goal, achieving freedom without frustrating the freedom of his fellow-beings and winning happiness without inflicting more suffering on the world. Otherwise, the struggle to secure the human rights for some can become an act of appropriating the human rights of others. By knowledge of, and practice in accordance with, the law of the Dharma, man can fulfill the basic requirement of, to use the words of a quote, "the intelligence in knowing how to wage the struggle for freedom without destroying it in the process." In the present study, the issue of human rights is dealt with in the context of, and as subordinate to, that of freedom.

Professor Saneh Chamarik, its author, has delineated how important the place of freedom is in Buddhism and how the path to freedom pointed out by the Buddha can lead, as a corollary, to the right solution of the problem of human rights, avoiding the dead end of the mere material interests and transcending the confines of the craving self. The work is an example of how Buddhism can be presented in such a way as to speak meaningfully to the world of today. Such pioneer works are needed in the various fields of human activities and academic disciplines through which Buddhism can prove it the real guide and the true help in the right solution of the problems or in the eradication of suffering of the modern man.

4

Buddhism and Animal Rights

Unlike the Judeo-Christian tradition, Buddhism affirms the unity of all living beings, all equally posses the Buddha-nature, and all have the potential to become Buddhas, that is, to become fully and perfectly enlightened. Among the sentient, there are no second-class citizens. According to Buddhist teaching, human beings do not have a privileged, special place above and beyond that of the rest of life. The world is not a creation specifically for the benefit and pleasure of human beings. Furthermore, in some circumstances according with their karma, humans can be reborn as humans and animals can be reborn as humans. In Buddhism the most fundamental guideline for conduct is ahimsa-the prohibition against the bringing of harm and/or death to any living being.

Why should one refrain from killing? It is because all beings have lives; they love their lives and do not wish to die. Even one of the smallest creatures, the mosquito, when it approaches to bite you, will fly away if you make the slightest motion. Why does it fly away? Because it fears death. It figures that if it drinks your blood, you will take its life.... We should nurture compassionate thought. Since we wish to live, we should not kill any other living being. Furthermore, the karma of killing is understood as the root of all suffering and the fundamental cause of sickness and war, and the forces of killing are explicitly identified with the demonic. The highest and most universal ideal of Buddhism is to work unceasingly for permanent end to the suffering of all living beings, not just humans.

EXAMPLES

The Buddha in a former life was reborn as a Deer-king. He offers to substitute his own life for that of a pregnant doe who is about to give birth. In another previous lifetime, the Buddha sacrificed his own life to feed a starving tiger and her two cubs, which were trapped in the snow. He reasoned that it would be better to save three lives than to merely preserve his own. It is better to lose one's own life than to kill another being.

THE RELATIVE VALUE OF ONE'S LIFE AND THE PRECEPTS

Question: If it is not a case of my being attacked, then the thought of killing may be put to rest. If, however, one has been attacked, overcome by force, and is then being coerced [by imminent peril], what should one do then?

Reply: One should weigh the relative gravity [of the alternatives]. If someone is about to take one's life, one [should] first consider whether the benefit from preserving the precept is more important or whether the benefit from preserving one's physical life is more important and whether breaking the precept constitutes a loss or whether physical demise constitutes a loss.

After having reflected in this manner one realizes that maintaining the precept is momentous and that preserving one's physical life is [relatively] unimportant. If in avoiding [such peril] one is only [able to succeed in] preserving one's body, [then] what [advantage]is gained with the body? This body is the swamp of senescence, disease and death. It will inevitably deteriorate and decay. If, [however], for the sake of upholding the precept, one loses one's body, the benefit of it is extremely consequential.

Furthermore, one [should] consider [thus]: "From the past on up to the present, I have lost my life an innumerable number of times. At times I have incarnated as a malevolent brigand, as a bird, or as a beast where I have lived merely for the sake of wealth or profit or all manner of unworthy pursuits. Now I have encountered [a situation where I might perish] on account of preserving the pure precepts. To not spare this body and sacrifice my life to uphold the precepts would be a billion times better than and [in fact] incomparable to safeguarding my body [at the expense of] violating the prohibitions." In this manner one decides that one should foresake the body in order to protect [the integrity] of the pure precepts.

THE BUTCHER'S SON AND THE KILLING PRECEPT

For example, there once was a man who was a srota-aapanna born into the family of a butcher. He was on the threshhold of adulthood. Although he was expected to pursue his household occupation, he was unable to kill animals. His father and mother gave him a knife and a sheep and shut him up in a room, telling him, "If you do not kill the sheep, we will not allow you to come out and see the sun or the moon or to have the food and drink to survive."

The son thought to himself, "If I kill this sheep, then I will [be compelled to] pursue this occupation my entire life. How could I commit this great crime [simply] for the sake of this body?" Then he took up the knife and killed himself. The father and mother opened the door to look. The sheep was standing to one side whereas the son was [laying there], already expired.

At that time, when he killed himself, he was born in the heavens. If one is like this, then this amounts to not sparing [even one's own] life in safeguarding [the integrity of] the pure precepts.

PRACTICES

The Rite of Liberating Living Beings is a Buddhist practice of rescuing animals, birds, fish and so forth that are destined for slaughter or that are permanently caged. They are released to a new physical and spiritual life. The practice exemplifies the fundamental Buddhist teaching of compassion for all living beings. A disciple of the Buddha must maintain a mind of kindness and cultivate the practice of liberating beings. He should reflect thus: 'All male beings have been my father and all females have been my mother. There is not a single being that has not given birth to me during my previous lives; hence all beings of the Six Destinies are my parents.

Therefore, when a person kills and eats any of these beings, he thereby slaughters my parents. Furthermore, he kills a body that was once my own, for all elemental earth and water previously served as part of my body and all elemental fire and wind have served as my basic substance. Therefore, I shall always cultivate the practice of liberating beings and in every life be reborn in the eternally abiding Dharma and teach other to liberate beings as well.' Whenever a *Bodhisattva* sees a person preparing to kill an animal, he should devise a skilful method to rescue and protect it, freeing it from its suffering and difficulties...

In China the Rite of Liberating Living Beings was very popular and has continued to be so to the present day. It also is practiced in the United States at the City of Ten Thousand Buddhas in Mendocino County and at other Buddhist centers.

VEGETARIANISM

All beings-human or beast-

Love life and hate to die.

They fear most the butcher's knife

Which slices and chops them piece-by-piece?

Instead of being cruel and mean,

Why not stop killing and cherish life?

In Buddhism adhering to a completely vegetarian diet is a natural and logical ramification of the moral precept against the taking of life. The *Bodhisattva* Precepts also explicitly forbid the eating of non-vegetarian food. Student: "...when you eat one bowl of rice, you take the life of all the grains of rice, whereas eating meat you take only one animal's life."

The [Venerable] Master [Hua] replied: "On the body of one single animal are a hundred thousand, in fact, several million little organisms. These organisms are fragments of what was once an animal. The soul of a human being at death may split up to become many animals. One person can become about ten animals. That's why animals are so stupid. The soul of an animal can split up and become, in its smallest division, an organism or plant. The feelings which plants have, then, are what separated from the animal's soul when it split up at death. Although the life force of a large number of plants may appear sizable, it is not as great as that of a single animal or a single mouthful of meat. Take, for example, rice: tens of billions of grains of rice do not contain as much life force as a single piece of meat. If you open your Five Eyes you can know this at a glance. If you haven't opened your eyes, no matter how one tries to explain it to you, you won't understand. No matter how it's explained, you won't believe it, because you haven't been a plant!

"Another example is the mosquitoes. The millions of mosquitoes on this mountain may be simply the soul of one person who has been transformed into all those bugs. It is not the case that a single human soul turns into a single mosquito. One person can turn into countless numbers of mosquitoes. At death the nature changes, the soul scatters, and its smallest fragments become plants. Thus, there is a difference between eating plants and eating animals. What is more, plants have very short life-spans. The grass, for example, is born in the spring and dies within months. Animals live a long time. If you don't kill them, they will live for many years. Rice, regardless of conditions, will only live a short time. And so, if you really look into it, there are many factors to consider, and even science hasn't got it all straight."

Mahakashyapa asked the Buddha, "Why is it that the Thus Come One does not allow eating meat?' The Buddha replied, "It is because meat-eating cuts off the seeds of great compassion."

CURRENT ANIMAL RIGHTS ISSUES

Although the following guidelines for working on animal rights issues follow clearly from fundamental Buddhist teachings, they are by no means exclusively Buddhist. My hope for this conference is that many of the participants, regardless of their religious views, will wholeheartedly embrace them in their future work for animal rights.

1. We should reduce the fear, hate, and thoughts of revenge generated by the torturing and killing of animals.
2. We should not be prey to negative emotions or violence. They compound the problem. Real solutions come from changing people's minds rather than from creating confrontation and friction.
3. We should not limit our compassion to the animals and to those of like mind, but extend it to all living beings, even if we feel that some are clearly in the wrong. Compassion should be the basis of all our interactions with others, regardless of their views and actions in the area of animal rights.

What does Buddhism have to say about animal rights? Among the world's hundreds of millions of Buddhists, there is disagreement about this basic issue. I first became interested in Buddhism because two of my favourite restaurants (Buddha's Vegetarian Foods and the Lotus Garden, both on Dundas Street West in Toronto) are Buddhist, and are very careful to serve only vegetarian food with no eggs. In one restaurant I was told that this was necessary because Buddhist monks and nuns eat there. This suggested to me that Buddhism takes the plight of nonhuman animals very seriously indeed. On the other hand, my fiancé and I have several friends who are Buddhist, but continue to eat meat and feel this is consistent with Buddhism.

Do Buddhists, or at least Buddhist nuns and monks, have to be vegetarian? What does Buddhism have to say about our treatment of animals in general? To resolve this controversy, it is necessary, I feel, to return to the Buddhist scriptures and see what (if anything) they have to say about the issue. So far, I have been frustrated in my attempts to purchase my own copy of the Bhuddist Pali scriptures-perhaps because they are eleven times as long as the Bible. The bookstores I have been to all stock large numbers of books about Buddhism, but not the scriptures themselves! These secondary (or worse!) sources about Buddhism shed little light on what the Buddha's own teachings about animals were.

However, I have been able to acquire a copy of an important part of the Pali scriptures, the *Dhammapada*. *Dhamma* (Dharma in Sanskrit), means "law, a moral law, a spiritual law of righteousness, the eternal law of the Universe, Truth;" and *pada* means "foot" or "step." So the *Dhammapada* are the steps we must take to live according to (Buddhist) moral and spiritual laws. According to scholar Juan Mascaró, "that the spirit of the *Dhammapada* is the spirit of Buddha is accepted both by his followers and by scholars." Therefore, it seems reasonable that we can derive at least a first approximation of the Buddhist approach to the question of animal rights from the basic moral foundation laid by Gotama Buddha in the *Dhammapada*.

NOT KILLING AND NOT HURTING

In Buddhism, there are five "precepts," which could be considered to play a similar rôle as the Ten Commandments do for Jews and Christians. These precepts provide moral guidance for lay Buddhists as well as monks and nuns. They are concisely summed up as follows:

He who destroys life, who utters lies, who takes what is not given to him, who goes to the wife of another, who gets drunk with strong drinks-he digs up the very roots of his life.

The injunction against destroying life is known as the First Precept. In addition, the Buddha also tells us not to "hurt" others, for example: He who for the sake of happiness hurts others, who also want happiness, shall not hereafter find happiness.

Probably because not killing and not hurting are so important, Buddha repeatedly asks us not to do either in many places throughout the *Dhammapada*.

The fact that the First Precept and other teachings forbid killing and hurting is not controversial among Buddhists. Where the controversy comes in is the question of whom Buddhists are forbidden to kill or hurt.

THE FIRST PRECEPT AND THE PROHIBITION ON HURTING

Do the First Precept and other passages against hurting protect non-human animals? Perhaps they, like the Judeo-Christian Commandment "Thou shalt not kill," were intended to apply only to humans. This possibility can be ruled out almost immediately, for in the *Dhammapada*, there are numerous explicit injunctions against killing or otherwise hurting "living beings," rather than "persons": But although a man may wear fine clothing, if he lives peacefully; and is good, self-possessed, has faith and is pure; and if he does not hurt any living being, he is a holy Brahmin, a hermit of seclusion, a monk called a Bhikkhu. (*Dhammapada*, 142)

The wise who hurt no living being, and who keep their body under self-control, they go to the immortal Nirvana, where once gone they sorrow no more. (*Dhammapada*, 225)

A man is not a great man because he is a warrior and kills other men; but because he hurts not any living being he in truth is called a great man. (*Dhammapada*, 405)

It seems clear that the Buddha has taken pains to make it clear that the injunction against killing or hurting is not confined to humans, but extends to other "living beings." Then we might wonder who or what are these "living beings"? Some have argued that the protection of "living beings" extends to plants as well as to animals, for they are also alive. If this were the case, then it could be claimed that for a Buddhist, eating a rabbit is no worse than eating a carrot.

Here I am at a disadvantage, as I have not yet learned Pali, nor do I have the scriptures as originally rendered in Pali. However, a beautiful passage suggests that the beings referred to be sentient beings:

All beings tremble before danger, all fear death. When a man considers this, he does not kill or cause to kill.

All beings fear before danger, life is dear to all. When a man considers this, he does not kill or cause to kill. (*Dhammapada*, 129-130.)

Here, the Buddha explains that we should not kill out of consideration for the feelings of fear and the love of life that beings experience. Moreover, he says all beings share these attributes, suggesting that the word which Mascaró has translated as "beings" really means "sentient beings."

Some skeptics may claim that nonhuman animals are not really sentient. However, in another passage, the Buddha alludes to the sentience of fish in a metaphor describing an unquiet mind:

Like a fish which is thrown on dry land, taken from his home in the waters, the mind strives and struggles to get free from the power of Death. (*Dhammapada*, 34.)

This passage suggests that, like the "beings" referred to in *Dhammapada* 130, the fish's life is dear to him-otherwise why would he "strive and struggle to get free from the power of Death" when removed from his aquatic home? If the Buddha believed fish to be sentient, it is highly improbable that he would deny that many of the other animals commonly killed and hurt by humans (e.g. mammals and birds) are not sentient. Therefore, at least fish, birds, and mammals could not be killed or otherwise hurt according to the First Precept and other teachings which protect sentient beings. It is quite possible that the First Precept covers other animals as well.

So why didn't the Buddha come right out and say that "animals" should not be harmed, rather than "living beings"? Perhaps it was because, when and where the Buddha lived, practitioners of other well-known religions such as Jainism were already conscientious about protecting animals and so it would have been obvious to the Buddha's students that not killing "living beings" meant not killing animals. Perhaps there was no word in Pali which would encompass both nonhuman and human animals, so that the term translated as "living beings" was needed to be inclusive. Or perhaps the Buddha wanted us to be more concerned about sentient animals, rather than any nonsentient animals which might exist. Since the Buddha's time, there have been enormous changes in the relationship between human and nonhuman animals. Practices such as vivisection and factory farming would have been unknown to the Buddha, and so of course they are not explicitly mentioned in the *Dhammapada*. Moreover, the *Dhammapada* is very concise, and does not catalogue all the possible misdeeds which could be committed against animals (note that includes humans as well as non humans!)

However, although the myriad harms to animals are not all explicitly mentioned in the *Dhammapada*, we can infer a great deal merely from the First Precept and the teachings against hurting other beings. It is clear that the Buddha does not want us to kill or hurt animals ourselves. Therefore, Buddhists cannot be hunters, fisherpeople, trappers, slaughterhouse workers, vivisectors, etc., nor can we "euthanize" homeless animals in so-called animal "shelters."

What about eating meat? Some might claim that, as long as people don't kill animals themselves, it is okay to eat meat. However, note that passages 129 and 130 in the *Dhammapada* specify that we should not "kill or cause to kill." When people buy products made from the bodies of dead animals, they must necessarily cause someone to kill those animals. Therefore, meat, leather, and fur are off limits. It is probably true that, in order to be economically viable, killing older, less productive animals is necessary to produce milk and eggs-certainly this is one claim of the egg and milk industries in justifying this practice. If so, then buying milk and eggs also necessarily causes killing, and thus should be avoided under the First Precept.

How about meat that someone else has bought? In most, perhaps all cases, by accepting meat served to us by someone else, we are causing killing. For example, if meat-eating friends invite us over for dinner, they will buy extra meat for us in anticipation of our visit, or if our visit was unplanned they are likely to buy extra meat to restock their larder after we leave. In either case, our acceptance of the meat has caused additional animals to be killed. So ideally, we should not accept meat served to us by others, and should let people know this in advance whenever possible.

Some claim that the contents of their stomach do not matter, only the contents of their mind. However, the Buddha points out that we should give thought to what we eat:

He who lives only for pleasures, and whose soul is not in harmony, who considers not the food he eats, is idle, and has not the power of virtue-such a man is moved by Mara, is moved by selfish temptations, even as a weak tree is shaken by the wind. (*Dhammapada*, 7)

Not to hurt by deeds or words, self-control as taught in the Rules, moderation in food, the solitude of one's room and one's bed, and the practice of the highest consciousness: this is the teaching of the Buddhas who are awake. (*Dhammapada*, 185)

Probably these passages refer to avoiding gluttony as well as vegetarianism. Certainly, people who find the thought of "giving up" meat (or other products of animal killing) distressing should also consider if they have allowed themselves to become too attached to material pleasures, and heed the words of the Buddha:

He who does what should not be done and fails to do what should be done, who forgets the true aim of life and sinks into transient pleasures-he will one day envy the man who lives in high contemplation.

Let a man be free from pleasure and let a man be free from pain; for not to have pleasure is sorrow and to have pain is also sorrow. (*Dhammapada*, 209-210.)

Although the ideal of detachment does not mean we are forbidden to experience material pleasures, clearly allowing one's attachment to, say, the taste of meat to override adherence to the First Precept is contrary to the spirit of the *Dhammapada*.

Many people have tried to justify killing animals because of the (alleged) benefits it brings, whether economic benefits to people who work in animal-killing occupations, or potential medical benefits which might arise from vivisection. But the Buddha says:

He who for himself or others craves not for sons or power or wealth, which puts not his own success before the success of righteousness, he is virtuous, and righteous, and wise. (*Dhammapada*, 84)

That is, doing the righteous thing (obeying the Precepts) has a higher priority over worldly "success." Moreover, the Buddha cautions against being overly attached to our current bodies:

Consider this body! A painted puppet with jointed limbs sometimes suffering and covered with ulcers, full of imaginings, never permanent, and forever changing.

This body is decaying! A nest of diseases, a heap of corruption, bound to destruction, to dissolution. All life ends in death. Look at these grey-white dried bones, like dried empty gourds thrown away at the end of the summer. Who will feel joy in looking at them? A house of bones is this body, bones covered with flesh and with blood. Pride and hypocrisy dwell in this house and also old age and death.

The glorious chariots of kings wear out, and the body wears out and grows old; but the virtue of the good never grows old... (*Dhammapada*, 147-151).

Although the Buddha does not ask that we harm our body, either directly or by neglecting our bodies' needs (this would be pointless), he emphasizes that the body is impermanent, and we should be more concerned about being virtuous than about preserving the body. Therefore, killing animals (a violation of the First Precept), cannot be justified by the claim that it will prolong human life. Moreover, unlike the Judeo-Christian scriptures, the *Dhamma*pada does not claim that humans are superior to or more important than other animals.

Where does it end? It is a depressing fact of life that absolutely everything we buy has involved harm to sentient beings at some point in its production, simply because the vast majority of people are willing to harm nonhumans whenever it is expedient. For example, the vegetables we eat may have been fertilized with bone meal, plant-fibre clothing may have been treated with animal-derived products, and medications are currently required by law to be tested on animals. However, in buying products such as these which do not require killing for their production, it is not clear that we are causing others to kill-especially if we are also working to change the practices in these industries. Still, it is best to keep the consumption of all products to a minimum, both to minimize our monetary contribution to killing, and in keeping with the Buddhist ideal of detachment.

IMPLICATIONS OF THE DHAMMAPADA FOR ANIMAL RIGHTS ACTIVISTS

At a minimum, the *Dhammapada* is consistent with animal rights. Indeed, it seems to mandate many of the goals of the animal rights movement, for example the abolition of the meat industry and vivisection. Given that the *Dhammapada* is one of the core scriptures of Buddhism, it is difficult to see how Buddhists who do participate in activities which kill animals can justify the discrepancy between their practice and the words of the Buddha.

However, animal rights activists should note that killing of animals in "shelters" is also forbidden. This is a logical consequence of animal rights as well as Buddhism, however it is an unfortunate reality that many who consider themselves part of the animal rights movement still see killing of homeless cats and dogs as legitimate or perhaps even necessary. Also, although the goals of animal rights are by and large consistent with Buddhism, too often the actions taken to achieve these goals are not. Many animal rights advocates speak harshly of those who oppress animals, but what good does that do? The Buddha reminds us to

Never speak harsh words, for once spoken they may return to you. Angry words are painful and there may be blows for blows. (*Dhammapada*, 133.)

So how are we to work to liberate our fellow sentient beings from suffering? We would do well to reflect frequently on the following:

Overcome anger by peacefulness: overcome evil by good. Overcome the mean by generosity; and the man who lies by truth. (*Dhammapada*, 223.)

It is sufficient merely to tell the truth about what is happening to animals-there is no need to attack the character of the people committing these actions as well. And striving to live peacefully will teach the world more about compassion than hostile ranting. Of course, this isn't easy! I don't claim to have mastered this myself, although it is something I continue to strive for. Buddha acknowledges the difficulty, but encourages us to keep striving:

If he makes himself as good as he tells others to be, then he in truth can teach others. Difficult indeed is self-control. (*Dhammapada*, 159.)

At times when this ideal seems pointless, and frustrating, and futile, let us try to set aside our rage and despair at what our fellow humans are doing to animals, and focus on the love for animals which motivates our animal rights work: For hate is not conquered by hate: hate is conquered by love. This is a law eternal. (*Dhammapada*, 5.)

5

Buddhism and Ecology

Deep ecology is based on Buddhist principles. It calls for a holistic strategy, what can the earth sustain for the long term? Where will our natural resources come from even in a thousand years? Who are we really? The page below touches and elaborates with some additional description on the points made by Rev. Castro from the Seattle Betsuin in the video clip, this page is a process and it will continue to evolve.

This text looks at 6 Buddhist concepts and how they relate to ecology:

- Interdependence
- Emptiness
- Impermanence
- Selflessness
- Non-duality
- Middle Path

INTERDEPENDENCE

Interdependence as illustrated by the analogy of Indra's net. Each intersection of the net holds one jewel reflecting all the others through infinity. Pulling the strand in one place in the web affects everything else, similar to a ripple effect. How hard it is to comprehend the vast net of causes and conditions that brought us here! When you look at what brought you here, you can see that there is no such thing as a "self-made man".

If any of your ancestors had not been there, you would not be here now.

To understand Interdependence or interbeing, the contemplative Buddhist traditions use what is called deep looking. Thich Nhat Hanh is well known for his poetic analogy of the seeing the cloud in the chapter. When we pick up a piece of paper we don't usually think of the drops of water that evaporate, turn into clouds, rain on the forest which grows through the sun, which then gets logged by the logger, who then transports the logs to the factory, both factory and transport use other people, fuels, trucks and so forth, which is run by yet more people who turn the pulp into paper, which goes to the store.

This helps you understand reality through a poem, or perhaps helps you get a job through a resume. This is a simplified example, but it does bring home the point that you can't really say anything is completely independent. Just as when you physically die, the ripple effect of your life will however minutely and subtle affect life around you. With deep looking one realizes that boundaries from mere observations become blurry and downright dissolve from a deeper perspective.

EMPTINESS

Buddhists say "Form is Emptiness, Emptiness is form". Emptiness means empty of a separate self nature, an unchanging identity, something that stands alone and is fixed and permanent. Everything is a process. "Life is consuming life" as Joseph Campbell says. "To be empty of a separate self, means to be full of everything, to be alive" says Thich Nhat Hanh. Once this is understood, the ideas of birth and dying are also overcome, and the fear of death disappears naturally.

IMPERMANENCE

All phenomenon's are continuously changing, constantly created and destroyed, but the emptiness is not born and destroyed. Although we don't see this impermanence necessarily in all things on a superficial level, if we look on a geologic scale, we can see how even mountains wear down into dust. We tend to cling to permanence, as in clinging to gain, fame, praise, etc, causing us great suffering when we loose things, or when we cling to an impermanent identity or ego. While it might sound rather depressing that everything is impermanent, it is also a cause for joy, as in this example. How can a child grow up if it isn't impermanent, how can a seed of corn turn into your corn flakes, unless its state is impermanent?

SELFLESSNESS

As said previously, the ignorance that gave rise to the attachment to a fictitious self, ruled by fears and desires, creates a separation and disconnect with everything else, resulting in conflict, an alienation from your authentic self, or "friction with impermanence" as Dr. Nobuo Haneda puts it. There now is the distinction between this "me" and everything else "out there".

Realizing selflessness dissolves this artificial boundary and suddenly there is connection with everything else, there is interbeing, no more inner conflict, struggle. This is also called our "true Self" or True nature. Can you show your original face before your parents were born? An analogy is to imagine each of us a separate cell in a body. This Body also needs each separate cell to be a whole. The healthier and in touch each cell is with their body, the healthier the whole body. If the cell looses its touch and sense of place, we call that cancer. These cancerous cells treat the body as somehow other than themselves.

NON-DUALITY

The previous example of a person feeling separate is an example of dualistic discursive thinking. Buddhist practice is about transcending duality, being "transparent to transcendence", and cultivating a non-dual awareness that allows the practitioner to see things as they are, rather than his/her thoughts about what reality is. It is said that when opposites arise (in one's thinking) the Buddha mind is lost.

As soon as our minds come up with "good", then automatically the opposite arises, "evil". Confusing conceptual dualities for reality can easily turn "us and them" into "Us vs them". An example is to look at war time cartoons, usually, the "enemy" is portrayed as the devil, and lumped together with all the people of a country, this makes it much easier to go out and kill and get voter support to kill and torture.

MIDDLE PATH

The path that Buddha laid out, that rides in between the opposites, such as existence and non-existence, being and non-being, this middle path is not affected by these opposites. The historical Buddha went through both opposites himself before choosing the middle path. His life started out as a prince being groomed to become a king, he had all the comforts and luxuries, very self affirming and complacent. He renounced this life once he found out about old age, sickness and death; even his comforts would be impermanent. He got inspired by seeing a yogi ascetic. Becoming an ascetic himself, he went into self-denial, the extreme opposite of self affirmation. When he finally became enlightened, he extinguished his self-preoccupation, and so blew out, or extinguished his selfish attachments, this is called Nirvana.

Nonviolent ecology refers to a society which is economically and socially just, ecologically sustainable, and non-killing and compassionate in relating to its environment. This chapter draws on principles and insights from Buddhism as one foundation for developing a nonviolent ecology. But first some preliminary comments are needed about the violence which some suppose to be inherent and pervasive in nature and in human nature. One major point is that violence and nonviolence are relative rather than absolute conditions. Some regions are prone to violent forces in nature such as hurricanes or earthquakes; however, there is other a region in which such violent forces is negligible or even absent. Competition and predation between animal species can be violent; however, there are also nonviolent relations between species such as mutualism.

Within our own species, individuals and groups can be very violent in their social interactions; however, most interactions are nonviolent. Such considerations lead to the conclusion that there are environments and societies which are nonviolent, and thus a nonviolent ecology is not limited to romantic or utopian ideals. While there may well be more than one way to cultivate a nonviolent ecology, Buddhism can certainly be pertinent for such an effort.

Disregarding the variation in Buddhist orthodoxy and orthopraxy, at the generic level there are several important principles inherent in Buddhism which can be applied by individuals and societies for the creation and maintenance of a nonviolent ecology. Of course these principles are most relevant to Buddhist individuals and societies. Granted, these principles may not be sufficient, but they provide one useful place to start. Here they are offered as possibilities for consideration rather than as any rigid doctrine. It should be noted that here the interpretation of these principles is influenced by the authors' background in Western philosophy, anthropology, and ecology.

BUDDHIST PRINCIPLES FOR A NONVIOLENT ECOLOGY

UNITY AND INTERDEPENDENCE

Buddhism is ecocentric rather than anthropocentric since it views humans as an integral part of nature. As Kaza (1990) explains, Buddhism focuses on the interaction of mind and nature through the three practices of direct knowing, discriminating awareness, and deep compassion: By cultivating these three practices, one's actions in relation to the environment come to be based in relationship and interconnectedness, rather than in dualistic subject-object modes of separation. Through this approach, one's orientation to the world is fundamentally altered from dominant species to member of a community, from part to process. With interdependence as a core understanding, an environmental ethic becomes a practice in recognizing and supporting relationships with all beings.

The Buddhist transcends separateness from nature and instead identifies with the welfare of all beings. Nirvana (the awakening into a state of bliss) is reached when the boundary separating the finite self from its surroundings and also all mortal craving are extinguished. Accordingly Kaza (1990:25) recognizes that: An environmental ethic is not something we apply outside ourselves; there is no outside ourselves. We are the environment, and it is us.

From this recognition of the unity of human and nature it follows that the laws of nature apply to humans as well as to other living beings. Thus the *Dhamma* includes the discovery of the nature of things which encompasses the character and processes of the environment as system.

LIMITS AND SUSTAINABILITY

While environmentalism emphasizes that natural resources are limited, Buddhism is more direct in encouraging individuals to limit their resource consumption to the optimal satisfaction of the four basic needs of food, clothing, shelter, and medicine. This vantage point renders ecology a very concrete and personal matter following the Middle Way, one life and progresses in accord with the principles of detachment and moderation. In short, the Middle Way avoids the extremes of denial (asceticism) and overindulgence (consumerism). This is the "rationed life". (This contrasts with the emphasis in materialist consumer societies on the maximal satisfaction of needs, wants, and desires). Thus Buddhism points to the fundamental distinction between need and greed.

Implicit in the Middle Way is also moderation in population reproduction as well as in economic production and consumption. In such ways Buddhism can contribute to ecological sustainability as well as economic and social justice. Similarly, biologist Kozlovsky (1974:106) identifies as "the fundamental rule" of human ecology: "Live as simply and as naturally and as close to the earth as possible, inhibiting only two aspects of your unlimited self; your capacity to reproduce and your desire for material things."

COMPASSION FOR DIVERSITY

Although in recent years conservationists have shifted their emphasis from individual species to whole ecosystems, Buddhism has long advocated reverence and compassion for all life. In the case of animals this encompasses invertebrates as well as vertebrates.

For meditation Buddhists seek a natural and peaceful environment, the highest expression of which is the forest. Thus traditionally temples were often built in forests, and by association the surrounding forest became sacred space to be preserved rather than exploited. Traditionally this would tend to promote the conservation of all the species diversity within the surrounding ecosystem. It is noteworthy that the greatest diversity and complexity of life is found in tropical rain forests.

EXISTENCE AND RIGHTS

Buddhism considers the intrinsic value of both humans and nature as providing a more meaningful way of living. This is in contrast to extrinsic value, the economic valuation of nature for resource exploitation for the market economy. An individual should limit personal use of natural resources to obtaining optimal satisfaction of basic needs.

Instead of the use of nature, the Buddhist is more concerned with the contemplation of nature, especially through meditation. All life forms have a natural right to existence as functional components of the ecosystem; thus the Buddhist should avoid the use of pesticides and other unnecessary destruction of life.

Thich Nhat Hanh (1988:41) writes: We should deal with nature the way we should deal with ourselves! We should not harm ourselves; we should not harm nature. Harming nature is harming ourselves, and vice versa. If we knew how to deal with our self and with our fellow human beings, we would know how to deal with nature. Human beings and nature are inseparable. Therefore, by not caring properly for any one of these, we harm them all.

THOUGHT AND ACTION IN RELATION TO RESPONSIBILITY

The key to Buddhist ethics is the primacy of the mind. The *Dhammapada* (sayings of the Buddha) begins with the words: "All we are is the result of what we have thought". From positive thoughts flow positive actions and positive consequences, whereas from negative thoughts flow negative actions and negative consequences. Furthermore, the actions of an individual in the present life can influence the next one as well. The source of suffering is in the individual, and likewise the source of happiness is in the individual. Enlightenment derives from the understanding of this elemental reality. Thus ignorance rather than sin is the problem.

Wisdom and morality are mutually reinforcing. Accordingly, Buddhism would encourage the cultivation of environmental understanding through education as well as the practice of environmental ethics as a basis for a nonviolent ecology. As Kaza (1990:25) cogently explains: The qualities of our thoughts and actions are inextricably linked and have a powerful impact on the environment. It is here that Buddhism can offer a great gift to the world. The root of the environmental crisis lies in the habits of mind as much as the destructive habits of behavior.

Also relevant to responsibility are the first of both the negative and positive precepts which are complementary. Non killing (the first negative precept) means to abstain from taking life. *Karuna,* (the first positive precept), is deep and universal compassion or loving kindness toward all life. Since the first negative precept extends to all life, it includes forms such as insects which are not usually identified as a concern of environmentalists.

Also because of this precept normally Buddhists would not be involved in the kind of violence which is sometimes practiced by radical environmentalists. A nonviolent ecology would realize its ideals through its actions toward all life forms, even those which are violent towards humans or nature. Education and persuasion rather than violent confrontation would be used to reach those humans who degrade or threaten other humans and/or nature.

INDIVIDUAL DEPENDENCE

Because the locus of either happiness or suffering is in the individual, it is up to each individual to cultivate positive thoughts from which will flow positive actions from which will flow positive consequences. This action rests on the realization of the Four Noble Truths and the pursuit of the Noble Eightfold Path. It also depends on following the Middle Way of detachment and moderation, while satisfying basic needs and avoiding greed. Meditation in nature is an important part of this process of reaching *nirvana*-the union with nature through the extinction of ego and of all mortal cravings. Thus Buddhism would not blame the ecocrisis on science, technology, industry, business, advertising, government, or some other amorphous scapegoat.

Rather it would view the ecocrisis as the product of the collective behavior of individuals who are driven by circumstance, ignorance, and/or greed instead of by wisdom, need, moderation, compassion, and nonviolence. If Buddhists followed the above principles as a basis for environmental ethics in their daily actions, then it seems likely that the consequences would promote a nonviolent ecology. As Bodhi writes: With its philosophic insight into the interconnectedness and thoroughgoing interdependence of all conditioned things, with its thesis that happiness is to be found through the restraint of desire in a life of contentment rather than through the proliferation of desire, with its goal of enlightenment through renunciation and contemplation and its ethic of non-injury and boundless loving-kindness for all beings, Buddhism provides all the essential elements for a relationship to the natural world characterized by respect, care, and compassion.

To some degree there are Buddhist societies which have a nonviolent ecology, but less so in the present than in the past. As Berry (1987:6) observes: The smaller Buddhist countries of South and Southeast Asia, in their pre-modern period, had minimal impact upon the life systems of their regions because of limited populations, village modes of life, and few large urban centers- supported, of course, by a spirituality that exalted a lifestyle detached from earthly possessions. Part of the problem is that in any religious and/or philosophical doctrine, there is often an embarrassing discrepancy between ideals and practices.

Moreover, in many Buddhist societies modernization has greatly increased this discrepancy. The ubiquity of this discrepancy suggests that good ideals are not enough, but that other factors such as material circumstances are also important. This is one reason why a nonviolent ecology must also be economically and socially just. Despite the discrepancy between ideals and actions, in recent years there has been "a kind of Buddhist revolt against the deterioration of nature" in countries like Thailand, according to Sulak Sivaraksa. Thus in Sri Lanka, Thailand, USA, and Brazil and among other countries Buddhists are environmental activists and applying the principles of Buddhist ethics and ecology.

The multiplicity, variety, and energy of these revitalization movements offers hope that it may not be too late to develop a nonviolent ecology. As Shrader-Frechette (1981:28) notes: "How to view man's relationship to the environment is one of the great moral problems of our time." Buddhism offers some insights for the solution of this problem, especially for Buddhist individuals and societies. Buddhism has endured for more than 2,500 years because people have found it meaningful. However, there are discontinuities as well as continuities in its history. In the future Buddhism will continue to adapt as it helps humans adapt to new circumstances and challenges.

6

Buddhism and Abortion

Most Western and Japanese Buddhists come away believing in the permissibility of abortion, while many other Buddhists believe abortion to be murder- James Hughes.

Buddhists believe that life should not be destroyed, but they regard causing death as morally wrong only if the death is caused deliberately or by negligence. Traditional Buddhism rejects abortion because it involves the deliberate destroying of a life. Buddhists regard life as starting at conception. Buddhism believes in rebirth and teaches that individual human life begins at conception. The new being, bearing the karmic identity of a recently deceased individual, is therefore as entitled to the same moral respect as an adult human being. Modern Buddhists, however, are more divided about the morality of abortion.

BUDDHISM AND KILLING

According to the teachings of Buddha, five conditions must be present to constitute an act of killing.

- The thing killed must be a living being
- You, the killer, must know or be aware that it is a living being
- You must have the intention to kill it
- There must be an effort to kill
- The being must be killed as the result

Here's an example of how an abortion might constitute an act of killing:

- When a baby is conceived, a living being is created and that satisfies the first condition. Although Buddhists believe that beings live in a cycle of birth death and rebirth, they regard the moment of conception as the beginning of the life of an embodied individual.
- After a few weeks the woman becomes aware of its existence and that meets the second condition.
- If she decides she wants an abortion that provides an intention to kill.
- When she seeks an abortion that meets the fourth condition of making an effort to kill.
- Finally the being is killed because of that action.

Therefore the First Precept of Buddhism - not to kill - is violated and this is tantamount to killing a human being.

KARMA

While it's pretty obvious why abortion generates bad karma for the mother and the abortionist it may not be so obvious why it generates bad karma for the foetus.

The foetus suffers bad karma because its soul is deprived of the opportunities that an earthly existence would have given it to earn good karma, and is returned immediately to the cycle of birth, death and rebirth. Thus abortion hinders its spiritual progress.

LIVES IN THE BALANCE

Buddhists face a difficulty where an abortion is medically necessary to save the life of the mother and so a life will be lost whether there is or isn't an abortion. In such cases the moral status of an abortion will depend on the intentions of those carrying it out. If the decision is taken compassionately, and after long and careful thought then although the action may be wrong the moral harm done will be reduced by the good intentions involved.

ABORTION FOR THE SAKE OF THE BABY

There are cases where not having an abortion may result in the birth of a child with medical conditions that cause it to suffer. Traditional Buddhist thinking does not deal with these cases, but it has been argued by some Buddhists that if the child would be so severely handicapped that it would undergo great suffering, abortion is permissible.

The Dalai Lama has said:

Of course, abortion, from a Buddhist viewpoint, is an act of killing and is negative, generally speaking. But it depends on the circumstances.

If the unborn child will be retarded or if the birth will create serious problems for the parent, these are cases where there can be an exception. I think abortion should be approved or disapproved according to each circumstance.

It's Personal

Buddhists are expected to take full personal responsibility for everything they do and for the consequences that follow. The decision to abort is therefore a highly personal one, and one that requires careful and compassionate exploration of the ethical issues involved, and a willingness to carry the burden of whatever happens as a result of the decision. The ethical consequences of the decision will also depend on the motive and intention behind the decision, and the level of mindfulness with which it was taken.

JAPAN

Japanese Buddhists have had to make significant efforts to reconcile abortion with their religion, as abortion is common in Japan, and has been used as a form of birth control. Some followers of Japanese Buddhism who have had an abortion make offerings to Jizo, the god of lost travellers and children. They believe that Jizo will steward the child until it is reborn in another incarnation. They do this in a *mizuko kuyô*, a memorial service for aborted children that became popular in the 1970s. (The service can also be used in cases of miscarriage or still birth.) The ritual includes elements of folk religion and Shinto as well as Buddhism.

The writer William R. Lafleur has pointed out some difficulties with this tradition:

> ...within the Japanese Buddhist community the discussion of abortion is now limited largely to criticisms of those temples and temple-like organizations which employ the notion of 'foetal retribution' to coerce the "parents" of an aborted foetus into performing rituals that memorialize the foetus, remove its 'grudges,' and facilitate its rebirth or its Buddhahood.

Many Buddhists find repugnant such types of manipulation of parental guilt - especially when expressed in the notion that a foetus in limbo will wreak vengeance (*tatari*) on parents who neglect to memorialize it. The U.S. has struggled with the issue of abortion for many years without coming to consensus. We need a fresh perspective, and I believe the Buddhist view of the abortion issue may provide one.

Buddhism does consider abortion to be the taking of a human life. At the same time, Buddhists generally are reluctant to intervene in a woman's personal decision to terminate a pregnancy. Buddhism may discourage abortion, but it also discourages imposing rigid moral absolutes. This may seem contradictory. In our culture, many think that if something is morally wrong it ought to be banned. However, the Buddhist view is that the rigid following of rules is not what makes us moral. Further, imposing authoritative rules often creates a new set of moral wrongs.

First, the Buddhist view of abortion does not include a concept of rights, either a "right to life" or a "right to one's own body." In part this is because Buddhism is a very old religion, and the concept of human rights is relatively recent. However, approaching abortion as merely a "rights" issue doesn't seem to be getting us anywhere. "Rights" are defined by the Stanford Encyclopedia of Philosophy as "entitlements (not) to perform certain actions or be in certain states, or entitlements that others (not) perform certain actions or be in certain states." In this argument, a right becomes a trump card that, when played, wins the hand and shuts down all further consideration of the issue. However, activists both for and against legal abortion believe *their* trump card beats the other side's trump card. So nothing is settled.

I'm going to address this question with a personal observation that is not necessarily Buddhist but is not, I think, contradictory to Buddhism. My understanding is that life doesn't "begin." Scientists tell us that life got to this planet, somehow, about 4 billion years ago, and since then life has expressed itself in diverse forms beyond counting. But no one has observed it "beginning." We living beings are manifestations of an unbroken process that has been going on for 4 billion years, give or take. To me, "When does life begin?" is a nonsensical question.

And if you understand yourself as a culmination of a 4-billion-year-old process, then is conception really more significant that the moment your grandfather met your grandmother? Is any one moment in those 4 billion years really separable from all the other moments and couplings and cell divisions going back to the first macromolecules to life's beginning, assuming life had a beginning?

You might ask, What about the individual soul? One of the most basic, most essential, and most difficult teachings of Buddhism is *anatman* or *anatta*-no soul. Buddhism teaches that our physical bodies are not possessed of an intrinsic self, and our persistent sense of ourselves as separate from the rest of the universe is a delusion. Please understand that this is not a nihilistic teaching. The Buddha taught that if we can see through the delusion of the small, individual self, we realize a boundless "self" that is not subject to birth and death.

Our judgments on issues depend heavily on how we conceptualize them. In western culture, we understand individuals to be autonomous units. Most religions teach that these autonomous units are invested with a soul. I've already mentioned the doctrine of *anatman*. According to this doctrine, what we think of as our "self" is a temporary creation of the *skandhas*. The skandhas are attributes-form, senses, cognition, discrimination, consciousness-that come together to create a distinctive, living being.

As there is no soul to transmigrate from one body to another, there is no "reincarnation" in the usual sense of the word. "Rebirth" occurs when the karma created by a past life carries over to another life. Most schools of Buddhism teach that conception is the beginning of the process of rebirth and does, therefore, mark the beginning of a human being's life.

THE FIRST PRECEPT

The First Precept of Buddhism-*Panatipata veramani sikkhapadam samadiyami*-often is translated "I undertake to refrain from destroying life." The literal translation of the Precept makes no distinction between humans and horses, spiders and spinach. Although human life is most important, the Precept cautions us to refrain from taking life in *any* of its countless manifestations. That said, there is no question that terminating a pregnancy is an extremely serious matter. Abortion is considered to be taking a human life and is strongly discouraged in Buddhist teachings. However, I do not believe any school of Buddhism absolutely forbids it.

Buddhism teaches us not to impose our views on others and to have compassion for those facing difficult situations. Although some predominantly Buddhist countries, such as Thailand, place legal restrictions on abortion, many Buddhists do not think the state should intervene in matters of conscience.

THE BUDDHIST APPROACH TO MORALITY

Buddhism does not approach morality by handing out absolute rules to be followed in all circumstances. Instead, it provides guidance to help us see how what we do affects ourselves and others. The karma we create with our thoughts, words and actions keeps us subject to cause and effect. Thus, we assume responsibility for our actions and the results of our actions. Even the Precepts are not commandments, but principles, and it is up to us to decide how to apply those principles to our lives.

Karma Lekshe Tsomo, a professor of theology and a nun in the Tibetan Buddhist tradition, explains,

"There are no moral absolutes in Buddhism and it is recognized that ethical decision-making involves a complex nexus of causes and conditions. 'Buddhism' encompasses a wide spectrum of beliefs and practices, and the canonical scriptures leave room for a range of interpretations. All of these are grounded in a theory of intentionality, and individuals are encouraged to analyze issues carefully for themselves.... When making moral choices, individuals are advised to examine their motivation- whether aversion, attachment, ignorance, wisdom, or compassion- and to weigh the consequences of their actions in light of the Buddha's teachings."

Our culture places great value on something called "moral clarity." Moral clarity rarely is defined, but I infer it means ignoring the messier aspects of complex moral issues so that one can apply simple, rigid rules to solving them. If you take all facets of an issue into account, you risk not being clear. Moral clarifiers love to rework all ethical problems into simple equations of right and wrong, good and bad. There is an assumption that an issue can have only two sides, and that one side must be entirely right and the other side entirely wrong. Complex issues are simplified and oversimplified and stripped of all ambiguous aspects to make them fit into "right" and "wrong" boxes.

To a Buddhist, this is a dishonest and unskillful way to approach morality. In the case of abortion, often people who have taken a side glibly dismiss the concerns of any other side. For example, in much anti-abortion literature women who have abortions are portrayed as selfish or thoughtless, or sometimes just plain evil. The very real problems an unwanted pregnancy might bring to a woman's life are not honestly acknowledged. Moralists sometimes discuss embryos, pregnancy and abortion without mentioning women at all. At the same time, those who favor legal abortion sometimes fail to acknowledge the humanity of the fetus.

THE FRUITS OF ABSOLUTISM

Although Buddhism discourages abortion, we see that criminalizing abortion causes much suffering. The Alan Guttmacher Institute documents that criminalizing abortion does not stop it or even reduce it. Instead, abortion goes underground and is performed in unsafe conditions. In desperation, women submit to unsterile procedures. They drink bleach or turpentine, perforate themselves with sticks and coat hangers, and even jump off roofs. Worldwide, unsafe abortion procedures cause the deaths of about 67,000 women per year, mostly in nations in which abortion is illegal.

Those with "moral clarity" can ignore this suffering. A Buddhist cannot. In his book *The Mind of Clover: Essays in Zen Buddhist Ethics*, Robert Aitken Roshi said, "The absolute position, when isolated, omits human details completely. Doctrines, including Buddhism, are meant to be used. Beware of them taking life of their own, for then they use us."

He said,

"My understanding is that an individual is a phenomenon of life in the same way a wave is a phenomenon of ocean. When the wave begins, nothing is added to the ocean; when it ends, nothing is taken away."

Robert Aitken Roshi wrote in *The Mind of Clover*,

"Sorrow and suffering form the nature of samsara, the flow of life and death, and the decision to prevent birth is made on balance with other elements of suffering. Once the decision is made, there is no blame, but rather acknowledgment that sadness pervades the whole universe and this bit of life goes with our deepest love."

THE BUDDHIST APPROACH

In researching this chapter I found universal consensus among Buddhist ethicists that the best approach to the abortion issue is to educate people about birth control and encourage them to use contraceptives. Beyond that, as Karma Lekshe Tsomo writes,

"In the end, most Buddhists recognize the incongruity that exists between ethical theory and actual practice and, while they do not condone the taking of life, do advocate understanding and compassion toward all living beings, a lovingkindness that is nonjudgmental and respects the right and freedom of human beings to make their own choices."

It is quite clear from a variety of sources that abortion has been severely disapproved of in the Buddhist tradition. It is also equally clear that abortion has been tolerated in Buddhist Japan and accommodated under exceptional circumstances by some modern Buddhists in the U.S. Those sources most often cited that prohibit abortion are Theravaadin and ancient. By contrast, Japanese Buddhism as well as the traditions out of which a more lenient approach emerges are more recent and Mahayana traditions.

Superficially, the situation seems not unlike that of Roman Catholicism, where abortion, though disapproved of in the strongest terms by Church authorities drawing on the canonical tradition, is nonetheless practiced by a large number of devout Catholics and defended by at least a few, sometimes renegade, theologians and philosophers, as acceptable in some circumstances. Therefore, if it makes sense to speak of a possible Catholic defense of abortion, then it makes equally good sense to speak of a Buddhist defense of abortion, a defense made in full knowledge that one is swimming against the tide of conventional interpretation but still within the tradition.

In other words, I am not so much concerned to show that Buddhism has, do, or will support the choice to abort or one's right to make such a choice as I am to show that such a choice can be made in a manner consistent with Buddhist principles. Buddhism itself, therefore, speaks with more than one moral voice on this issue, and furthermore, the nature of the moral debate may have important applications for similarly situated others and constitute an enlargement of the repertoire of applicable moral theories and rationales.

One of the strongest antiabortion cases from a Buddhist perspective emerges in Damien Keown's wonderfully thorough and insightful analysis of Buddhism's bioethical ramifications in the book *Buddhism* and *Bioethics*. Keown argues that the preponderance of the Buddhist traditon is overwhelmingly antiabortionist. In support, he develops two lines of argument. The first relies on the nearly uniform rejection of abortion, especially in ancient Theravada texts, what Keown regards as the core of the tradition. Here I believe he is on fairly firm ground although I am uncertain regarding his preference for what he calls "Buddhist fundamentalism" and his concomitant emphasis on "scriptural authority."

The second line of argument concerns his interpretation of these sources and their connection to the basic tenets of Buddhism regarding the nature of personal identity and the *skandhas*, karma and rebirth, life and death. I find Keown's discussion of the sources that directly relate to the question of abortion fairly convincing. Especially in the *Pitakas*, or in Buddhagosa's commentaries, it seems quite clear that the practice of abortion is considered unacceptable. However, as Keown points out, the cases dealt with involve women seeking abortions for questionable, perhaps self-serving, reasons including "concealing extramarital affairs, preventing inheritances, and domestic rivalry between co-wives." In short, if these are the paradigm examples of abortion, then the case is heavily biased against the practice.

Keown does comment in an endnote that Buddhism would surely have sided with a woman seeking an abortion in order to save her own life, a position he attributes to Hindu jurists of the time. Why Buddhism would make such an exception is unclear, especially given the case Keown builds against the practice. For if abortion is always in violation of the First Precept against taking life, especially such karmically advanced life as that of a developing human being, then why should the mother's imperiled condition make a difference? Why prefer one life to another?

One might, of course, argue that abortion in such circumstances was a form of self-defense. Indeed, Keown seems to feel that killing in self-defense is not itself an example of taking life. But pregnancy and its associated dangers present a wholly different kind of situation from that of self-defense. In the case of a fetus, if the mother's life is in jeopardy, it is not because the fetus is in some manner attacking the mother as in most such cases. Rather, the mother's medical condition renders her unable to carry a fetus to term or give birth safely. Even if it is the fetus's medical condition that jeopardizes the mother, it is in no way analogous to a physical attack.

The fetus is not responsible for its medical condition and in no way intends to harm its mother. Hence, the question why such special exceptions to a general prohibition on abortion are acceptable remains unanswered. Correlatively, if such exceptions can be made, why not make them in other, perhaps less threatening but still serious, circumstances? Yet whether or not early Buddhism's condemnation of abortion is fully rationalized or not, the fact is that the scriptural evidence is against it. However, when it comes to connecting the apparent condemnation of abortion with the deeper inspirations of Buddhism, the case is less compelling and perhaps affords a toehold in the Theravada tradition for a different evaluation of abortion.

Keown argues that the First Precept and its prohibition against taking life is part of a much larger reverence for life, life being one of Buddhism's three basic goods-life, wisdom and "friendship" (Keown's spin on *karuna* and other associated qualities). While respect for life is undeniable, the abortion issue usually hinges on whether the fetus is indeed a life in the relevant sense, and one could challenge either Buddhism or Keown on this point. That is, as Keown makes quite clear, though Buddhism values life, it does not value all life equally, and human life as a karmically advanced stage is particularly important.

The fetus at any stage in its development is certainly in some measure living, but it is not obviously a recognizable human being at every stage. As a mere conceptus it lacks, of course, many of the attributes one might label distinctively human except its genotype. Therefore, unless one insists, reductionistically, that a certain genetic sequence just *is* the essence of our humanity, one cannot say that a fertilized egg is a karmically advanced human being just because it is a fertilized egg. In other words, one needs a theory as to what constitutes a human being, a human life, and therefore a thing worthy of the greatest possible protection.

This Keown attempts to provide through a discussion of the traditional *sk*and*ha* theory and its implications for the various embryonic stages of human development. With few exceptions, which I will return to, Keown argues that a fertilized egg is a fully human being because the ingredient most essential to such a life is already present-*vinnana* (in the Pali). *Vinnana,* usually translated as consciousness, is of course only one of five traditional components of a living being. The other four are the following: form (the body), feeling, thought, and character or disposition. Keown's argument for treating *vinnana* as the most essential group is perhaps best stated in his discussion and rejection of sentience as the basic moral criterion for respect as a living being.

He says, the most fundamental [category] is consciousness (*vinnana*), the fifth. To specify *vinnana,* the criterion of moral status is, however, simply to say that all living beings have moral status, since it is impossible to isolate *vinnana* from the psychosomatic totality of a living being. It is impossible to point to *vinnana* without in the same act pointing to a living creature, just as it is impossible to point to 'shape' without referencing a physical object.

Although he does add, perhaps inconsistently,

Overall, since neither *vinnana* nor any other of the five categories by themselves can adequately encompass the nature of a living being, there is reason to be suspicious of any view which claims to locate in any one of them what is essential in human nature. (Keown 36)

Earlier he claims that "although feeling and thought define the architecture of experience, it is... *vinnana* which constitutes it."

What I take Keown to be arguing here is that *vinnana* is the most important of the *skandhas* which, to my mind at least, seems most unBuddhistic. As he himself notes and the Pali canon repeats *ad nauseum,* it is the conjunction of all five of the groups that constitute a living being, at least by any meaning of constitute that I am aware of so, why the emphasis on *vinnana*? The above-stated reasons are, to my mind, weak. It is no less true that without a body, without sensation, without disposition (in the sense of a karmic past), one would not be a living, at least human, being.

That is, lacking form, a body, perhaps one could qualify as a hungry ghost, but the Pali texts are very clear that the "groups" form the basis of the human ego, or at least the illusion of an ego. "Accordingly, he [Buddha] laid down only five groups, because it is only these that can afford a basis for the figment of an ego or of anything related to an Ego".

Hence, no conjunction of the *skandhas,* no ego-delusion is possible; and furthermore, no basis, consequently, for what Keown identifies as an ontological individual apart from its various phenomenal qualities. In short, it is impossible to isolate any of these groups from "the psychosomatic totality of a living being."

That said, it is important to consider further what Keown means by the term *vinnana.* His chosen translation is not actually 'consciousness' but 'spirit' which I think rises if not anti Buddhist then at least unBuddhist associations and implications. Keown rejects the traditional "consciousness" translation of *vinnana* because "the experience of *vinnana* in this form [as consciousness]... is merely one of its many modes. It is better understood as functioning at a deeper level and underlying all the powers of an organism" (Keown 25). He goes on to remark that "*vinnana* resembles certain Aristotelian-derived notions of the soul in Christianity, namely as 'the spiritual principle in man which organizes, sustains, and activates his physical components.'" This then becomes the justification for the claim that 'spirit' is an appropriate translation of *vinnana.*

There are times, however, when the refusal to use the obvious English term hinders rather than helps the process of understanding. The term in question is 'spirit', and I do not think it would be misleading to refer to *vinnana* in certain contexts as the spirit of an individual. *Vinnana* is the spiritual DNA which defines a person as the individual they are. (Keown 25)

Rather confusingly, he compares the role of *vinnana* with that of the electricity in a computer in order to clarify the kind of constituting spirituality he has in mind. An electrical current flows through the computer and is invisibly present in every functional part. When the power is on, many complex operations can take place; when the power is off the computer is a sophisticated but useless pile of junk. Like electricity, *vinnana* empowers an organism to perform its function. (Keown 27)

The reason I find this association confusing is that rather than being "invisibly present," electricity is all too visibly present. Electricity is a physical, not a spiritual, phenomenon. And if *vinnana* is to be understood on such a model, then not only is it no longer ghostly but no longer fulfills the functional purpose of accounting for the "spiritual principle in man which organizes, sustains, and activates his physical components." Electricity may, in a loose sense, animate a computer, but it doesn't in any way organize its physical components. Keown seems to be entertaining two rather different conceptions of *vinnana*.

On the one hand, it is a quasi-Aristotelian soul-like entelechy that individuates and constitutes an ontological individual moving along the karmic ladder to eventual enlightenment. Ultimately, what I find unBuddhistic about such an interpretation is not the almost antithetical mixture of psychological and physical characteristics, but the purpose to which this hybrid is put and its association with the concept of a soul. That Keown intends to make such a connection is very clear, especially when he remarks that *vinnana* so understood acts "as the carrier-wave of a person's moral identity; in the stage of transition between one life and the next... [I]t may be referred to as 'spirit'. An alternative designation for *vinnana* in the state of transition between lives is the *gandhabba*, which will be translated as the 'intermediate being'" (Keown 26). Thus, *vinnana* is meant to account for individual moral responsibility across the various stages of karmic life, including rebirth, to eventual nirvana.

However, such an account of human life still does not square with Buddhism's rejection of the Ego or *atman*. Indeed, Keown's version of *vinnana* rather resembles a Vedantic understanding of *atman*. Elsewhere he argues that the "moral identity" he mentions is not what Locke, for example, would identify as 'personhood'. Keown's notion is much broader, while Locke's concept with its attendant qualities of rationality and self-consciousness is inappropriate for Buddhist anthropology. Such qualities or capacities flower at different times in the course of an individual's evolution; hence, if all stages of individual existence are morally significant because they are karmically continuous, then a suitably broad understanding of the individual is required in order to valorize the entirety of a human life so understood.

The strength of the *atman* concept lies in its transcendental vision of an individual life and support for a moral identity which holds across chains of rebirth. In short, the *atman* as it is traditionally understood accomplishes exactly these functions, preserving moral identity, while at the same time remaining irreducible to any particular human characteristic, including self-consciousness, as well as all human characteristics collectively. In other words, if Keown is looking for a translation of the term *vinnana* other than 'consciousness', the term 'soul' seems better suited than 'spirit'.

However, it is exactly such a principle or entity which the Buddhist *skandha* theory would deny. An individual as such, the *Pitakas* argue, is like a chariot, not really there. If presented a chariot, a Buddhist would ask, "Where, exactly, is the chariot?" Your majesty if you came in a chariot, declare to me the chariot... the word 'chariot' is but a way of counting, term, appellation, convenient designation, and name for pole, axle, wheels, chariot-body, and banner-staff.

Similarly, Nagasena is but a way of counting, term, appellation, convenient designation, and mere name for the hair of my head... brain of the head, form, sensation, perception, the predispositions, and consciousness. But in the absolute sense there is no Ego here to be found.

In other words, no *atman* whatsoever and, arguably, no ontological individual either. In fact, "strictly speaking, the duration of the life of a living being is exceedingly brief, lasting only while a thought lasts." Buddhists, even early Theravada Buddhists, seem to feel they can get along quite well without anything which might subtend the processes of existence, of *samsara,* and provide "moral identity," ontological continuity, or the spiritual DNA explaining anyone's present predicament.

The question really comes down to whether *vinnana* or any other quality need endure to explain personality or transmigrate in order to explain rebirth and karma. Keown seems to feel that logically something must and *vinnana* is the best candidate. However, the scriptural evidence is missing, and furthermore a non-substantialist and thoroughly non-Aristotelian explanation of rebirth can be given.

Supposing we understand rebirth not as the rebirth of someone but as a mere succession or process then in this view, all acts or events share some form of dependent connection (*paticca-samuppada*). Therefore, actions and events that take place now share intrinsic connections to actions and events in the past and in the future along any number of natural dimensions. In the case of human beings, these dimensions correspond to the *skandhas*. Form, sensation, and so on all represent various sorts of dependency between phenomena. Because there is no self, soul, or ego we can look at this process in two different manners corresponding to the difference between enlightenment and delusion.

On the one hand, we can look at the process as a mere empty process wherein nothing essentially happens, completely detached and hence freed from the bondage of desire or the expectations of life, and importantly, the anxieties of death. This represents an enlightened approach which is not an expectation of transmigration because there is nothing to be reborn. So, the Buddha claims, this death is his last. Or, we can look at the process from the standpoint of belief in a thing that perdures. From this perspective, there is rebirth as transmigration, the expectation of future lives, the existence of past lives, and so on. One must, perforce, explain the process as the biography of someone; hence the fiction of an ego becomes necessary. It is this last which tempts us to rely on such quasi-Aristotelian notions as souls, spirits, or "spiritual DNA."

To be fair, Keown is aware of these issues and argues at several points that *vinnana* is not really a soul not is it a "subject of experience" (Keown 26). He eloquently states Buddhism does not ground its ethics in a metaphysical soul or self, and denies that any such thing exists. According to Buddhism, the five categories are what remain when the 'soul' is deconstructed. (Keown 28)

To which I would simply add, why do we need to speak of "spiritual DNA" or "moral identity" in order to make sense of Buddhism? These categories themselves seem equally prone to fixation and quite contrary to the basic notion of *anatta*. In other words, I would argue that like all the other groups-form, sensation, and the like-*vinnana* also does not endure, either across or within lifetimes. None of the groups do, and this is the essential feature of the *anattaa* doctrine. Hence, I would not equate *vinnana* in the state of transition with anything, much less the *gandhabba*, simply because it is not transitional.

Keown makes much of the *gandhabba's* essential role in the process of conception as portrayed in various Buddhist sources, interpreting the descent of the intermediate being when biological conditions at the time of conception are just right as offering what looks very much like an account of ensoulment. Such a strategy then justifies Keown's claim that for Buddhists "in the overwhelming majority of cases individual life is generated through sexual reproduction and begins at fertilization" (Keown 91). Consequently, abortion is immoral because it deprives an individual of life and so violates the First Precept against the intentional taking of life.

In terms of a Buddhist defense of abortion, the main difficulty with Keown's analysis has to do with his understanding of the Buddhist view of life which subsumes abortion under the general heading of intentional killing. Given my understanding of *anatta*, I see no reason to subscribe to Keown's understanding of the Buddhist view of human life. For Keown, all biologically human life is normatively significant because it is animated by the descended *gandhabba*, thus conferring the singularity necessary to view it as ontologically individual. However, given the distinction between the groups, I see no reason why a committed Buddhist can't hold that just because one has a body, form or *rupa*; one doesn't necessarily have a human life, especially one worthy of the strongest protection.

A human life, in the moral sense, starts unambiguously when all the *skandhas* are in place, and the Buddha as well as the early Buddhist scriptures leaves room for a rather large number of interpretations as to exactly when such a condition occurs in the process of embryonic development. I suspect that much of Keown's enthusiasm for his interpretation stems from the ready parallels that may be drawn between the natural law tradition of Roman Catholicism and Buddhism if one's *vinnana* is identical to the soul-like *gandhabba* that pops into the development process. However, as we have seen, such an assumption provides Buddhism with a form of ensoulment that it goes to great lengths to avoid.

If *vinnana* does not in any way subtend the karmic process from individual to individual and may even be completely episodic within the context of an individual life, then (1) I see no reason to interpret *vinnana* as anything other than consciousness or some such equivalent, and (2) Buddhism need not take *vinnana* to be present at any particular point in the process of embryonic development. That is, *vinnana* or consciousness is present whenever one would customarily say it is and that could be just as well at viability as at conception.

In fact, we would generally hold consciousness to be present only when, minimally, the cerebral cortex develops and perhaps later. Thus, even though a Buddhist would hold that consciousness provides the platform for mind and body, making any conscious being a living being worthy of moral consideration, it is not clear exactly when such a point might first occur. Furthermore, even if scriptural sources would locate this point early on in the embryonic process, a Buddhist could still coherently question any such time designation as potentially arbitrary mainly because, as I have argued, Buddhism lacks any comprehensive theory or deep-level principle that requires the presence of consciousness or an intermediate being at any particular point in the biological process of human development.

In fact, Keown admits that a Buddhist could hold the above position as the Buddha laid down several conditions covering ontogeny, some strictly biological and mainly regarding coitus and the mingling of sperm and, mistakenly, "menstrual blood." That is, even on Keown's analysis, Buddhism traditionally separates the biological *basis* for life from the individual life itself. Thus, a fertilized ovum is arguably a necessary but not sufficient condition for a new life. Rather, one requires the presence of the full complement of groups including *vinnana* to complete the development of an individual life. However, this allows "the material basis for life to arise on its own" (Keown 81), which Keown admits seems to contradict the assumption that the biological and spiritual basis must always arise together. Keown replies that if an unanimated conceptus is possible, its long-term survival is not for it is not "a new individual," and therefore "from the standpoint of Buddhist doctrine it would seem impossible for it to develop very far."

The justification for this claim is the Buddha's statement "that if consciousness were 'extirpated' from one still young, then normal growth and development could not continue"

(Keown 81). Incidentally, this claim also forms the basis for Keown's view that PVS patients (those in a "persistent vegetative state") are still individuals worthy of moral protection and should not be ruled as dead, as some advocates of a higher-brain definition of death would allow. That is, their continued and stabilized biological existence (some can live on for decades) demonstrates the presence of *vinnana* and hence individual life.

However, a liberal Buddhist could claim that while the loss of *vinnana* might curtail growth and development, it is not clear that *vinnana's* never having arisen need affect the biological development of the material basis of an individual's life. Indeed, one might argue that (1) because "extirpation" of consciousness from one who already possesses it usually involves physical trauma, of course we would expect normal growth and development to stop; or (2) even though *vinnana* is essential to the life of an individual and its irretrievable loss signals the individual's demise, it doesn't follow that the mere biological platform and its growth and development signal the inevitable presence of *vinnana*.

That is, it doesn't follow that *vinnana*; however we interpret it, is essential to the life of the biological organism. Especially if, as Keown suggests, Buddhism allows the presence of the material basis of life without that of the gand*habba*, then I don't see how Buddhism can rule out the possibility of simply a more extended existence of that material basis without *vinnana*. The biological basis of life may be organically integrated in the manner of a functional organism, but it is not itself the same thing as an individual life. I see no compelling rationale, based on Buddhist principles as articulated in the early scriptures, absolutely requiring the 'individual life begins at conception' point of view of radically pro-life antiabortionism. I grant that the early Buddhist scriptures do seem to have a somewhat pro-life orientation.

Yet, on closer inspection, I'm not sure the footing is there mostly because of the lack of a theory of ensoulment. Furthermore, had Buddhists of the time faced the bewildering medical possibilities of the late twentieth century, I'm not at all sure how doctrine would have evolved. For example, anencephaly, PVS and various other comatose conditions where patients exist in only the most minimal sense and on life support, not to mention transplant surgery, the advances in human genetics, and so on surely pose a challenge to traditional ways of regarding the human body. Many of these cases are, to my mind, simply waved aside by Keown (or his version of Buddhism). To claim that the pro-life stance of Buddhism simply means that PVS patients are fully alive is not to do justice to the complexities of the cases or of Buddhism, both of which suggest that 'life' is an extremely complex 'dependently arisen' phenomenon.

If one keeps to the traditional translation/interpretation of *vinnana* as consciousness, rejects any kind of soul, spirit, *atman*, or ego as a subsistent core of individual being either for the course of many karmic lives or a single individual karmic life, then I see no reason why even a Theravada Buddhist could not adopt a socially liberal position on abortion as well as a variety of other biomedical issues. This is not to say abortion would be a trivial matter, but the idea that it necessarily demonstrates disrespect for present life would be undermined. Of course, since abortion does compromise future life, it is still a morally serious matter, but as such it does not of itself violate the First Precept. A prohibition on killing is not an injunction to "be fruitful and multiply" by bringing into existence as much future life as is possible.

Rather, as long as consciousness is not yet deemed present, we face the material basis of a life, not the individual life itself. In many ways, this version of the Buddhist view would echo what bioethicist Bonnie Steinbock has called the "interest view":

> On the interest view, embryos and preconscious fetuses lack moral status, despite that they are potentially people... the fact that a being has the capacity to develop into a person, does not mean that it has any interest in doing so, or any interests at all, for that matter. And without interest, a being can have no claim to our moral attention and concern.

However, Steinbock does go on to argue that one's potential personhood does make a moral difference in regard to interested beings. So, in her view, a human infant rates more highly than even a fully developed chimpanzee on the grounds that chimpanzees are not moral persons in any relevant sense.

The similarity to Buddhism rests on the role of consciousness or what is sometimes called "the developed capacity for consciousness." As Keown tirelessly point out, the presence of *vinnana* is the key to individual status. If *vinnana* is consciousness and represents the platform on which mind and body are conjoined, then the presence of *vinnana* signals a karmically significant stage, that of an individual life for which either release or rebirth are the twin possibilities marking moral success or failure. Thus, on the Buddhist view, human life consists of a physical body and various sensori-motor capacities, conjoined with a mind or intellect all sporting a karmically conditioned past, that is always in context; individuals do not have any non-contextual existence.

Consciousness is indeed the platform of mind and body. The body is not itself the mind, and there is no hint of physicalism or reductionism in this understanding of human nature. The mind, however, is always passing away; mind is identical to thoughts and these are fleeting. The stream of consciousness, one could say, is a Heraclitean river, never the same exact thing twice. Consciousness is the developed capacity for such a stream in a physical context. But does this not mean that consciousness, the mental stream of thoughts, the sensori-motor complex, or one's karmic context are themselves the subsistent individual? Rather, to the degree such elements co-arise we have an individual and the permanent absence of any of the groups is the loss of an individual.

Surely, there is at least *prima facie* plausibility in the claim that without your body you do not exist; without your consciousness you do not exist; without your mind you do not exist. But all of them together do not create some other thing we call the person which exists apart from these qualities, nor something that goes on after or existed before.

Hence, each and every one of us is egoless strictly speaking, though we still retain "moral identity" and so can be held accountable for our actions. In short, when it comes to individual identity, Buddhism takes a similar position to philosophical nominalism.

When it comes to marking the temporal boundaries of a human life, therefore, such Buddhist nominalism tolerates a fair degree of imprecision. The only way of working out a fairly acceptable answer to the question when does life begin and when does it end would probably be through the process of analogizing. We can say that each of us is a living, morally significant being. The question becomes how much like us are other beings. How similarly situated do we take them to be? My suspicion is that some of the variation one finds in Buddhist texts over whether to treat various life forms as deserving of compassion reflects differences in individual abilities to imaginatively extend such analogies so as to creatively identify with the pleasures and pains of other beings, especially animals. Does a fetus constitute a morally significant being?

The answer would depend on how like us any particular fetus is. Surely, a late term fetus is, not so certainly a fetus on the threshold of viability, and dubiously a conceptus. Of course, such an approach does not help too much in the process of line drawing. But there are other Buddhist resources that may assist the line drawer. Any such act would be a matter of conscience, a morally significant act for the individual reflecting on such distinctions, as perhaps in the process of contemplating an abortion. What is important in situations of this nature is to negotiate the pitfalls of attachment and desire.

Correct line drawing is not based in metaphysical distinctions regarding personhood, but in the moral fiber of the line drawer and the complex interweave of circumstance and motivation that color and inform practical judgments. Appropriate questions for reflection might be the following: What am I seeking to gain? Why am I having or not having this child? What sort of life is possible for this child? How do I feel towards this life, this new being? What kind of pain and suffering is involved in either life or abortion? In short, all those questions which people do typically seem to mull over when faced with unwanted pregnancies. In short, though Buddhism encourages compassionate action, the question as to what is compassionate in the case of an unwanted pregnancy cannot be peremptorily answered by metaphysical proclamations as to when life begins. Thus, without leaving the province of a conservative Theravada Buddhism, a traditionalist Buddhism, one need not embrace the radical antiabortionism of Keown's Buddhist.

Some confirmation of such a position can be found in testimony collected in William R. LaFleur's book *Liquid Life*. A Japanese woman and committed Buddhist reflect on the practice of *tatari* or propitiating the soul of a dead fetus in order to avert posthumous revenge. Buddhism has its origin in the rejection of any notion of souls... that souls cast spells... Of course we who are Buddhists will hold to the end that a fetus is "life." No matter what kind of conditions makes abortion necessary we cannot completely justify it. But to us it is not just fetuses; all forms of life deserve our respect. We may not turn them into our private possessions even rice and wheat shares in life's sanctity. Nevertheless as long as we are alive it is necessary for us to go on "taking" the lives of various kinds of such beings.

Even in the context of trying to rectify the contradictions and inequalities in our society, we sometimes remove from our bodies that which is the life potential of infants. We women need to bring this out as one of society's problems, but at the same time it needs to be said that the life of all humans is full of things that cannot be whitewashed over. Life is full of wounds and woundings. In Japan, however, there is always the danger of mindless religion. There are also lots of movements that are anti-modern and they are tangled up with the resurgence of concern about the souls of the dead.

It is, of course, arguable that this way of looking at the issue is fundamentally incoherent. Either we are intentionally taking life or we are not, and if we are, then we violate

Buddhism's First Precept. The response a Buddhist may make, such Ochiai Seiko's above, is in essence, "Yes, we should always avoid the ending of a life, no matter how insignificant it may seem." But 'life' is an ambiguous term, and the ending of one form of life in the service of others is not necessarily prohibited in Buddhism. And if one's intention is not so much to end a life as to rescue others, then we are not dealing with a simple case of intentionally killing. In other words, compassionate action will always involve weighing up the full range of circumstances that bear on a situation or action.

On this view, the point of the First Precept is to disqualify intentional killing where the clear purpose is to end an individual life. Such an action can never be compassionate in Buddhist eyes. However, questions as to the status and nature of the lives one weighs in such tricky situations where interests clash are obviously relevant. If we are talking about the lives and interests of mothers and fetuses, fetuses and families, or fetuses and communities (such as in times of famine), then we are directly faced with the issue of the relative moral standing of different sorts of life.

What I have argued here is that because Buddhism allows a distinction between the biological basis of life and its higher cognitive as well as affective aspects and insists that an individual human life requires the conjunction of all such aspects, no Buddhist need equate a presentient fetus with a sentient human. Thus, Ochiai's insistence that in dealing with the messiness of everyday living, abortion may qualify as a compassionate response need not contradict Buddhist principles. Especially if we are dealing with the material platform of an individual being before the point of cerebral development sufficient for the developed capacity for consciousness, then the moral seriousness of its claim to life may well be outweighed by other considerations.

BUDDHIST SCRIPTURES

There is a great multiplicity of Buddhist scriptures. The oldest ones are the most reliable. The oldest Buddhist scriptures are the Pali Canon; accepted as scripture by the Theraveda School of Buddhism (Burma, Thailand, Laos, and Cambodia). Scholars are sure that not all of the books in the Pali Canon (called the "Tripitaka" or "Three Baskets") are the authentic discourses of Buddha, but that they are the oldest works and thus the most reliable.

The Tripitaka consists of:

1. Vinaya *Pitaka* (a book of laws for monks and nuns)
2. *Sutta Pitaka* (the Discourses of the Buddha)
3. *Abhidhamma Pitaka* (the commentaries and interpreations from the early successors of the Buddha)

It is in the Pali Canon that abortion is dealt with and vehemently condemned.

The Buddha Himself spoke directly of abortion is His discourse called the *Dharani Sutra*. He said:

"There are five kinds of Evil Karma which are difficult to extinguish, even if one were to repent of them. What are the five kinds of offences? The first one is killing the father, the second one is killing the mother, the third one is abortion, the fourth one is to injure The Buddha, the fifth one is to create disharmony among the *Sangha* assemblies [i.e. create division and schism]. These five types of evil and sinful karma are difficult to extinguish."

In the Vinaya (guide for monks and nuns) there are "Four Disrobing Offences"; in other words, four offenses that can get a monk or nun "disrobed" (excommunicated). They are:

1. Engaging in sexual intercourse.
2. Stealing something of value.
3. Purposely killing a human being, or encouraging someone to commit suicide, or "convincing a woman to have an abortion"
4. Boasting that one has realized enlightment while knowing one has not yet realized it (i.e. lying about one's own spiritual station).

Other offences monks and nuns can do penance for, but not these four. These are excommunicable offences.

THE NOBLE EIGHTFOLD PATH

The symbol of Buddhism is a wheel with 8 spokes. This represents the Eightfold-Path. Each Buddhist is supposed to follow the "Noble Eightfold Path" which is:

1. Right Understanding
2. Right Thought
3. Right Speech
4. Right Action
5. Right Livelihood
6. Right Effort
7. Right Mindfulness
8. Right Concentration

Under Right Action is the principle of *ahimsa*; non-violence to all living things. One Buddhist publication states:

"This would include the unborn, so abortion is not an acceptable alternative for controlling the population; however, contraception is not an issue as far as Buddhists are concerned."

THE DALAI LAMA

The largest sect of Tibetan Buddhism sees as its spiritual head the Dalai Lama. The 14th Dalai Lama has been living in India since the Communists took over Tibet in the late 1940s. Many Baha'is revere the Dalai Lama because of many or most of his views corresponds with Baha'i principles of peace, justice, and equality. In 1995 the Dalai Lama wrote a book titled *The Power of Compassion* in which he condemned injustice, racial and ethnic hatred, inequality, and abortion. The Dalai Lama is quoted to have "denounced abortion as a sin against 'non-violence to all sentient beings.'"

BUDDHISM IN JAPAN

Many Buddhist sects in Japan practice *Kuyo Mizuko*; which is a rite which some Buddhist priests perform for women and parents of aborted fetuses. It is believed that the *mizuko* (aborted child) will take retribution against the parents unless a rite is performed where the Buddhist priest prays to a *bohisattva* (saint) in order to get the saint to apply some of his virtuous merit (earned while a mortal) toward the aborted child in order to qwell the wrath of the fetus by assuring the child Nirvana or at least another birth in better circumstances.

The Pure Land Sect of Japanese Buddhist (known as *Jodo Shinshu*) absolutey condemns *kuyo mizuko*. Helen Hardacre writes:

"A childhood death, still birth, miscarriage, and abortion are all treated in the same manner as any human death in Jodo Shinshu. A fetus is recognized as fully human from the moment of conception (and thus abortion is wrong), and if a fetus should die, regardless of the circumstances, it is ritualized on the same model, though on a smaller scale, as adult deaths."

One of Japan's modern Seers is Taniguchi Seicho; the founder of the "House of Life" sect. William R. La Fleur writes:

"In writings of Taniguchi Seicho, head of House of Life, the equality of the fetal life with life forms outside the womb is stressed. The only difference is a metter of comparative size and the fact that the fetus is connected to the mother by an umbilical cord."

Regarding Buddhism and abortion, Prof. L.O. Ling writes:

"Abortion- Act of A., i.e. terminating life of the foetus, is explicitly mentioned in Buddha canonical scriptures, in the Vinaya -*Pitaka*, as a grave offence. If A. is brought about by Buddha monk, or if he is in any way a party to the procuring of an A., by offering advice as to the method, or supplying abortive medicine, penalty is expulsion from monkhood. This is in accord with Buddha view that destruction of life is a moral transgression."

Sundo Tachibana, in *The Ethics of Buddhism*, writes: "As far as the human being is concerned, even the abortion of an embryo which was just conceived is regarded as a crime."

Prof. Matsunami Kado writes: "According to Buddhist scriptures the fetus in the womb is supposed to be cared for and brought safely into this world...."

Abortion is Japan takes place, and some Buddhist temples make lots of money by performing ceremonies in which it is believed that the sin of abortion (and the wrath of the aborted child) can be eliminated. However, the main Japanese Buddhist sects look upon this practice as mere simony (like the selling of indulgences), and say that the sin of abortion cannot be negated from such rituals that have no basis in Buddhist scripture or orthodox Buddhism.

Abortion is legal in Japan. In 1970 the Japanese High Court declared: "A fetus is part of a mother's body until it is born, and is not by itself a person."

Although, most Japanese are Buddhists (at least partly or traditionally so) and their notion that a fetus is not human but a part of the mother's body comes not from Buddhism but from the Shintoism. The ancient religion of Japan was Shintoism; the belief that nature contains many spirits called *Kami*. Even rocks, stones, trees, lakes, mountains, etc., have kamis, and they need to be placated. Ancient Shintoism included human sacrifice (including infants) and ritual suicide.

Before World War II the Militaristic Imperial Japanese government made Shintoism the official religion of Japan, and did all they could to suppress Buddhism; including jailing Buddhist monks and leaders. The Imperialist Japanese were responsible for the deaths of millions of innocent human beings, and conducted medical experiments on tens of thousands of Chinese men, women, and children which rivalled the Nazis in cruelty and horror. Even though Shinto was no longer the official state religion after 1945, its influence is still strong in some circles; including Japanese courts.

ABORTION IN BUDDHIST COUNTRIES

Thailand, Burma, Nepal, and Taiwan are all Buddhist countries, and abortion is very restrictive in all of them. Illegal abortions do take place, but they are not nearly as numerous as abortions in countries where abortion-on-demand is legal. Japan can be called a "Buddhist" country, but Shintoism still has a strong influence. Communist China can be called a "Buddhist" country since so many Chinese who live in the People's Republic are Buddhist. However, the Communist Chinese government instituted a "one child per couple" policy in an effort to reduce and control the population. The pressure to have a son among the Chinese is great, and if a couple doesn't have a son they sometimes kill or abandon the female child (or children) until a son is born.

The orphanages in China are overflowing with girl infants; the great majority of them healthy, but abandoned. Many Chinese women who already have one child are forced by the government to have an abortion, or be heavily fined or threatened with jail. The very words of a Manifestation of God, the Buddha, in one of His oldest discourses equate abortion with killing one's own parents. Can anything else be clearer? Baha'is believes that the Words of a Manifestation of God are the Words of God Himself.

As we all know, bio-ethics is currently one of the most active areas in Western religious and philosophical discourse. Although Eastern countries are facing the same bio-ethical issues as we are in the West, on the whole, Eastern religious leaders have not systematically dealt with the problems raised by the collision between ancient traditions and explosively advancing medical techniques. In Buddhist circles, for example, the work is just beginning. Dr Pinit Ratanakul of Mahidol University in Bangkok published a book in 1986 entitled Bioethics. Although a Thai Buddhist, Dr Pinit's doctorate is from Yale, and his very interesting study is fundamentally written from a Western point of view.

He does note, however, that: Thailand and Thai medicine confront in general the same ethical questions which have been raised in the West; what has been lacking is the systematic, interdisciplinary attention to and discussion of them that has begun in the West through the discipline of Biomedical Ethics. It is time that discussion of a more systematic and intensive nature... be developed in Asian societies. In many sections of this book, there are valuable comments from a Buddhist point of view, and the appendix called 'The Buddhist Concept of Life, Suffering and Death and their Meaning for Health Policy' is a valuable contribution to the Asian discussion he calls for. Shoyo Taniguchi's pioneering 1987 Master of Arts thesis, A Study of Biomedical Ethics from a Buddhist Perspective, which attempts to develop a Pall text based approach to the field, also notes that although little has been done up to now, Buddhists have much to contribute to the discussion.

An attempt has been made to advance the discussion by presenting some Buddhist theoretical and practical responses to the ethical and religious problems raised concerning abortion. It is based both on textual study and on field observations and interviews in Hawaii, Japan, The People's Republic of China, Taiwan, and Thailand from 1987 through 1989.

SOME BUDDHIST ETHICAL PRINCIPLES

Let us begin with some basic Buddhist principles to put the question of abortion in a wider context. First, anything that exists exists only in relationship with everything else that exists. That is, nothing has independent self-being.

You and I- anything that is-exist only as the result of temporary, contingent causal relationships with other similarly changing, unsubstantial, suffering beings. Therefore, all ethical problems must be considered globally and rationally as problems in co-conditioned causality. The Buddha's great insight into the interrelatedness of all phenomena (co-conditioned causality), which is perhaps the first principal of Buddhism, has two major expressions. First is the ultimate truth that all things are fundamentally empty, which leads inevitably to the second, relative truth, compassion. The wise person, knowing the truth of the contingency and complete interdependence of all beings, can only regard their frenzied grasping for selfish ends with compassion.

Practically, wisdom leads to selfless action for the sake of others. Thus prajna or wisdom and karuna or compassion are the two major Buddhist ideals, the first relating to the realm of ultimacy and the second to the world of day-to-day existence. Without ultimate wisdom one will be defective in *upaya* or skilful means for helping others. Witless compassion, the bungling attempt to do well without the wisdom to affect it, is extremely dangerous. Moral behaviour in Buddhist systems then, is not an absolute in itself; it is a means towards a religious end, the transcendence of those selfish cravings which bind all beings to an unending round of suffering.

Accordingly all moral acts are understood either to be *kusala* karma, skilful deeds which are beneficial to self and others, or a*kusala* karma, unskilful deeds which harm self and others. Everything in the phenomenal world is relative. Human behaviour, therefore, is to be judged not on an absolute scale of good and evil but rather on a relative scale of skilful and unskilful. Skilfulness, of course, is understood in regard to the ascent of the path of the Buddha out of this world of suffering. This means that the precepts of morality laid down by the Buddha also are not absolute commandments. They are clearly understood as 'rules of training' which the individual undertakes in order to advance along the religious path.

In fact, so little are they absolute commandments, that the precepts have been used since the earliest days of the Buddhist community as temporary vows, freely assumed by individuals for specified lengths of time. A lay meditator, for example, might follow the rule of training to abstain from the misuse of sensual pleasures for the period of a retreat. The relativity of the precepts is further demonstrated by the fact that there are traditionally five for the ordinary person, eight for the advanced laity, and 10 for monks and nuns. It is taught that, for advanced Mahayana practitioners and especially for Vajrayana adepts, the precepts can be violated if done for the benefit of others. However, it is cautioned that it takes a very wise person, far along in prajna to make this judgement. Others had better stick with the rules or they will reap the whirlwind.

Although Buddhist morality is contextual and relative, it is not generally antinomian. On the level of relative truth, one's deeds or karma obey fixed laws of causality which determine one's destiny. Basically the moral consequences of an act are determined by the will or motivation (*cetana*) of the actor. If the will behind an act is driven by greed, hatred, or delusion understand as the three fundamental aspects of selfish craving, then the act is *akusala* or unskilful. It works in the following way. Every act involves body, speech, and mind working in conjunction. Mind starts a train of activity, and if mind is motivated by greed, hatred, or delusion, then the speech and bodily activity which follow are doomed to be unskilful.

Unskilful acts always have negative consequences for the actor and generally for the recipient of the act. The precepts are designed to provide guidelines for skilful activity and when followed will minimise negative karmic consequences. From the Buddhist vantage point of the middle way, there are two basic errors one could fall into on this issue. If one denies the reality of karmic consequences, one has adopted the nihilistic extreme view, which tends towards antinomianism. The eternalistic extreme view would involve the reification of moral precepts, resulting in inflexible dogmatic positions.

Application to Abortion From the very earliest days, the theory of co-conditioned causality, or *pratitya-samutpada*, the doctrine of the interrelatedness of all phenomena, was interpreted embryologically. In the form which came to be the standard, dependent origination was expressed as a circle of 12 causal factors or links, which seem to operate simultaneously. As applied to the foetal development of an individual, the first three links of the chain are ignorance, which gives rise to the *karma* foundations, which in turn give rise to consciousness or *vijnana*.

Vasubandhu, an outstandingly brilliant fourth or fifth century exegete, clarifies this very well: *Avidya* [ignorance] is in the previous life the condition of passion... All the passions in effect accompany ignorance, entering into activity through ignorance. It is just the same as they say, 'When the king comes, you understand that his courtesans accompany him'. *Samskaras* [karma foundations] are in the previous life the condition of the act. The series of the previous existence, in so far as it accomplished a good act or a bad one and so on, is what is understood by the karma foundations. *Vijnana* [consciousness] is the skandhas [the physical and mental components of a being] at conception.

The five *skandhas* are within the womb at the moment of reincarnation or of birth-of-existence. Thus, vijanana in this context is sometimes translated as 'rebirth consciousness'. In short, what all this boils down to is that Buddhists traditionally have understood that the human being begins at the instant of conception when sperm, egg, and *vijnana* come together. As Taniguchi puts it, "there is no qualitative difference between an unborn foetus and a born individual". Therefore, the precept against taking life applies in the case of abortion.

Buddhaghosa, a fifth century Theray, da commentator who is Vasubandhu's only equal though of another school, has an extensive commentary on this precept: 'I undertake to observe the rule to abstain from taking life.'... 'Taking life' means to murder anything that lives. It refers to the striking and killing of living beings... 'Taking life' is then the will to kill anything that one perceives as having life, to act so as to terminate the life-force in it, in so far as the will finds expression in bodily action or in speech. With regard to animals it is worse to kill large ones than small. Because a more extensive effort is involved.

Even where the effort is the same, the difference in substance must be considered. In the case of humans the killing is the more blameworthy the more virtuous they are. Apart from that, the extent of the offence is proportionate to the intensity of the wish to kill. Considered externally, then, abortion is a serious unskilful act as it involves violence against a presumably virtuous foetal human being. From the point of view of motivation, the most important factor in Buddhist ethical evaluation, abortion again involves several grievous errors. Greed, hatred, and delusion, the three root drives of unskilful men and women, seem to apply all too well to abortion decisions. Greed, that is passionate attachment, would lie behind persons' considering only their own interests or pleasures in the situation. It would also solidify the notion that an 'I' owned the foetus and could do with it what 'I' would.

Hatred would motivate one to strike out to eliminate the perceived cause of discomfort, the foetus. Delusion might cloud one's understanding and lead to denial that the foetus is a living being. It also could result in a condition of apathy where one, avoiding responsibility for oneself, followed advice to terminate the pregnancy. Underlying these three 'poisons' of greed, hatred, and delusion are even more fundamental errors. The three poisons arise through lack of insight into the interconnectedness of all beings, a misguided sense of difference between me and other. When prajna is so lacking, then so too karuna or compassion will also fall short, and *upaya* or skilful means will not be conspicuous. In light of co-conditioned causality, the moral consequences of abortion do not only concern the relationship between the pregnant woman and the foetus.

Abortion also entails physical and mental trauma to the woman and has karmic consequences on the technicians, advisors, friends, and family involved. Additionally the situation which leads one to consider abortion is often caused by some previous error involving the precept concerning sexuality, which as explained by Buddhaghosa is: 'I undertake to observe the rule to abstain from sensuous misconduct.'... The offence is the more serious, the more moral and virtuous the person transgressed against. Four factors are involved: someone who should not be gone into, the thought of cohabiting with that one, the actions which lead to such cohabitation, and its actual performance. There is only one way of carrying it out: with one's own body.

Sensuous misconduct leads to an awkward pregnancy, which leads to abortion being contemplated. One unskilful act tends to lead to another as long as one lives unmindfully. This leads us back to the religious context of this discussion. What Buddhists aim to do is to perfect themselves by following the path that the Buddha blazed for them. It involves replacing unwholesome roots of action, namely the selfish drives of greed, hatred, and delusion, with wholesome motives: loving-kindness, compassion, joy for others, and equanimity. Morality, meditation, and wisdom constantly work together in this path of *prajna* and *karuna*.

From this point of view any pregnancy could be taken as an opportunity to help one in perfecting selfless compassion. Ratanakul closes his book with a very fine reminder of the high religious ideals of the "voluntary sacrifice of one's claims or rights" that are at the heart of Buddhism and Christianity. At any rate, whatever one does, and one's acts will ripen, with those skilful acts that are beneficial to self and others bearing good fruit while those unskilful acts that harm self and others yielding bad fruit. It should also be mentioned that contraception, if the methods used do no harm to foetus or the lovers, is considered to be skilful means. Obviously, then, from the Buddhist point of view, preventing unwanted pregnancies is far better than terminating them.

ABORTION AND BUDDHISM IN THAILAND

Buddhism is generally depicted as an extremely tolerant tradition which does not seek to impose its teachings on individuals. On March 20, 1988, the CBC interviewed Dr Sugunasari, the President of the Buddhist Council of Canada, to solicit a Buddhist view on the current national abortion dilemma. Dr Sugunasari noted that although abortions involve lack of skill in two of the fundamental Buddhist precepts, the abstention from taking life and the abstention from going astray in sensual pleasures, Buddhists do not think that the state should intervene in matters of conscience. Further he advocated compassion for the individuals involved. In Thailand, a Theravada kingdom where Buddhism is the state religion, there is a very complex and intricate interrelationship amongst the king, the military, the government, the universities, the religious orders, and the people.

The Thais, unlike the Canadian Buddhists, are not shy about trying to build their legal system on Buddhist principles. As they recognise the foetus as a human being from the moment of conception and take the precept against killing as primary, their law against abortion is quite restrictive. Abortions are legal only when there is a serious threat to the health of the mother and in cases of rape. Strictly speaking, it would seem to me that even the outrage of rape, even though it includes both violence and sensuous misconduct, should not be adequate dharmic grounds to allow abortion, which always involves killing a relatively innocent sentient being. That is, one unskilful act does not justify another. The point is to break the chain.

At any rate, the vast majority of Thais think that abortion is a*kusala* karma and are pleased with the restrictive law. Legal abortions are very rare; only five per year on average were reported in the mid 1960s. Nonetheless, the law is widely broken. Virginity is highly valued and there is a heavy social stigma against unmarried mothers so that fear and shame drive many single pregnant women to illegal abortions. They are unable to face the social consequences of their situation and thus sacrifice their Buddhist principles against taking life. Some rationalise that a very small foetus is not yet conscious and thus an abortion does not involve killing. However, as we have seen, this is contrary to the traditional Buddhist understanding. Some medical professionals more or less discretely advertise for abortion business, but many abortionists are untrained, which leads to the usual dreadful consequences.

The Buddhist community in Thailand is divided on the abortion issue. Some leaders like Major General Chamlong Srimunang, the political head of Bangkok, are firmly opposed to any liberalization of the abortion law, basing their position on the absolute sanctity of life in the Buddhist tradition. Others, including some monastic leaders, take a much more global view, pointing out that in Buddhist morality the intent of the action has much to do with the karmic result of the act. Therefore, in some cases, for example when the mother's life is endangered by the pregnancy, abortion could be a skilful act. Dr Pinit Ratanakul's study Bioethics, while it does not offer a complete Buddhist discussion on the abortion question, looks at issues in subtle and complex ways.

While the precept against killing counsels against easy abortion decisions, many factors have to be taken into account in coming to a skilful judgement. Professor Siralee Sirilai of the Faculty of Social Sciences and Humanities at Mahidol University, Bangkok, points out that the main Buddhist criterion for moral decisionmaking is whether or not the act has wholesome motivation. A skilful deed should work against greed, hatred, and delusion, and thus will be for the good of self and others. However, there are also secondary criteria such as "wholesome-unwholesome, usefulness-unusefulness, trouble-untrouble, admirability-blameworthiness". She thinks that for the world renouncers, only the first criterion can be taken into account, but that for the Buddhist layperson the secondary can also come into play. Therefore, in some circumstances, abortion could perhaps be morally permissible.

ABORTION AND BUDDHISM IN CHINA

In Taiwan, where Chinese Buddhism is currently in a very strong resurgence, abortion is condemned in Buddhist theory, for the same reasons as mentioned earlier. However, in traditional Buddhist thought abortion was less culpable than other forms of taking human life. The law in Taiwan is very restrictive, with induced abortion being illegal for any reason and with strong penalties both for the technician and woman involved. Since chastity for unmarried people is very highly valued in both theory and practice, abortions, therefore, are mainly confined to married women who already have the desired number of children. Although illegal, abortion is both widespread and tolerated. It does not seem to be of particular public concern in Taiwan to Buddhists.

In mainland China from my observations been reduced to an adjunct to the tourist industry. Chinese traditional religions are permitted only the most marginal sort of half life, and all religious bodies are expected to restrict themselves to ritual activities within the confines of their buildings. Religious participation in political or legal issues has been unthinkable. Indeed, very few citizens have any interest in traditional Buddhist thought. Therefore, Buddhist objections to abortion are neither voiced nor would they be listened to in the People's Republic of China and the government has a free hand in its one-child policy which relies on abortion for enforcement. Incidentally, the People's Republic and Taiwan are very similar in their attitudes towards sexual chastity.

ABORTION IN JAPAN

Since 1948 Japan has had a liberal abortion law and has had a rather high rate of legal abortions, in 1980 running at 22.5 per 1000 women of child-bearing age. In the same year, for comparison, that rate in the USA was 29.3, Canada 11.5, and the Soviet Union 180, the worlds highest. As is true in many countries, it is thought that the actual rate of medically supervised procedures is much higher than the officially reported rate, and there are still an unknown number of illegal abortions. Although contraception is increasing in Japan, abortion remains the major form of birth control. In part, this is because the government has refused to certify the pill and IUDs as medically safe.

Cynics argue that the medical profession has opposed these means of contraception to protect their highly lucrative abortion trade, but it is true that the pill and IUDs do involve medical risks.

Buddhist Responses to Abortion in Japan

In 1987, Kamakura visited, one of the great centres of Buddhist culture. It was in the grounds of one of Kamakura's exquisite temples, the Hasedera dedicated to Kannon (also known as Kanzeon in Japanese, Kuan Yin in Chinese, *Bodhisattva* Avalokitesvara in Sanskrit) and containing a monumental wooden statue of him, that I came across an extraordinary sight. There were thousands of statues of Jizo Bosatsu lining the walkways and filling courtyards. Stone, porcelain, and plastic Jizos of various sizes were grouped together. None of particular artistic merit, they came in about a half dozen varieties. The mass of these little statuettes was somehow very touching, and the pathetic effect was greatly intensified by the way many of them were decorated.

Very often they were dressed with a red bib or a little red hand-knit cap. Some had soothers on a ribbon around their necks; some had pinwheels or rattles to play with. What was going on here? The vast majority of the statues are for aborted mizuko. At this particular temple, so many women commissioned statues that they continually were clearing away old ones to make room for the new. A major part of the income of the temple came from these services.

The cheapest figurine cost the equivalent of US$80 and memorial services, which many clients ordered, were extra. In the literature given out by Hasedera temple, the images of Jizo were explained as commemorating stillborn and miscarried children, but not aborted ones, even though they did note that Jizo was the protector of aborted foetuses. Jizo Bosatsu's connection with aborted foetuses in Japan has a revealing history. Originating in India as the *Bodhisattva* Ksitigarbha (womb of the earth, or earth store), Jizo vowed to roam all six realms of existence in this dark time between Gautama, the historical Buddha, and Maitreya, the Buddha of the future. Because of this vow, in Japan his images sometimes appear in groups of six slightly different statues, each one representing his activities in one of the realms of reincarnation.

In his wandering, Jizo aids all suffering creatures towards their ultimate salvation. Although introduced to China and Japan as one of the celestial *Bodhisattva*s of Vajrayana or esoteric Buddhism, he became very popular in the folk religion due to his connection with the hells. In Japan he became connected with a folk belief concerning the fate of water-babies and very young children who die. Such youngsters are neither good enough to enter a paradise nor bad enough for a hell, so they find themselves on a deserted river bank called Saino-kawara in Meido, the ghostly realm of gloom. During the day there, they try to make the best of it and play with the pebbles they find, stacking them into the form of little *pagodas*.

This play is more than it seems as their building of *pagodas*, for the benefit of their surviving relatives, is a powerful act of merit. However, when night falls, they become cold and afraid of the dark, and to make things worse malicious demons come and destroy their little structures. Jizo, who has vowed to help all creatures no matter how sad the circumstances, then appears. He is pictured as dressed in the robes of a monk and carrying a staff with six jingling rings on it, each ring representing one of the six realms that he constantly patrols. The jingling of the rings reassures the children, and they are comforted by sheltering in his robe, which gently glows, dispelling the dark.

To his long sleeves cling the infants, Smile in response to his smiling, Glad in his beauteous compassion. Although the image of Kannon in the Hasedera temple was the art treasure that drew the tourists, it was the Jizos in the courtyard that fulfilled a religious need of the people. In dedicating a statuette and commissioning services for their aborted foetuses believers can accrue religious merit. Donations to temples and performing services are excellent ways to improve one's *karma*, to compensate for the unskilfulness in sexual conduct and violence that accompany an act of abortion. Also, whether taken literally or metaphorically, the notion of Jizo comforting the lost mizuko would be very comforting to the mourning survivors.

Jizo has a very large place in the hearts of the Japanese, and little shrines to him appear all over the country, often in unexpected sites: I recall one image nestled amongst a display of valves and piping in a plumber's display window. Often they have little stacks of pebbles before them, recalling the meritorious play of the departed water-babies. The outdoors votive images of Jizo tend to be very simple, stylised figures with him dressed as a Hinayana monk. Although I did not notice it at the time, these figures have an undoubtedly phallic appearance. Indeed, when the Japanese adopted Jizo, he partly supplanted the ancient indigenous Dosojin, Earth Ancestor Deity or Road Ancestor Deity, a god of sexuality in the form of a husband-and-wife couple, who previously had the function of protecting children.

His images were often carved onto ancient phallic representations of Dosojin and, to my eye at least, his usual folk form reflects this origin. In this light, the little images in the courtyard of the Hasedera temple, dedicated to so many mizuko are even more poignant as symbols of human frailty and futility. Religion's wonderful power to express our deepest illusions, as in this case that sexuality can conquer death, is no doubt one of the reasons it has such a hold on humanity. Not all temples display their votive Jizo figures in the casual mode of Hasedera, where they almost seem like mushrooms growing in profusion from the soil. In 1989 I observed a very different style at the Kannon memorial temple in Kyoto. In this modern temple, which dates from the 1950s, the Jizos are encased neatly in numbered rows in glass cases.

All of the figures are the same, and the overall effect reminded me of a sterile department store. However, there were rows of pinwheels for the mizuko as well as racks for toys, in which one also sees some of the more traditional Jizo images.

An American Buddhist Response to Abortion

In Honolulu I attended and eventually joined the Diamond *Sangha*, a Zen group led by an American Roshi, Robert Airkin. He is a leading figure in the 'engaged Buddhism' movement, an informal grouping of North American Buddhists who are trying to formulate theory and practice for applying Buddhist insights and traditions to the social situation of North American practitioners. Roshi Aitken's reflections on abortion are found in the context of his discussion of the first precept, to abstain from killing: Perhaps the most intimate and agonizing test is faced by the woman considering abortion. Over-simplified positions of pro-life and pro-choice do not touch the depths of dilemma.

Usually she experiences distressing conflict between her sexual/reproductive drive and the realities of her life... and indeed, she faces such realities for any child she may bring to term... I get the impression that when a woman is sensitive to her feelings, she is conscious that abortion is killing a part of her and terminating the ancient process, begun anew within her, of bringing life into being.

Thus she is likely to feel acutely miserable after making a decision to have an abortion. This is time for compassion for the woman, and for her to be compassionate with herself and for her unborn child. If I am consulted, and we explore the options carefully and I learn that the decision is definite, I encourage her to go through the act with the consciousness of a mother who holds her dying child in her arms, lovingly nurturing it as it passes from life.... Once the decision is made, there is not blame, but rather acknowledgement that sadness pervades the whole universe and this bit of life goes with our deepest love.

This position seems to hold them to the middle way very skilfully. The moral consequences of the precepts are fully recognised, but the persons involved are treated compassionately rather than judgementally. For those who so desire, the Diamond *Sangha* marks these deaths with a public ceremony based on the Japanese funeral services for mizuko. From my experience I believe that this or a similar ceremony could be very useful in dealing with such a loss, which in our culture usually remains hidden and difficult to resolve. Here it should be mentioned that in Japan, due to the disgrace surrounding abortion, both as a function of sexual misconduct and killing, such services do not seem to involve a public, community recognition of the unhappy event.

In Thailand and Taiwan there also is no formalised religious consolation for people involved in abortions. It is a private hidden grief. Furthermore, in Theravada countries there is no tradition of revering *Bodhisattva* Ksitigarbha. In China this *bodhisattva*, known as Titsang, is neither widely worshipped, nor is he particularly connected with 'water babies'. Finally, my research confirms earlier studies. Where religious prohibitions result in highly restrictive abortion laws, illegal abortions are frequent.

When social pressure to limit family size or to avoid the disgrace of unmarried pregnancy conflicts with religious principles then religion loses out. It seems that the gaps between religious theory and practice are often fruitful places for investigation.

7

Thai Buddhist Perspective on Euthanasia

In few areas have the advances in scientific knowledge and the new medical technologies raised more basic questions about the very nature, meaning and value of human life than in the whole area of death and dying. That health care professionals find themselves in conflict over ethical dilemmas in this area is not surprising, since there is a lack of public consensus on what is morally acceptable. Already in the West, there has begun a groundswell of cultural change in which traditional attitudes and ideas about death and the dying process are being modified or rejected by many and the same development is occurring now in Thai society. In this society, undergirded by the teachings of Theravada Buddhism, the replacement of traditional medicine with high technological medicine has raised new ethical issues that traditional Thai morality and accepted practices cannot adequately deal with.

The new life-support technologies have blurred the line between prolongation of life and prolongation of the dying process, and have raised questions about the adequacy of the traditional definition of death as the cessation of all vital signs. At what moment in the dying process should we declare that "death" has occurred? Shall we continue the traditional definition of "death" or declare "death", when the new measuring devices detect the cessation of higher brain activity, or when both the higher and lower brain activities cease to function spontaneously, unassisted by machines or procedures like hyperalimentation?

There are also other questions such as: Is the refusal of life-preserving treatment by artificial means a morally acceptable option or does it constitute a kind of suicide prohibited by Buddhist teachings? Is it morally wrong for doctors, nurses and families to withdraw life-preserving treatments or to stop such treatment, once these have begun? Are such actions the same as "killing" patients or are there important ethical distinctions to be made between "letting-go-of-life" by withholding or stopping treatment, and actual "killing" or causing death?

The lack of public and professional consensus on these questions creates the possibility for emotionally laden moral conflicts within the general public, between families and their doctors and even among medical professionals themselves. Therefore it is necessary for Thai Buddhists to make systematic review of Buddhist morality and traditionally accepted practices concerning death and dying, and to rethink or reinterpret Buddhist ethics in its application to these new issues that are not so far clearly defined in Buddhism.

It is clear that active euthanasia including assisted suicide is against the Buddhist teaching. This is because in Buddhist psychology, "mercy killing" cannot be carried out without the ill-will or feeling of repugnance (*dosa*) of the perpetrator toward the fact of the patient's suffering. Even though the motivation behind this action may have been good, i.e. to prevent further suffering of the patient, but as soon as such thought becomes action to terminate life it becomes an act of aversion. So when a doctor performs what, he believes is "mercy-killing", actually it is due to his repugnance of the patient's pain and suffering which disturb his mind.

Subsequently the doctor experiences negative emotions toward this disturbance and projects it on the suffering of the patient. But he disguises his real feeling (i.e. repugnance) as a morally praiseworthy deed to justify to himself "mercy-killing". If he understands this psychological process he would recognize the hidden hatred that arises in his mind at the time of performing the lethal deed, and would not deceive himself with the belief that this deed was motivated by benevolence alone. Therefore from the view of Buddhist psychology "mercy-killing" is not really a benevolent act. It is done from ill-will and thus has bad karmic effects both for the doctor and the patient. However, the Buddhist teaching of compassion complicates the issue, for to end the suffering of others is the goal of this Buddhist ethical value.

In health care, compassion implies two obligations doctors have towards their patient i.e. to do all they can in their power to enhance the well-being and health of their patients, and to do no further harm to the patients by preventing and alleviating their harm and suffering. Accordingly doctors and nurses are obligated not to expose their patients to further harm and suffering because of their lack of knowledge, inadequate skills or negligence. In case of terminal patients, compassion is limited to giving drugs in sufficient quantities to relieve intense pain, as that experienced by cancer patients, as a last resort when no hope of recovery is possible and the patient is dying. This is the farthest that compassion can go. Beyond this point the precept against taking of life is violated.

The position of "passive euthanasia" is more difficult to resolve in Buddhist terms. In this case the ethical waters become muddier. Because of its complexity involving scarce medical resources, the high costs of treatment and medical uncertainty the majority of lay Thai Buddhists are more cautious in their approach to "passive euthanasia". Despite their belief in the law of karma for some of them withdrawing life support systems can be justified in a case when, by the best medical wisdom and through rigid testing, there has occurred in the patient total brain death which means irreversible coma and no hope for recovery. Some Thai Buddhists recognize that there is a real moral distinction between "letting die" or allowing a patient to die and directly and intentionally taking life. For them, allowing a patient to die does not violate the precept and is considered an altruistic action for those involved.

In Buddhist ethics intention is crucial in determining actions as right or wrong, but with regard to euthanasia other factors are also important. There can be mixed motivations behind the intention to act in seemingly good ways. The intent of family members and the doctor to let the patient die may be motivated by selfish as well as altruistic desires. For example, for family members there may be the desire to relieve the suffering of a patient and the desire to inherit his fortune. In the case of the doctor he may have the desire to end the pain and suffering of one patient and the desire to have a viable organ for transplantation in another patient.

A hospital can have a policy accepting passive euthanasia with both a desire to relieve the suffering of patients and families and to contain medical costs. For these reasons lay Thai Buddhists are cautious about extending the grounds for "letting-go-of-life" by the withdrawal of medical technologies beyond the strict and narrow grounds in the case just mentioned above. And because of many factors entering into decisions about withdrawing life-support treatments such decisions have to be made on a case to case base. They also recognize that sometimes in real life human choices are only between two evils.

Yet even in this tragic life situation one still has responsibility to choose the lesser evil. But for such agonizing decisions there has been little guidance culled so far from Buddhist sources to help Buddhists and to ease their conscience. As generally known, Buddhism encourages each person to face the troubles by relying on oneself alone, without expecting any divine power to intercede and help.

Choosing among evils requires wisdom (*panna*) or insight arising from the regulated mind (*samadhi*), right understanding (*sammadhithi*) of the real nature of existence characterized by conditionality (*paticca-samuppda*), impermanence (*anicca*), suffering (*dukkha*) and unsubstantiality (*anatta*), and from continuing learning (*sikkha*). With *samadhi* and *sammadithi* one is able to make a realistic evaluation of a given situation and to act unselfishly. *Sikka* enriches *panna* diminishing the number of mistakes made. Since there have been cases especially with younger people where remarkable recoveries have occurred even after doctors pronounced them terminally ill or as being in irreversible coma, Thai lay Buddhists also are unwilling to see general policies adopted accepting passive euthanasia. As there are always risks and uncertainties, they would favor risking in favor of life and not against it.

The problems surrounding the euthanasia issue are complex. It involves the expanded use of hi-tech medicine, doctor's traditional values, patient's autonomy, medical costs, family's desires and religious teachings. There are also many cases of moral conflicts between doctors and families over the continued life or death of patients and between nurses and doctors. The fact of medical costs for serious illnesses weighs differently on the rich and the poor. Distribution of scarce and expensive high-tech medical treatments follows no rule of justice. Lay Thai Buddhists in general are opposed to euthanasia considering it to be against the Buddhist precept of taking life.

At the same time they have become aware of the many aspects of the issue which make it not that clear cut. For example, through the newspapers they have become aware of cases such as that of a 94 year old woman, kept alive by artificial means for over a year at the cost of bankruptcy of her family. Another case was that of an 11 year old girl in irreversible coma for years, again at high cost to the family. To these lay Buddhists, questions are raised if when asked whether economic factor, the age of the patient and the quality of life would make any important difference in their decisions regarding the use of life-support systems, none could give a definite Buddhist answer. Some say yes and some no, but they could not find grounds in Buddhism to support their answers.

The reality is that some forms of euthanasia are currently being practiced in some hospitals by doctors who make life and death and decisions alone without any directives whether these are ethical, religious, moral or legal. If such practice it is allowed to continue unchecked, public suspicions and therefore mistrust of medical professionals will increase to the detriment of all, patient, families and doctors. Central Buddhist teachings must be reinterpreted to deal with the issue of euthanasia which is a new challenge arisen as a result of the discovery and expanded use of modern technological medicine.

BUDDHIST PRINCIPLE FOR EUTHANASIA DECISIONS

Perhaps the Buddhist concept of mutual dependency and interrelatedness (*paticca-samuppada*) should be applied to the field of medicine. This concept affirms the interdependence of all beings. When all beings depend on other beings, none of them is primary, and concern for other, co-operation and harmony are crucial human values in social relationship. Suicide or assisted suicide as a "right to die" cannot be absolute because people do not live lone but there are also members of communities who might be injured by their death or by a social policy that encourages such death.

With regard to life and death decisions doctors and other medical personnel should not decide and act by themselves but in partnership with patients, their families and/or surrogates when making decisions on treatment, including the use of life-sustaining technologies. Accordingly doctors ought to include in their professional ethics the need to have the consent of their patients or surrogates for any treatment. When conflicts between doctors and patients or surrogates arise, some form or structure of mediation is needed.

Lacking such mediational means, resolution of conflicts depended upon the good will of the two sides to find a compromise. Such good will or possible compromise may not always be present and a law might be enacted to regulate decision-making in cases of conflict. But the law tends to be a blunt instrument, unable to deal with the individual differences and nuances that mark human interactions especially in matters of life and death. Rather, the public must be more educated about what is involved in such decisions. Similarly doctors and nurses must be educated to change their roles to be more of a partner and facilitator in helping patients and surrogates make decisions.

Apart from this, while keeping their primary image as healers, dedicated to preserving and prolonging the life of all patients under their care, they have to develop a new approach to death and dying, so that when death becomes imminent they would become graceful acceptors of the inevitable, without considering the hopeless condition of the dying patient as representing the failure of their skills and knowledge. They should instead turn their full attention now to the compassionate care of the dying. Their main concern of course is to relieve the suffering of patients and families and ensure a "good death". To make these changes a long process is required but it is a needed one to minimize conflicts, and pitfalls.

Especially in regard to euthanasia, there are grounds in Buddhism for hospice care. This is because in Buddhist tradition death is accepted as the natural end of life and one is not encouraged to either hasten it or to save it all costs. Buddhism is also known for its holistic approach to health care focusing on the entire person, and for its emphasis on the last stage of life as being of great importance and, on the practice of compassion on the part of doctors and nurses to provide a special care for the dying. The ideal is to help them to die in a calm, conscious state, so that possible good rebirth is obtained.

Hospice care provides humane treatment, comfort, consolation and companionship to the dying either in their own homes or in special units at hospitals staffed by specialists specially trained to deal with all kinds of suffering that people and families endure at the end of life, involving physical, mental, emotional, moral and spiritual. These hospice specialists have successfully demonstrated not only that no one needs to suffer from unbearable pain toward the end of life, but that most people can be maintained at a level of pain-relief which does not impair their faculties or cloud consciousness, but permits them to have meaningful lives at the end. Such care obviates much of the concern for euthanasia and is in conformity with the Buddhist teaching about life and death and the practice of compassion.

The success in pain-relief and the atmosphere and policies of hospice movement indicate that no one needs die neglected, alone, shunted aside by doctors and nurses, busy with the living yet unconscious and hooked to machines, kept from their families and that death with dignity and humane treatment is still possible in our time. The question of the use of artificial means to keep alive does not arise in hospice care, for the acceptance of death is one of the main tenets of the hospice movement when dying is the only option open.

Euthanasia is an agonizing problem of Thai society as more and more high-tech treatments are being used by doctors. It has raised many unresolved ethical problems as the issue is further complicated because of the increased of the practice of organ transplantation. The question being raised now is whether the Buddhist compassion as practiced by doctors should go beyond their concern for their own immediate patients to those patients whose lives could be saved by their own dying patients' organs, as Buddhist compassion is impartial and is directed to all involved in a given situation. There should be extensive dialogue between members of the public and medical profession about this issue. Doctors, patients and the public alike will be benefited by this discussion of the reality and possibility of organ transplantation.

While active euthanasia violates the Buddhist first precept against killing passive euthanasia presents a complex ethical challenge to Buddhist morality. Doctors cannot prolong the use of life-support systems indefinitely because of complicated factors involved such as medical cost for family members, scarce medical resources, medical uncertainty, and the resulting quality of patients' lives saved or sustained. Contemporary emphasis upon patients' autonomy, that patient should have the right to choose and refuse treatment and the possibility of conflicts between patients and doctors, doctors and family members are the other factors that complicated the issue. But the situation is even more aggravated when cases involved incompetent patients such as seriously defective infant (e.g. spina bifida babies, and anencephalics) who may be spared the agony of short but futile life by stopping life-sustaining treatments. In this case it is not the length of life that is really significant in making life and death decision it is the infants' own agony and the futility of treatment that matter.

Suggestions are given by some Thai Buddhists that one can draw a distinction between "killing" and "letting-go-of-life" is worthy of serious consideration because in Buddhist ethics the motivation and intention behind actions are morally significant factors not simply the end result. If there really is such distinction Thai Buddhists may feel that letting-go-of-life does not constitute a breach of the Buddhist first precept, and Buddhism can offer a "middle way" between the two extremes i.e. active euthanasia including assisted suicide and the position of sustaining life at all costs and under all circumstances. However for general public there is still uncertainty about distintinguishing between "killing" and "letting-go-of-life", and passive euthanasia remains problematic for them.

It is even more problematic for the doctors who strongly believe that sustaining the lives of their patients is their primary duty and obligation. Therefore the question of to save or let-go-of-life is a continuing ethical issue as Thai Buddhists grapple with the reality of existence in the modern world and the need to be faithful to Buddhist teachings. More and more elderly Buddhists, monks and lay people alike, express their wishes to be allowed to die in the last stage of their lives accepting death as a natural end simply because, they believe, this is the Buddhist way of facing the inevitable death.

The themes of impermanence, decay and death are omnipresent in Buddhist literature. In many Asian cultures Buddhism is identified as the authority par excellence on matters pertaining to death, and is closely linked to the rites and ceremonies associated with the transition from this life to the next. Buddhist literature emphasises the importance of meeting death mindfully since the last moment of one life can be particularly influential in determining the quality of the next rebirth.

General reflections on death will be found in Philip Kapleau's 1972 anthology The Wheel of Death and his 1989 The Wheel of Life and Death. Stephen Levine is the author of several books dealing with the subject of death from a Zen perspective while a contemporary Tibetan perspective is provided by Sogyal Rinpoche's popular Tibetan Book of Living and Dying, Glenn H. Mullin (1986) and John Powers. James Whitehill (1974) discussed what can be learned from the death of the Buddhist masters, and the development of a corpus of "Great Death" stories of various Buddhist masters is examined by LaFleur (1974). Other writings on death in Buddhism include Smart (1968), Amore (1974), and Bowker (1991).

In a 1993 monograph on the subject of death in Buddhism, Becker asserts that the Buddhist tradition, especially in Japan, is very tolerant of suicide and euthanasia. Evidence of this is the Buddha's tolerance of suicide by monks and Japanese stories praising suicide by monks, samurai and laypeople. Becker suggests that Buddhism values self-determination and praises those who decide when and how they will die when they do so in order to have a dignified conscious death. Becker also concludes that the key point is not whether there is still warmth or reflexes (as suggested by some readings of the *Visuddhimagga*) but whether the patient's *skandhas* have permanently left, i.e. the patient is permanently unconscious. In other words, Buddhism would endorse a brain death definition of death. On the understanding of death in Japanese religion see also Picken (1977).

A number of issues in medical ethics turn upon the problem of defining death, but few writers have addressed the question of a Buddhist definition of death directly. Only van Loon (1978), Keown (1995), and Mettanando (1991) have argued for a specific definition: van Loon equates death with neocortical death whereas Keown and Mettanando support the "whole brain" criterion.

There has been considerable resistance to the adoption of the brain death standard in Japan, both from the public and within the medical profession, due in no small measure to its association with organ transplantation. The brain death criterion allows organs to be harvested with the minimum delay, thereby enhancing the prospects for a successful transplant. Japanese tradition, however, requires the performance of rituals over a lengthy period before an individual is regarded as having passed on, and is also reluctant to countenance plundering the bodily organs of future ancestors.

Some commentators suggest that public acceptance of brain death is growing as professional groups and universities develop criteria, and as pressure from potential beneficiaries grow. Also, countries such as the Philippines have raised objections to Japanese patients going abroad for transplants rather than building an organ retrieval system of their own. The best analysis available (in English) of the Japanese situation is Hardacre (1994), but relevant material may also be found in Lock and Honde (1990), Feldman (1988), Becker (1990), and Nudeshima (1991).

A more positive attitude towards transplantation is revealed in Tsomo (1993). The author surveyed teachers from many different traditions about their attitudes to donation. All were very positive, and emphasized that the corpse is merely an empty vessel, and that to give of oneself is a great thing, and an act of compassion.

EUTHANASIA

There are no monographs devoted specifically to euthanasia in Buddhism. There are a few periodical articles and the subject is dealt within one or two books. Relevant issues are the distinction between various forms of euthanasia (e.g. "active" and "passive") and the use of narcotics in palliative care which may cloud the mind and interfere with the process of dying. Kapleau's volume The Wheel of Life and Death (1989) contains a short discussion of euthanasia in conjunction with suicide and it is suggested that Buddhism would reject the practice of either.

Ratanakul concurs, reporting "a growing consensus among the Thai public that euthanasia (passive or active) is morally unjustifiable" (1990:27). Keown and Keown (1995) explore Buddhist and Christian attitudes to euthanasia and suggest both oppose it for similar reasons. Nakasone, however, is of the opinion that "Evidence indicates that Buddhists would favor the 'right-to-die' position" (1990:76). Jennifer Green's short article "Death with Dignity: Buddhism" (1989:40-41) discusses only the practicalities of funeral arrangements and does not mention euthanasia. Neuberger (1987) is likewise concerned with practical as opposed to moral issues.

Euthanasia has been a special feature in two Buddhist magazines, Raft, and Tricycle. London-based Raft, the Journal of the Buddhist Hospice Trust, devoted its No. 2 Winter 1989/90 issue to Euthanasia. Sixteen pages in length it contains short pieces by authors such as Elisabeth Kubler-Ross, Ajahn Sumedho, Dame Cicely Saunders and David Stott, exploring the cases for, against, and in terms of a middle way. A similar range of opinions will be found in the Winter 1992 edition of *Tricycle*, which contains short articles by Patricia Anderson, Jeffrey Hopkins, Philip Kapleau, Chogyam Trungpa, and an interview with author Stephen Levine.

In a number of contexts, the discourses of the Buddha that have come down to us in the four Pali *Nikayas* present the act of killing a living being as an unwholesome (*akusala*) act and, as such, to be avoided.

The first of the ten courses of unwholesome action (*akusala-kammapatha*) is "to kill living beings." The third of the eight elements that make up the Buddha's eightfold path is "right action"; one of the three forms that right action takes is "refraining from killing living beings." The first of the five precepts or "rules of training" (*sikkhapada*) that are undertaken by all lay Buddhists takes the form, "I undertake the rule of training to refrain from harming living beings."

The ten courses of unwholesome action, the eightfold path, and the five precepts are all standard elements in the teaching of the Buddha as presented in the Pali *Nikayas*. But we also find the injunction not to kill or harm living beings spelled out in other ways and in specific contexts. Let me cite just two of the many possible examples. In the Brahmajala Sutta we are told how the Buddha "refrains from killing living creatures, discards sticks and swords, and is considerate and full of concern, remaining sympathetic and well disposed towards all creatures and beings." And a verse from the *Suttanipata* states, "Laying aside violence in respect of all living beings in the world, both those which are still and those which move, he should not kill a living creature, not cause to kill, nor allow others to kill." In the C*u*lla-*Kamma*vibhanga Sutta we are told of the results of killing living beings:

Some man or woman kills living beings and is murderous, has blood on his hands, is given to blows and violence, is without pity for living beings. Because of performing and carrying out such action, at the breaking up of the body, after death he reappears in a state of misfortune, an unhappy destiny, a state of affliction, hell. The well known Metta Sutta or "discourse on friendliness," a text frequently chanted in Buddhist ritual and considered one that brings protection or safety (*paritta*), sums up the positive corollary of not killing living beings as follows:

One should not wish another pain out of anger or thoughts of enmity. Just as a mother would protect with her life her own son, her only son, so one should cultivate the immeasurable mind towards all living beings and friendliness towards the whole world.

So, prima facie, the picture is clear: killing living beings-any living being-is a bad thing that leads to an unpleasant rebirth; following the Buddha's path involves refraining from killing living beings, laying aside weapons, and cultivating the compassion of the Buddha-end of story. But, one might ask, are all kinds of killing the same? Is there not a difference between killing a human being and squashing a mosquito and what of our motivations in killing? Is "putting down" an ailing cat or dog not rather different from, say, hunting animals for sport? What of acts of "mercy-killing" or euthanasia in the case of the sick and dying? What of abortion? What of war? While not all these questions are directly and explicitly addressed in traditional Buddhist writings, a number of statements and discussions in the Pali texts touch on these issues in various ways.

In recent years a number of scholars have drawn on some of these discussions in order to try to begin to map out something of the traditional Buddhist approach to some of the ethical issues surrounding the act of killing, and also to introduce a Buddhist perspective into the contemporary discussion of such issues as abortion, euthanasia, and general bioethics. While this work has certainly succeeded in clarifying Buddhist thinking on ethical issues, I also think that by too readily transposing Buddhist discourse into the framework of contemporary ethical discourse it has sometimes inadvertently distorted what I see as the distinctively Buddhist psychological take on ethical issues.

The scholars working in this area have got their Buddhist ethics wrong, but rather that they tend at crucial points to force Buddhist texts to conform to the idiom of contemporary ethical discourse, rather than allowing them their own distinctive voice. One reason for this, I think, is because existing discussions do not pay sufficient attention to the Pali commentaries and Abhidhamma framework in which their discussions of the finer points of Buddhist thought are set.

The basic relevance of the Abhidhamma to what in the Western intellectual tradition is called "ethics" was in fact recognized a century ago by Mrs. Rhys Davids when she translated the first book of the *Abhidhamma Pitaka* under the title of *Buddhist Psychological Ethics*. The present chapter is in part an attempt to follow her lead and consider more fully some details of the treatment found in the Theravada *Abhidhamma* and Pali commentaries of one particular unwholesome course of action and the related training rules in the Vinaya.

THE VINAYA RULES

The monastic code for Buddhist monks includes 227 rules; these are divided into groups according to the seriousness of the offence that follows from breaking the rule. The first four, the *parajikas,* are the most serious: breaking any one of them involves the monk in "defeat" (expulsion from the order). The third of the *parajika* offences is a rule against intentionally killing another human being:

Whatever bhikkhu should intentionally deprive a human being of life, or seek a weapon for him for taking [life], or should utter praise of death, or should urge him towards death saying, "Good man, what use to you is this miserable life? Death is better than life." Or, having such thoughts and intentions in mind, should in several ways utter praise of death, or should urge him towards death, he too becomes defeated, is not in communion.

Killing a living being other than a human being is distinguished as a lesser offence (pacittiya sixty-one): "If any bhikkhu should intentionally deprive a living being of life, there is an offence entailing expiation." Two things are clear in the formulation of these rules: (1) that whether or not we do things intentionally and with full consciousness is a crucial determinant of responsibility in the Buddhist view of things; (2) killing a human being is to be distinguished from killing other living beings.

Of course, we must tread carefully here. The canonical and commentarial Vinaya texts are not simply concerned with ethical issues and matters of morality; they are also concerned with legal questions-with how to determine whether or not a monk or nun has broken one of a set of 227 or 311 rules. As the texts are well aware, breaking a rule of law may or may not be the same thing as doing a moral wrong. The ancient Buddhist texts make a clear distinction between that which is loka-vajja and that which is pannatti-vajja-deeds that offend against a universally accepted moral principle and those that offend against a conventionally designated rule. I shall return to this distinction presently.

If we examine the Vinaya texts and the "case histories" (*vinîta-vatthu*) that accompany the various rules, the question of a monk's intentions and of his state of mind is raised again and again in determining whether or not a rule has been broken: accidentally killing someone or killing someone when one is in a confused state of mind is quite a different matter from deliberately and consciously killing someone.

Of course, the importance of intention in the Buddhist understanding of what constitutes moral or immoral action is brought out in an often quoted statement of the Buddha's: "It is intention that I call action (*kamma*); having formed an intention one acts." In other words, actions that carries moral responsibility-which will lead to pleasant or unpleasant results-are those which one does with clear intention. As in a modern court of law, intentions and state of mind are important considerations.

The old Vinaya exposition (*vibhanga*) of the third *parajika* offence also gives us some other details and clues: encouraging someone to commit suicide who then does so, carrying out an abortion or intentionally being instrumental in an abortion are both considered as constituting intentional killing of a human being and hence an offence involving "defeat" or "expulsion" (*parajika*).

THE COMMENTARIAL DISCUSSION

There are two main contexts in which the Pali *atthakathas* provide an analysis of the act of killing a being: (1) commenting on the list of ten *akusala-kammapatha*; (2) commenting on the third *parajika* rule and *pacittiya* sixty-one.

Let us turn first to the commentarial analysis of the "courses of action." In their treatment of the courses of action, the commentaries imply a distinction between *kamma* in general-any good or bad action that carries some degree of moral responsibility and which will have a desirable or undesirable result-and *kamma-patha*-a complete course of action. This last expression characterizes a completed and fully intentional morally good or bad action. The distinction at work here is perhaps comparable to the distinction made between venial and mortal sin in medieval Christian theology. So what do the commentaries have to say about what is involved in the course of action of killing a living being? The following passage occurs in at least five places in the *atthakathas,* which no doubt indicates that it has been drawn from the earlier Sinhala commentaries as an authoritative statement of the relevant issues.

In part it seems in turn to have drawn on and developed discussions found in the canonical Vinaya analysis of the third *parajika*. The word "living creature" means, in conventional discourse, a being; in the ultimate sense it is the faculty of life. Killing a living creature is the intention to kill in one who perceives a living creature as such, when this occurs through the door of either the body or of speech and produces the exertion that cuts off the life-faculty [of that living being].

In the case of living creatures without [moral] virtues, such as animals, [the act of killing] is less blameworthy when the creature has a small body, and more blameworthy when the being has a large body. Why? Because of the greater effort [required] in killing a being with a large body; and even when the effort is the same, [the act of killing a large-bodied creature is still more blameworthy] because of its greater physical substance. In the case of beings that possess [moral] virtues, such as human beings, the act of killing is less blameworthy when the being is of little virtue and more blameworthy when the being is of great virtue. But when the body and virtue [of creatures] are equal, [the act of killing] is less blameworthy when the defilements and force of the effort are mild, more blameworthy when they are powerful.

The act of killing has five components: a living being, the perception of the living being as such, the thought of killing, the action, and the death [of the being] as a result. There are six means: one's own person, giving orders, missiles, stationary devices, magical spells, and psychic power. So for the killing of a living being to be classified as a *kamma-patha,* five conditions need to be fulfilled. If any one of the five conditions is not fulfilled, then it is not a completed course of action, although it may still be an unwholesome or immoral act of some sort and degree.

From this idea it would seem to follow that any intentional killing of any living being whatsoever should be regarded as an unwholesome course of *kamma,* and as morally blameworthy. I will return to the question of intention presently. First I wish to consider briefly the three factors the commentary singles out as affecting the degree of seriousness or moral blameworthiness of the deed:

- Size: in the case of animals, the bigger the animal, the more serious the act of killing.
- Virtue: in the case of humans, the more virtuous the human, the more serious the act of killing.
- The intensity of the desire to kill coupled with the effort involved in the actual act of killing.

These criteria have been briefly discussed by Damien Keown. His discussion seems to assume that these factors are offered as a more or less exact way of calculating the relative blame that accrues to unwholesome deeds. But to read them in this way may land us in unnecessary difficulties. I would prefer to take them as articulating what is in many ways a "common sense" attitude towards the relative blameworthiness of different unwholesome acts-an attitude that has much in common with the attitudes of a contemporary court of law.

The first criterion is something that I would argue is taken for granted in contemporary society. Most of us would regard the swatting of a fly or a mosquito as different and qualitatively distinct from the killing of a mouse or rat; most would regard the killing of a mouse or a rat as different and qualitatively distinct from the killing of a horse, gorilla, or elephant. As long as we take the question of size as a general rule of thumb, and not as a strict and exact method of calculating moral blame, it would seem to work. Of course, some might want to argue that although we certainly do regard the killing of mosquitoes in a different light from that in which we regard the killing of, say, horses or humans, this difference is really just a measure of our moral confusion: in truth we really should not, since all life is of equal moral worth.

At first sight the second is more difficult and, some might feel, a more morally dangerous if not positively morally repugnant idea because it might be taken as allowing us to conclude that those whom we consider as morally degenerate are somehow morally less valuable, and so can be disposed of with impunity. I would suggest that this is the wrong conclusion. The view expressed here is that killing living beings is always wrong, and never right. What the commentary is trying to get at, I think, is the psychological attitude, the quality of intention that might be involved in killing different human beings: that is, we tend to feel differently about and find it harder to understand-and perhaps regard as more blameworthy-the killing of innocents than we do the killing of some serial murderer, for example.

Think for a moment of the murder of "a sweet old lady" who had never done anyone any harm and of the murder (or execution) of some notorious criminal; imagine for a moment the assassination of Adolf Hitler or Joseph Stalin alongside that of Mahatma Gandhi or Martin Luther King. The third criterion seems to have to do with the interplay between the viciousness and depravity of the act of killing; compare killings that are acts of uncharacteristic and sudden anger with those that are premeditated, sadistic acts. The relationship between effort and the intensity of the defilements is no doubt of some complexity: a casual act of killing without any thought for the victim might involve little effort and thought, yet that very fact might be taken as an indicator of deep-rooted and strong defilements.

Of course, in matters of morals we like to think that we can find universals, and the preceding discussion raises all sorts of questions about the extent to which we have to do here with socially and culturally conditioned values as opposed to universal human and moral values. Different cultures, different societies, have quite different attitudes towards certain animals. But whatever we precisely think of the moral suitability of the criteria suggested, we at least can see that the commentary are attempting to articulate an attitude which views killing living beings as in all circumstances an unwholesome *kamma*, an action leading to unpleasant results in future births, but nevertheless allows that some acts of killing are worse than others.

THE ABHIDHAMMA PERSPECTIVE

The particular detail of the commentarial analyses that I wish to focus on in the present context is the way that "killing a being" is defined not as the actual act of killing itself but as the mental intention or will (*cetana*) that prompts the act of killing:

Killing a living being is the intention to kill in one who is aware of a living being as a living being when this occurs through either the door of the body or of speech and produces the exertion that cuts off the life-faculty.

Or, as the *Samantapasadika* puts it, "The intention to kill as a result of which one produces the activity that cuts off [a being's] life-faculty is called 'killing a living being'; 'the one who kills a living being' should be understood as the person possessing that intention."

In both these commentarial passages, in line with the general tendency in Buddhist thought, the emphasis is on an unwholesome action (*kamma*) as consisting at least in part in the underlying mental intention (*cetana*). While the commentaries do not state the intention to kill as a sufficient condition for the course of action that is killing a living being, they do clearly state it as one of the five necessary conditions (*sambhara*): a living being, awareness of the living being, a mind that intends to kill, the exertion, and death as a result.

In the present context, what I wish to establish is the Theravada analysis of the nature of the mind that might produce in someone the intention or will to kill: what kinds of motivation might characterize the mind at the time of killing?

In fact, within the general framework of Abhidhamma psychology, the commentarial analysis of the nature of the intention to kill (*vadhaka-citta/vadhaka-cetana*) seems clear and unambiguous. After the initial analysis of the ten a*kusala kammapathas,* the commentarial analysis sets out five ways for defining (*vinicchaya*) their nature: by way of intrinsic nature (*dhamma/sabhava*), grouping (*kotthasa*), object (*arammana*), feeling (*vedana*), and root (m*u*la).

For present purposes, it is the definition by way of feeling and root that is particularly relevant. The definition by way of intrinsic nature reaffirms the point already made, namely that the act of killing is essentially the intention to kill. When it comes to the definition of killing a being by way of feeling, it is stated that it "has painful feeling, for even though kings presented with a thief say with a smile, "Go and execute him," nevertheless the decisive intention is only associated with painful feeling." As to root, killing a living being has two roots, namely hate and delusion. This set of definitions keys the *kamma*-pathas quite precisely into the Abhidhamma system of classes of consciousness.

The fact that intention to kill is accompanied by only painful feeling and has as its roots hate and delusion means that it can only be constituted by two of the standard list of eighty-nine classes of consciousness: the two classes of sense-sphere consciousness rooted in hate and accompanied by unhappiness. The possibility that the intention to kill might ever be constituted by one or other of the eight classes of sense-sphere consciousness rooted in lack of greed, lack of hate, and lack of ignorance is apparently simply excluded. In other words the intention to kill is understood as exclusively unwholesome, and the possibility that it might ever be something wholesome prompted by thoughts of compassion is not countenanced.

Of course, one might try to argue that wholesome minds are not included here by definition: what is under discussion here are the ten courses of unwholesome action, and if one kills a living being out of compassion it is by definition not an unwholesome course of action and hence not "killing a living being" (*patipata*). But, as we shall see, the way in which the Vinaya does allow for the fact that some rules can be broken with wholesome (*kusala*) and undetermined (*avyakata*) consciousness seems to exclude this interpretation. In the Sutta context, the point is that there simply is no wholesome course of action that is killing a living being.

The two older extant commentaries to the Vinaya, the *Samantapasadika* and the *Kankhavitaranî*, give a set of eight categories by which to analyze each rule of the *Patimokkha*. These categories concern (1) the nature of the "arising" or "origin" of an offence (*samutthana*); (2) whether it arises from activity (*kiriya*) or inactivity; (3) whether there needs to be full awareness (*sañña*) of what one is doing (or not doing) for something to constitute an offence; (4) whether the mind (*citta*) is involved in the offence's arising or origin; (5) whether an offence constitutes something that is universally a fault (*loka-vajja*) or whether it is something that is merely a fault by designation (*pannatti-vajja*) as such in the Vinaya; (6) whether an offence concerns an act (*kamma*) of body, speech, or mind; (7) whether at the time of committing an offence one's mind is constituted by unwholesome consciousness, or by either wholesome or undetermined consciousness; and (8) whether the mind at the time of committing an offence will be associated with unpleasant feeling, pleasant feeling, or neutral feeling.

The seventh and eighth categories in this list once again key into the Abhidhamma classification of consciousness. The *Samantapasadika* makes this quite explicit:

> There are wholesome rules, unwholesome rules and undetermined rules. For just thirty-two classes of consciousness can produce an offence: the eight wholesome sense-sphere consciousnesses, the twelve unwholesome and ten *kiriya* sense-sphere consciousnesses, and the two wholesome and kiriya higher knowledge consciousnesses. A rule which one breaks with wholesome consciousness is [classified as] wholesome, [those which one breaks] with the other kinds are classified accordingly.

What this makes clear is that for the *Samantapasadika,* while in many circumstances Vinaya rules will be broken, as one might expect, when the mind is constituted by unwholesome consciousness and motivated by some combination of greed, hatred, and delusion, at least certain rules in certain circumstances may be broken when the mind is constituted by wholesome consciousness and motivated by nonattachment, friendliness, and wisdom. Moreover, this being the case, it is explicitly stated that again at least certain rules in certain circumstances may be broken when the mind is constituted by various classes of undetermined or kiriya consciousness.

In other words, the Vinaya commentary recognizes that in certain circumstances a purely wholesome (*kusala*) intention will lead someone to break a Vinaya rule; even arahats in certain circumstance will-quite rightly and properly in that they are acting from the motivations of nonattachment (*alobha*), friendliness (*adosa*), and wisdom (*amoha*)-break Vinaya rules. In the course of commenting on the 227 rules of the *Patimokkha* the *Samantapasadika* and *Kankhavitaranî* spell out which rules can be broken when the mind is constituted by these different types of consciousness. Commenting on the third parajika, the *Samantapasadika* states:

As for arising, etc., this rule has three arisings (it arises from body and mind, from speech and mind, and from body, speech and mind); it concerns activity, it is rendered void by [the absence of] full awareness, it is associated with the mind, it concerns a universal fault, it is an act of the body, or an act of speech, it is connected with unwholesome consciousness, and painful feeling. For even when a king seated on his throne enjoying the pleasure of political power responds to the news that a thief has been arrested with a smile, saying, "Go and execute him!," it should be understood that he does so only with a mind associated with unhappiness. But because this unhappiness is mixed with pleasure and is also not sustained, it is difficult for ordinary people to notice.

In the case of Pacittiya sixty-one, *Samantapasadika* makes the following comment:

In the context of this rule, "living creature" refers only to animals; whether one kills a small or large creature, there is no variation in the offence, but in the case of a large animal there is more unwholesomeness because of the greater effort [involved]. Perceiving a living creature as such means that even when in the course of cleaning one's mattress one perceives just a bedbug egg as a living creature and without compassion removes it by crushing it, there is an offence entailing expiation. Therefore by establishing compassion in such circumstances, one who is heedful will fulfil his obligations. The rest should be understood in exactly the same way-with the [same] arisings, etc.-as has been stated in the case of killing a human being.

The fact that the Vinaya commentary does not allow for the possibility that one might break these two Vinaya rules when the mind is constituted by anything other than unwholesome consciousness and associated with anything other than painful feeling makes it clear that it considers only two of the eighty-nine classes of consciousness as relevant to the breaking of these rules: the two sense-sphere consciousnesses rooted in aversion/hate (*dosa*) and accompanied by unhappiness. As we are here dealing with the motivations for breaking a legal rule rather than for an ethical rule, the possibility that wholesome consciousness is not considered as a motivation by definition, as in the case of the unwholesome courses of *kamma*, seems to be excluded.

The case of the laughing king cited here was also cited in the commentarial analysis of the *kamma-patha*. Its significance might be interpreted in two slightly different ways: (1) even a king who takes pleasure in ordering the execution of criminals, at the moment he orders the execution does so with unwholesome consciousness motivated by aversion; (2) even a king merely carrying out the duties of government, at the moment he orders the execution of a criminal does so with unwholesome consciousness motivated by aversion.

According to Abhidhamma theory, beings may smile or laugh with any of the thirteen sense-sphere consciousnesses accompanied by happy feeling: four unwholesome, four wholesome, and five *kiriya*. The four unwholesome are rooted in greed (happy feeling never accompanies consciousness rooted in aversion); the four wholesome are rooted in nonattachment and friendliness or nonattachment, friendliness and wisdom, likewise four of the five kiriya; arahats and Buddhas may in addition smile with the unmotivated consciousness that produces smiles.

The point the commentary seems to want to make here-and, as we saw above, in the context of the unwholesome course of *kamma* that constitutes killing a living being-is that while unwholesome consciousness rooted in greed and accompanied with happy feeling may arise close to the time of the intention to kill and thus superficially appear to be directly and immediately associated with an act of killing, this is not strictly the case: the actual intention that directly leads to the act of killing is always motivated by some kind of aversion and hence accompanied by unhappy feeling. What is revealed here then is what, in the Abhidhamma view of things, is a fundamental principle of the way in which the mind and intention operate.

The Abhidhamma appears quite uncompromising here: it is a psychological impossibility, a psychological contradiction in terms that one should, when motivated by nonattachment, friendliness (and wisdom), intentionally kill another living being. The Abhidhamma and Theravadin exegetical tradition just do not seem to countenance the possibility.

COMPASSION AS A MOTIVE FOR KILLING

Given that in contemporary discussions of euthanasia (both in the case of sick animals and dying human beings) and abortion, a motivation of compassion is at least partly appealed to by those seeking an ethical justification, it seems worth trying to pursue the question of just why the Abhidhamma traditions puts forward what might appear a somewhat uncompromising view. How does this view fit within the broader framework of the values that underpin Buddhist thought and practice? The case histories that the canonical Vinaya appends to each of the rules of the *Patimokkha* outline several situations that are potentially relevant to the issue of euthanasia.

These have been discussed by Damien Keown and others. In the present context I would like to focus on the one instance where the motivation associated with the breaking of the third parajika offence is explicitly stated to be compassion (*karuña*):

At that time a certain monk was ill. Out of compassion monks spoke in praise of death to him, and the monk died. Those monks were full of regret, thinking, "The Blessed One has laid down a precept. What if we have committed an offence involving defeat?" They informed the Blessed One of the situation. [He said,] "Monks, you have committed an offence involving defeat.

In his analysis of this case, Damien Keown argues that since the Buddha rules that the monks are guilty of a parajika offence despite their having acted out of compassion, it shows that the motivation of an act-here the good motivation of compassion-is an insufficient condition for determining whether an act is moral or immoral in Buddhist thought. Since the monks' motivation is good, their wrongdoing must lie in something else. Keown suggests that the solution to the puzzle is to be found by employing a legal distinction between motivation and intention: the monks' motive (compassion) is good, but what they intend (the death of the sick monk) is bad.

Intending the death of the sick monk is bad because "it involves intentionally turning against a basic good," the basic good in question being "karmic life." So, while motive is of great importance in Buddhist ethics it does not by itself guarantee moral rightness. If it did, it would be impossible to do wrong from a good motive. We see here that the Buddha felt this was only too possible.

It seems to me that Keown's analysis of this case is a prime example of the problem I referred to at the beginning of this chapter: distorting Buddhist ethical discourse by slipping into a contemporary idiom in which the categories are derived from a quite different and specific tradition of ethical discussion. A concept such as "basic good" is not found in the Pali Buddhist texts; by using it and driving a wedge between "moral rightness" and "motive," Keown begins to talk in terms and categories that lack a firm foundation in Buddhist thought, at least as expounded in the Pali canon and its oldest extant commentaries.

For these texts, the concepts of moral right and moral wrong can only meaningfully be discussed in terms of what is *kusala* and a*kusala*, what is wholesome and unwholesome. And the terms *kusala* and a*kusala* are not applied with reference to "basic goods" such as "karmic life" in Buddhist thought; they are applied to the particular mentalities (*cetasika*) that motivate the mind and thus lead to acts of body and speech. In order to determine an act as "moral" or "immoral" in the framework of Buddhist thought assumed by the Pali commentarial tradition, we have to ask whether it is *kusala* or a*kusala*, and this is a question about the nature of the motivations (*hetu*) that function as the roots (m*u*la) of and so underlie the intention or will (*cetana*) to act, nothing else.

The Theravadin Abhidhamma defines these motivations or roots as essentially six in number: greed (*lobha*), hatred (*dosa*), and delusion (*moha*) on the unwholesome or a*kusala* side; and lack of greed (alobha), lack of hatred (*adosa*), and lack of delusion (amoha) on the wholesome or *kusala* side.

The latter three are understood as positive virtues equivalent to generosity (*dana*), friendliness (*metta*) and wisdom (*pañña*). What I wish to argue is that, contrary to Keown, for Theravada Buddhist thought it is indeed impossible to do wrong (such as perform an act that is a*kusala*) from an immediate motive that is good (*kusala*).

In his discussion of the Vinaya case referred to above, Keown cites the *Samantapasadika's* comments, although he does not quote these in full, and, in part as a consequence, his understanding of these is, I think, flawed. The following is a full translation:

Out of compassion: seeing that he was in great pain as a result of his illness, those monks felt compassion and, wanting his death yet not realizing that his death is what they wanted, spoke in praise of death, saying, "You are virtuous and have done wholesome deeds. Why should you be afraid of dying? For someone who is virtuous certainly the only thing that can follow from death is heaven." And as a result of their praising death, that monk stopped taking his food and died prematurely. Therefore they committed the offence. But that they spoke in praise of death out of compassion is said by way of the common way of speaking. So even now a wise monk should not speak in praise of death like this to a sick monk.

For if after hearing him praise [death] the sick monk makes the effort to stop taking food and as a result dies prematurely, even if all that remains to him of life is one process of impulsion, then it is he who has brought about the sick monk's death. However, a sick monk should be given the following sort of instruction, "For one who is virtuous the path and fruit can arise unexpectedly, so forget your attachment to such things as the monastery, and establish mindfulness of the Buddha, *Dhamma*, *Sangha* and the body, and pay attention to [the manner of] bringing [things] to mind." But even when death is praised, if the person makes no effort [to die] as a result of the praise and dies according to his own nature in accordance with his own life-span and the natural course of events, then for this reason the person who speaks in praise of death is not to be accused of an offence.

The term antara, which I have translated as "prematurely," Keown renders as "shortly after." But as A Critical Pali Dictionary points out, antara can have the connotation of "untimely," and the specific background to the *Samantapasadika's* comments here is surely the technical notion of timely *(kala)* and untimely death (*akala-marana*). As the *Visuddhimagga* states, one of the factors in determining death as timely or untimely is the exhaustion or otherwise of a being's natural lifespan (*ayus*). Only if one understands antara as "prematurely" does the sense of the statement about one course of impulsion being all that remains of life (*eka-javana-*

varavasese pi ayusmim) become clear-and also the point made subsequently (which Keown omits) about the monk dying in accordance with his lifespan (*yathayuna*).

Having cited the *Samantapasadika's* comments on this Vinaya case, Keown himself goes on to comment that the monks' motivation in speaking in praise of death in the present context "is not in question since we are explicitly told that they acted out of compassion." However, the *Samantapasadika* precisely does question the motivation of compassion here, in the first place with the following significant clause: *maranatthika va hutva maranatthika-bhavam ajananta.* Keown renders this "they made death their aim...although ignorant of the state of being one who makes death his aim," explaining in a note that "this is because no case of this kind had arisen hitherto, and the implication of their actions occurred to them after the death of the patient." I think this rendering represents a misunderstanding.

Above, I have rendered this clause "wanting his death yet not realizing that his death is what they wanted." The subcommentaries explain the clause as meaning that the monks in question did not know their own state of mind of intending death, and were thus not aware of the nature of the consciousness that had arisen in their own minds. In other words, they wanted the sick monk's death, but lacked the self-awareness to see that this is what they wanted. This view of the matter is consonant with the observation regarding the king who superficially appears to be ordering the execution of a criminal with a mind accompanied by pleasant feeling, when in fact according to the psychological analysis of Abhidhamma; the decisive state of mind must be accompanied by unpleasant feeling.

In precisely the same way the commentary and subcommentaries want to suggest that although the monks in the present case think they are acting out of compassion and only have the dying monk's welfare at heart, if they were able to see their motivations more clearly they would see that in fact this was not so. Thus the commentary goes on to state quite explicitly that when it is said the monks spoke in praise of death out of compassion, this is said "by way of the common way of speaking" (*vohara-vasena*). Significantly, Keown omits this sentence from his quotation. But, in the light of our earlier discussion, it is quite clear why the *Samantapasadika* says this.

For the *Samantapasadika*, it simply cannot be that the mind that directly intends the death of a living being is other than one of the two classes of unwholesome consciousness rooted in aversion; and the mental factors (*cetasika*) of friendliness (*adosa, metta*) and compassion (*karuna, karuñña*) cannot be associated with such a consciousness. As the subcommentaries explain, that these monks acted out of compassion is said with reference to their earlier motivation, because compassion is absent at the moment of the decisive intention in one who intends death; so the present case is precisely not like the setting free out of compassion of a boar caught in a trap.

While it is impossible to demonstrate conclusively that the *Samantapasadika's* and subcommentaries' understanding of the situation conforms to the spirit of the original Vinaya case, it is clear that Keown's suggestion that this case shows that for Buddhism "a good motive is thus a necessary but not a sufficient condition for a moral act" does not hold good for the Theravadin Abhidhamma and exegetical tradition. Indeed, I think his attempt to employ a legal distinction between motive and intention ("if I kill you from the motive of compassion... I nevertheless intend to kill you") in the present context is misconceived. I am not suggesting that the distinction is necessarily an invalid one in a Buddhist Abhidhamma framework, merely that in that framework it is considered psychologically impossible to intend to kill someone when motivated by compassion. Thus I am not convinced that there is a concept of "karmic life" as a "basic good" in mainstream Indian Buddhist thought as he maintains.

The manner in which the commentary understands the present case as an instance of parajika is clear: it fulfils the conditions for being classified as an unwholesome course of action. There is a living being, the monks are fully aware that he is a living being, they intend that the sick monk should die, they carry out the necessary action in speaking in praise of death to the sick monk, and the sick monk dies as result of their action. Moreover the commentary simply does not allow that the decisive (*sanitthapaka*) intention or motivation is one of compassion (karuñña). The decisive intention in this case-as in all cases of intentionally killing a living being-is to be understood in terms of one of the two classes of consciousness rooted in aversion and accompanied by unpleasant feeling.

It is important to note, however, that this does not mean that in the Abhidhamma view of things the motive of compassion is necessarily completely divorced from each and every act of killing. The example adduced by the commentaries of a laughing king ordering the execution of a criminal reveals an understanding that allows for the rapid change from pleasant feeling to unpleasant feeling, and hence from greed to aversion in the motivations of the mind.

Such a model of the way consciousness processes work suggests the possibility of situations where there is a similarly rapid change from wholesome consciousness to unwholesome consciousness, and if that is so the Abhidhamma model can accommodate the possibility of wholesome consciousnesses rooted in non attachment and friendliness (with or without in addition wisdom) being relatively closely associated in time with an act of killing-indeed, as we have seen, this appears to be how the subcommentaries understand the Vinaya case we have just been considering. Thus it can appear-when the rapid flow of different consciousnesses is not closely examined-that in certain circumstances a being is killed simply out of compassion.

Nevertheless, the possibility of the decisive (*sanitthapaka*) intention being motivated by these wholesome roots is simply ruled out. So while it is possible, on this view of the matter, that an act of killing a living being may in part be associated with compassion, the Abhidhamma wants to exclude the possibility that such an act could ever be wholly so: the arising of consciousness rooted in aversion at the decisive moment is a necessary condition of all intentional acts of killing. Hence that an awakened being-whether *sammasambuddha* or *arahat*-might intentionally kill a living being is not countenanced.

So why is it that the Theravada exegetical tradition wants to exclude compassion as the simple motivation for killing a living being? What is wrong with compassion as a motive for killing a living being? An initial answer to this question is apparent in the advice about what kind of instruction should be given to a sick monk. What the commentary suggests is that it is quite proper to recommend death to the dying as an occasion when there is a special opportunity for making crucial advances on the path: it is a time when the paths and fruits of stream-entry, once-return, never-return or even arahatship might be attained. But this opportunity is grasped not by actively hastening death, by willing the advent of death, but rather by renewing one's commitment to one's practice and cultivating mindfulness.

In taking up Keown's discussion of the case of the sick monk, Peter Harvey gives only a partial rendering of the commentary's advice; nonetheless, the conclusion he draws from it seems basically sound: This suggests that a person should use the process of dying as an opportunity for reflection, so as to see clearly the error of attachment to anything which is impermanent, be it the body, other people, possessions, or worldly achievements. Dying presents the reality of the components of body and mind as impermanent, *dukkha*, and not-Self in stark form; it is thus an opportunity for gaining insight into these.

As Harvey's observations suggest, the answer to why mainstream Indian Buddhist thought does not allow compassion as a motive for killing seems in part to lie with very fundamental Buddhist principles. As the first of the four truths or realities (*sacca*), suffering or dukkha is something that must be fully comprehended (*pariññeyya*). And indeed the *Nikayas'* shorthand definition of dukkha is the five *upadanakkh*andh*as*. Death, the breaking up of the *kh*andh*as*, is an opportunity par excellence to understand the nature of dukkha, its arising, its ceasing, and the way leading to its ceasing. If in the case of deliberately hastening a sick being's death, compassion and wisdom are excluded by the Abhidhamma from being considered the decisive motivations, then what we are left with as motivations are aversion and delusion.

The answer must surely be aversion towards the being's suffering, which amounts to a refusal to face the reality of suffering with true compassion and wisdom. Killing the being is certainly a solution to the problem of suffering in this situation: by getting rid of the being who is suffering, it gets rid of the suffering. But in the Abhidhamma view of things it can hardly be a wise solution: it is rather a quick fix that precisely avoids confronting the problem of suffering, which precisely avoids looking at its true nature. So while on the Abhidhamma psychological model it is possible to envisage situations where at least some of the consciousnesses associated with an act of killing might be wholesome and genuinely motivated by the two or three wholesome roots, it would seem that the decisive motivation in such a case would be regarded as some form of refusal to face the reality of suffering-a reality that real wisdom and compassion faces up to.

The understanding that I have been trying to articulate on the basis of the ancient texts has been recently quite precisely stated in an essay on Thai Buddhist perspectives on euthanasia:

In Buddhist psychology, "mercy killing" or active euthanasia cannot be carried out without ill-will or feeling of repugnance (*dosa*) of the perpetrator toward the fact of the patient's suffering. Even though the motivation behind this action may have been good, namely to prevent further suffering for the patient, as soon as it becomes action to terminate life it becomes an act of aversion. So when a doctor performs what, he believes is "mercy-killing," actually it is due to his repugnance of the patient's pain and suffering which disturb his mind.... If he understood this psychological process he would recognize the hidden hatred that arises in his mind at the time of performing the lethal deed and would not deceive himself with the belief that this deed was motivated by benevolence alone.

THE SIGNIFICANCE OF METTA

In the context of contemporary ethical discourse (and contemporary attitudes), the Abhidhamma analysis might seem rather bleak-almost heartless. If Abhidhamma Buddhist thought denies that euthanasia is ever a truly wholesome solution, does it offer an alternative approach-other than simply to sit and witness the death throes of some poor creature? I think in fact that an alternative approach is indeed taken for granted by the texts-but this approach, I would guess, is likely to appear at best somewhat idealistic and at worst hopelessly naive to modern sensibilities. For this alternative highlights what I think amounts to a crucial difference in perspective between the worldview of ancient Buddhist texts and contemporary ethical and philosophical discourse. Put simply, in Buddhist discourse *metta* and *karuna* are regarded as potentially rather more powerful and effective responses to suffering than contemporary ethical discourse would normally allow.

At the beginning of this chapter I quoted the Metta Sutta:

One should not wish another pain out of anger or a notion of enmity. Just as a mother would protect with her life her own son, her only son, so one should cultivate the immeasurable mind towards all living beings and friendliness towards the whole world.

What I want to suggest is that in the Buddhist (and to some extent general Indian religious) framework, cultivating friendliness and compassion in the face of suffering is seen not simply as a question of the religious contemplative turning inward and refusing to act or intervene, but also in a certain sense as a very practical response to the problem of suffering brought about by sickness and old age. A recent essay by Lambert Schmithausen focuses on the Buddhist attitude towards the dangerous and fearful in nature, and considers how the cultivation of friendliness (*maitrî/metta*) is presented as offering some kind of protection. Schmithausen's study is primarily concerned with friendliness as a means of giving oneself protection from dangers rather than as a means of helping others.

Having reviewed the "snake charm" of the Upasena *Sutra* and Khandha Paritta, followed by the Vedic background, he concludes that in its "typically Buddhist form" the cultivation of friendliness as a means of protection against potentially dangerous creatures "is the cultivation of a friendly mind with regard to them, which is supposed to engender a similar attitude in the addressee(s)". It seems to me that this entails a further dimension to the protective power of friendliness envisaged by traditional Buddhist texts. As Schmithausen notes, the cultivation of friendliness are seen as not only having the power to protect oneself, but as also having the power to engender friendliness in others.

And if this is so it has the potential to engender its beneficial effects in others-such beneficial effects as those listed as the eleven benefits that come to someone who develops the liberation of the heart through friendliness (*metta*ya *ceto-vimutti*): he sleeps happily; he wakes happily; he dreams no bad dreams; he is dear to human beings; he is dear to nonhuman beings; the gods protect him; fire, poison and weapons do not harm him; his mind easily attains concentration; the expression on his face is serene; he dies unconfused; and if he reaches no higher he is born in the world of Brahma. Of course, this old list of the benefits of friendliness is understood as presenting the benefits that come to one who cultivates *metta* as a subject of meditation practice (*kammatthana*), but the list assuredly points to an attitude that assumes friendliness to be generally beneficial to all concerned. But there are in the canonical and commentarial texts incidents recounted where the power of friendliness and compassion is in effect employed to the benefit of those who are suffering and in pain.

There is a story repeated in at least three places in the *atthakatha* literature that tells of what happened when a young boy's mother fell seriously ill:

It is told that when he was still a boy Cakkana's mother fell ill, and the doctor said that she needed fresh hare's meat. So Cakkana's brother sent him off to wander through the fields. Off he went and at that time a hare had come there to eat the tender young crop. When the hare saw him, it ran off fast and got caught in a creeper and cried out. Following the sound Cakkana grabbed the hare thinking that he could make the medicine for his mother. Then he thought, "It is not right that I should take the life of another for the sake of my mother's life." So he let the hare go, saying, "Go and enjoy the grass and water in the woods with the other hares." When his brother asked him if he had caught a hare, Cakkana told him what had happened. His brother scolded him. Cakkana went to his mother and stood [by her] affirming a truth, "Since I was born I am not aware that I have intentionally taken the life of a living creature." Immediately his mother recovered from her illness.

Here then the boy's firm, unwavering commitment to not harming a living creature provides the basis for an affirmation of truth (*sacca-kiriya*) that has the effect of curing his mother. It is worth noting that Cakkana's unwavering commitment to avoiding killing is precisely not presented by the commentaries as a blind, uncompromising adherence to the first precept. In the commentarial understanding there are three ways in which one can refrain from unwholesome action through the arising of wholesome consciousness: (1) one can naturally refrain from wrong action, etc., when the opportunity for wrong action, etc. has arisen; (2) one can refrain because one has previously undertaken the precepts; or (3) one can refrain by cutting off all desire for wrong action, etc. by reaching the noble path. The story of Cakkana is told as an illustration of the first kind of circumstance.

Interestingly Cakkana's words here echo almost precisely another famous affirmation of truth, that of the serial murderer "reborn" as an arahat, Angulimala. Wandering in Savatthî for alms, Angulimala comes across a woman struggling with the pains of birth. He is moved, saying to himself, "How beings suffer! How beings suffer!" A little later he tells the Buddha who instructs him to return to Savatthî and utter the words: "Lady, since I was born into the noble birth I am not aware that I have intentionally taken the life of a living creature. By this truth may you be safe, may your child be safe." And indeed the woman was safe, the child was safe. These two stories show the power of what is in effect *metta*-a commitment to not harming living creatures-being employed by means of an affirmation of truth to help someone who is sick and in pain by in one case an arahat and in the other just a boy.

THE SARVASTIVADA AND THE UPAYAKAUSALYA SUTRA

While it goes beyond the scope of the present chapter (and of my competence) to attempt to explore in depth the issue under discussion in the Sarvastvadin-Vaibhasika Abhidharma, it is perhaps worth pointing out that its understanding of the principles involved seems to be for the most part consonant with the Theravada. Thus the *Abhidharmakosa* distinguishes two types of "origin" for acts: the general cause (*hetu-samutthana*) and the immediate cause (*tatksana-samutthana*); the latter seems to correspond more or less to the Theravada notion of the decisive intention (*sanitthapaka-cetana*). The Kosa also distinguishes between the courses of action (karma-patha) proper and preliminary (*samantaka*) or preparatory (*prayoga*) acts.

On this basis the Kosa goes on to point out that the acts that form the preliminary to each ten *akusala-kamma-patha* may be motivated by any of the three basic unwholesome causes: greed (*lobha*), hatred (*dvesa*), or wrong-view (*mithya-driti*), and gives examples of this in the case of killing a living being. However, the *kamma-patha* proper of killing a living being is exclusively accomplished by hatred. An understanding that corresponds more or less to the Theravada account of the five necessary conditions (*sambhara*) for the course of action is also found. Having considered the Abhidhamma and commentarial analysis of the act of killing a living being, it is perhaps worth briefly turning to a well known story where the *bodhisattva* is represented as killing a living being apparently out of compassionate motives.

The *Upayakausalya Sutra* tells the story of how the *bodhisattva* in a life when he is indeed called "Great Compassion" kills a man in order to prevent him from killing 500 others-also *bodhisattvas*. The motivation for this act is thus compassionate on two accounts: by killing the man he prevents him from killing others and thus prevents him from committing an unwholesome act that would result in his being reborn and suffering in hell; the *bodhisattva* also by his act saves the lives of the 500 others. Interestingly the way in which the *bodhisattva*'s act of killing is presented seems to accept the basic outlook that I have presented above: acts of killing are instances of unwholesome karma. Thus in deciding to kill the man the *bodhisattva* is presented as accepting that this is an unwholesome act, the unpleasant consequences of which he will have to suffer in hell. Thus the *Sutra* does not, initially atleast; try to justify the act as one that is kusala.

However, the *Sutra* goes on to relate how the *bodhisattva* in fact avoided the sufferings of rebirth in hell; much later, as a Buddha, he lets his foot be pierced by a thorn in apparent retribution for this act of killing. There are perhaps two ways of reading this: (1) the *bodhisattva*'s compassion was such that it was able to transform the unwholesome nature of the act and render it an entirely wholesome act such that it had no unpleasant results whatsoever; (2) alternatively the compassionate component of the act was strong enough to override its unwholesome elements such that their ripening was indefinitely delayed allowing the *bodhisattva* to avoid the karmic fruit despite the fact that certain aspects of the act were in actual fact akusala.

Whichever way we read it though, it seems to me that the story should be understood in the context of the kind of Abhidhamma and commentarial analysis of the act of killing that I have tried to set out above. For while I have been presenting the details of the specifically Theravada viewpoint,

I think the evidence of the Abhidharmakosa is sufficient for us to conclude that it represents the mainstream approach of Indian Buddhist thought to the act of killing. The *Upaya*kausalya *Sutra* thus perhaps represents a deliberate challenge to mainstream Buddhist ethics.

In the course of this chapter I have tried to show, taking the act of killing a living being as an example, how an appreciation of the Abhidhamma framework is crucial in assessing the Pali commentarial approach to ethical questions. I have argued, contrary to Keown's claim that for Theravada Buddhist thought the motivation underlying the intention or will to act is sufficient to determine an act as "moral" (*kusala*) or "immoral" a*kusala*. In the particular case of killing a living being, I have argued that for Theravada Buddhist thought-and probably mainstream Indian Buddhist thought-intentionally killing a living being can never be considered wholly an act of compassion.

Although the Abhidhamma model of the way in which the mind works can accommodate a set of circumstances where genuine compassion might play some part in an act of killing a living being, it does not allow that the decisive intention leading to the killing of a living can ever be other than unwholesome and associated with some form of aversion (*dosa*). I have suggested two reasons why such an outlook should be characteristic of the Buddhist perspective on "mercy killing." The first is that the very idea that killing a living being might be the solution to the problem of suffering runs counters to the Buddhist emphasis on dukkha as the first of the four truths. As the first truth, its reality must be fully understood (*pariññeyya*).

The second is that the cultivation of friendliness and compassion in the face of suffering is seen as an appropriate and even practical alternative that can bring beneficial effects for self and others in a situation where it might seem that compassion should lead one to kill. I would like to finish with a general comment about the nature of Buddhist ethics. Abhidhamma-and hence I think mainstream Buddhist ethics-is not ultimately concerned to lay down ethical rules, or even ethical principles. It seeks instead to articulate a spiritual psychology focusing on the root causes that motivate us to act: greed, hatred, and delusion, or nonattachment, friendliness, and wisdom. Thus that intentionally killing a living being is wrong is not in fact presented in Buddhist thought as an ethical principle at all; it is a claim about how the mind works, about the nature of certain mental states and the kinds of action they give rise to.

It is a claim that when certain mental states (compassion) are in the mind it is simply impossible that one could act in certain ways (intentionally kill). For the Theravada Buddhist tradition there is in the end only one question one has to ask to determine whether an act is wholesome (*kusala*) or unwholesome (a*kusala*): is it motivated by greed, hatred, and delusion, or is it motivated by nonattachment, friendliness, and wisdom. So if one were to respond to the Abhidhamma claim that an act of intentional killing motivated by compassion is a psychological impossibility, that it simply runs counter to actual experience, then what the Abhidhamma analysis offers is a kind of psycho-ethical puzzle or riddle.

If you can intentionally kill out of compassion, then fine, go ahead. But are you sure? Are you sure that what you think is friendliness and compassion is really friendliness and compassion? Are you sure that some subtle aversion and delusion have not surfaced in the mind? In the end ethical principles cannot solve the problem of how to act in the world. If we want to know how to act in accordance with *Dhamma*, we must know our own minds. In the words of the *Dhammapada*, "ceasing to do all that is bad, accomplishing what is wholesome, and purifying the mind-this is the teaching of the Buddha's."

8

Buddhism Returns to the Market Place

Two thousand years ago, Plato, in The Republic, wrote one of the first essays on politics and started a search for an ideal society which has continued to the present day. Plato built his ideal society on the assumption that early societies grew from a rational decision to secure well-being, but if we look at the course of history, can we say that rational thinking has truly been the guiding force in the evolution of civilization? The reader is invited to imagine the beginnings of human society: groups of Stone Age humans are huddled together in their caves, each looking with suspicion on the group in the next cave down. They are cold and hungry. Danger and darkness surround them. Suddenly one of them hits on a brilliant idea: "I know, let's create a society where we can trade and build hospitals and live in mutual well-being!"

Such a scenario is not likely. Early humans, and the first societies, were probably bound together more by their deep emotional needs for warmth and security than any rational planning. And over the millennia, our societies have evolved to a large extent at the directives of these emotional needs. To be sure, rational thinking has played some part in the process, but if we take an honest look at our so-called advanced society, we must admit that our needs for security today are not so different from the cave men. While our societies are certainly more complex, the propelling force is still emotion, not reason.

If we are to honestly discuss economics, we must admit that emotional factors-fear and desire and the irrationality they generate-have a very powerful influence on the market place.

Economic decisions-decisions about production, consumption and distribution-are made by people in their struggle to survive and prosper. For the most part, these decisions are motivated by an emotional urge for self-preservation. There is nothing inherently bad about fear and irrationality; they are natural conditions that come with being human. Unfortunately, however, fear and desire drive us to our worst economic excesses. The forces of greed, exploitation and overconsumption seem to have overwhelmed our economies in recent decades. Our materialistic societies offer us little choice but to exploit and compete for survival in today's dog-eat-dog world. But at the same time, it is obvious that these forces are damaging our societies and ravaging our environment.

In the face of such problems, the science of economics adopts a rational approach. The job of economists is to devise well-reasoned models to help society rise above fear, greed and hatred. Rarely, however, do economists examine the basic question of fear and the emotional needs for security that drive human beings. As a result, their theoretical models remain rational solutions to largely irrational problems, and their economic ideals can only truly exist in books. Perhaps a little idealism is not so harmful; but there is a danger to the purely rational approach. At its worst, it is used to rationalize our basest, most fear-ridden responses to the question of survival. We see this tendency in the corporate strategists, policy advisors and defense analysts who logically and convincingly argue that arms production is in our best interests.

When rationalism turns a blind eye to the irrational, unseen irrational impulses are all the more likely to cloud our rationality. The book you are reading takes a different approach-a spiritual approach. As such, it does not delve into the technical intricacies of economics. Instead it examines the fundamental fears, desires and emotions that motivate our economic activities. Of all the spiritual traditions, Buddhism is best suited to this task. As we shall see, the Buddhist teachings offer profound insights into the psychology of desire and the motivating forces of economic activity. These insights can lead to a liberating self-awareness that slowly dissolves the confusion between what is truly harmful and what is truly beneficial in production and consumption. This awareness is, in turn, the foundation for a mature ethics.

Truly rational decisions must be based on insight into the forces that make us irrational. When we understand the nature of desire, we see that it cannot be satisfied by all the riches in the world. When we understand the universality of fear, we find a natural compassion for all beings. Thus, the spiritual approach to economics leads not to models and theories, but to the vital forces that can truly benefit our world-wisdom, compassion and restraint. In other words, the spiritual approach must be lived. This is not to say that one must embrace Buddhism and renounce the science of economics, because, in the larger scheme of things, the two are mutually supportive.

In fact, one needn't be a Buddhist or an economist to practice Buddhist economics. One need only acknowledge the common thread that runs through life and seek to live in balance with the way things really are. In a discussion of Buddhist economics, the first question that arises is whether such a thing actually exists, or whether it is even possible. The image of a Buddhist monk quietly walking on alms round does not readily come to mind as an economic activity for most people. Skyscrapers, shopping centers and the stock market would more accurately fit the bill. At present the economics that we are acquainted with is a Western one.

When talking of economics or matters pertaining to it, we use a Western vocabulary and we think within the conceptual framework of Western economic theory. It is difficult to avoid these constraints when talking about a Buddhist economics. We might find ourselves in fact discussing Buddhism with the language and concepts of Western economics. Even so, in the course of this book, I hope to at least provide some Buddhist perspectives on things that can be usefully employed in economics. While economic thinking has been in existence since the time of Plato and Aristotle, the study of economics has only really crystallized into a science in the industrial era.

Like other sciences in this age of specialization, economics has become a narrow and rarefied discipline; an isolated, almost stunted, body of knowledge, having little to do with other disciplines or human activities. Ideally, the sciences should provide solutions to the complex, interrelated problems that face humanity, but cut off as it is from other disciplines and the larger sphere of human activity, economics can do little to ease the ethical, social and environmental problems that face us today. And given the tremendous influence it exerts on our market-driven societies, narrow economic thinking may, in fact, be the primary cause of some of our most pressing social and environmental troubles.

Like other sciences, economics strives for objectivity. In the process, however, subjective values, such as ethics, are excluded. With no consideration of subjective, moral values, an economist may say, for instance, that a bottle of whiskey and a Chinese dinner have the same economic value, or that drinking in a night club contributes more to the economy than listening to a religious talk or volunteering for humanitarian work. These are truths according to economics. But the objectivity of economics is shortsighted. Economists look at just one short phase of the natural causal process and single out the part that interests them, ignoring the wider ramifications. Thus, modern economists take no account of the ethical consequences of economic activity.

Neither the vices associated with the frequenting of night clubs, nor the wisdom arising from listening to a religious teaching, are its concern. But is it in fact desirable to look on economics as a science? Although many believe that science can save us from the perils of life, it has many limitations. Science shows only one side of the truth, that which concerns the material world. By only considering the material side of things, the science of economics is out of step with the overall truth of the way things are. Given that all things in this world are naturally interrelated and interconnected, it follows that human problems must also be interrelated and interconnected.

One-sided scientific solutions are bound to fail, and the problems bound to spread. Environmental degradation is the most obvious and dangerous consequence to our industrialized, specialized approach to solving problems. Environmental problems have become so pressing that people are now beginning to see how foolish it is to place their faith in individual, isolated disciplines that ignore the larger perspective. They are starting to look at human activities on a broader scale, to see the repercussions their actions have on personal lives, society, and the environment.

From a Buddhist perspective, economics cannot be separated from other branches of knowledge. Economics is rather one component of a concerted effort to remedy the problems of humanity; and an economics based on Buddhism, a "Buddhist economics," is therefore not so much a self-contained science, but one of a number of interdependent disciplines working in concert toward the common goal of social, individual and environmental well-being. One of the first to integrate the Buddha's teachings with economics (and indeed to coin the phrase "Buddhist economics") was E. F. Schumacher in his book *Small is Beautiful.*

In his essay on Buddhist economics, Mr. Schumacher looks to the Buddhist teaching of the Noble Eightfold Path to make his case. He affirms that the inclusion of the factor of Right Livelihood in the Eightfold Path, in other words the Buddhist way of life, indicates the necessity of a Buddhist economics. This is Mr. Schumacher's starting point. Looking back, we can see that both the writing of *Small is Beautiful,* and the subsequent interest in Buddhist economics shown by some Western academics, took place in response to a crisis. Western academic disciplines and conceptual structures have reached a point which many feel to be a dead end, or if not, at least a turning point demanding new paradigms of thought and methodology. This has led many economists to rethink their isolated, specialized approach.

The serious environmental repercussions of rampant consumerism have compelled economists to develop more ecological awareness. Some even propose that all new students of economics incorporate basic ecology into their curriculum. Mr. Schumacher's point that the existence of Right Livelihood as one of the factors of the Noble Eightfold Path necessitates a Buddhist economics has a number of implications. Firstly, it indicates the importance given to Right Livelihood (or economics) in Buddhism. Secondly, and conversely, it means that economics is taken to be merely one amongst a number of factors (traditionally eight) that comprise a right way of life, that is, one capable of solving the problems of life.

Specialization can be a great benefit as long as we don't lose sight of our common goal: as a specialized study, economics allows us to analyze with minute detail the causes and factors within economic activities. But it is a mistake to believe that any one discipline or field of learning can in itself solve all problems. In concert with other disciplines, however, economics can constitute a complete response to human suffering, and it is only by fully understanding the contributions and limitations of each discipline that we will be able to produce such a coordinated effort. Unfortunately, as it stands, economics is grossly out of touch with the whole stream of causes and conditions that constitute reality. Economics, and indeed all the social sciences, are, after all, based on man-made or artificial truths.

For example, according to natural laws, the action of digging the earth results in a hole. This is a fixed cause and effect relationship based on natural laws. However, the digging which results in a wage is a conventional truth based on a social agreement. Without the social agreement, the action of digging does not result in a wage. While economists scrutinize one isolated segment of the cause and effect process, the universe manifests itself in an inconceivably vast array of causes and conditions, actions and reactions. Focused as they are on the linear progression of the economic events that concern them, economists forget that nature unfolds in all directions. In nature, actions and results are not confined to isolated spheres. One action gives rise to results, which in turn becomes a cause for further results. Each result conditions further results. In this way, action and reaction are intertwined to form the vibrant fabric of causes and conditions that we perceive as reality. To understand reality, it is necessary to understand this process.

THE TWO MEANINGS OF DHAMMA

For many people, the term "Buddhist economics" may evoke the image of an ideal society where all economic activity-buying and selling, production and consumption-adheres to strict ethical standards. But such an idealized image, attractive as it may sound, does not convey the full depth of the Buddha's teachings. The Buddha's teachings point to *Dhamma*, or truth. In Buddhism the term *Dhamma* is used to convey different levels of truth, both relative truths and ultimate truth. Those truths regarding ethical behavior-both on a personal day-to-day basis and in society-are called *cariyadhamma*.

These are the truths related to matters of good and evil. *Dhamma* in its larger sense is *saccadhamma*, truth, or *sabhavadhamma*, reality: it includes all things as they are and the laws by which they function. In this sense, *Dhamma* is used to describe the entire stream of causes and conditions, the process by which all things exist and function. Unlike the narrower scope of *cariyadhamma*, which refers to isolated ethical considerations, *sabhavadhamma* points to nature or reality itself, which is beyond concerns of good and evil. In this all-encompassing sense, *Dhamma* expresses the totality of natural conditions that which the various branches of science seek to describe. Thus, the Buddha's teachings give us more than just ethical guidelines for a virtuous life.

His teachings offer a grand insight into the nature of reality. Given the twofold meaning of the term *Dhamma*, it follows that an economics inspired by the *Dhamma* would be both attuned to the grand sphere of causes and conditions and, at the same time, guided by the specific ethical teachings based on natural reality. In other words, Buddhist economists would not only consider the ethical values of economic activity, but also strive to understand reality and direct economic activity to be in harmony with "the way things are." Ultimately, economics cannot be separated from *Dhamma*, because all the activities we associate with economics emerge from the *Dhamma*.

Economics is just one part of a vast interconnected whole, subject to the same natural laws by which all things function. *Dhamma* describes the workings of this whole, the basic truth of all things, including economics. If economics is ignorant of the *Dhamma*-of the complex and dynamic process of causes-and-effects that constitutes reality-then it will be hard pressed to solve problems, much less produce the benefits to which it aims. Yet this is precisely the trouble with modern economic thinking. Lacking any holistic, comprehensive insight and limited by the narrowness of their specialized view, economists single out one isolated portion of the stream of conditions and fail to consider results beyond that point.

An example: there exists a demand for a commodity, such as whiskey. The demand is supplied by production-growing grain and distilling it into liquor. The whiskey is then put on the market and then purchased and consumed. When it is consumed, demand is satisfied. Modern economic thinking stops here, at the satisfaction of the demand. There is no investigation of what happens after the demand is satisfied. By contrast, an economics inspired by *Dhamma* would be concerned with how economic activities influence the entire process of causes and conditions.

While modern economics confines its regard to events within its specialized sphere, Buddhist economics would investigate how a given economic activity affects the three interconnected spheres of human existence: the individual, society, and nature or the environment. In the case of the demand for a commodity such as whiskey, we would have to ask ourselves how liquor production affects the ecology and how its consumption affects the individual and society. These are largely ethical considerations and this brings us back to the more specialized meaning of *Dhamma*, that relating to matters of good and evil. It is said in the Buddhist scriptures that good actions lead to good results and bad actions lead to bad results.

All of the Buddha's teachings on ethical behavior are based on this principle. It is important to note here that, unlike the theistic religions, Buddhism does not propose an agent or arbitrating force that rewards or punishes good and evil actions. Rather, good and evil actions are seen as causes and conditions that unfold according to the natural flow of events. In this regard, *Dhamma* (in the sense of ethical teachings) and *Dhamma* (in the sense of natural reality) are connected in that the Buddhist ethical teachings are based on natural reality. Ethical laws follow the natural law of cause and effect: virtuous actions naturally lead to benefit and evil actions naturally lead to harm, because all of these are factors in the stream of causes and conditions.

Given its dynamic view of the world, Buddhism does not put forth absolute rules for ethical behavior. The ethical value of behavior is judged partly by the results it brings and partly by the qualities which lead to it. Virtuous actions are good because they lead to benefit; evil actions are evil because they lead to harm. There is a belief that any method used to attain a worthy end is justified by the worthiness of that end. This idea is summed up in the expression "the end justifies the means." Communist revolutionaries, for instance, believed that since the objective is to create an ideal society in which all people are treated fairly, then destroying anybody and anything which stands in the way of that ideal society is justified. The end (the ideal society) justifies the means (hatred and bloodshed).

The idea that "the end justifies the means" is a good example of a human belief which simply does not accord with natural truth. This concept is a human invention, an expedient rationalization which contradicts natural law and "the way things are." Beliefs are not evil in themselves, but when they are in contradiction with reality, they are bound to cause problems. Throughout the ages, people with extreme political and religious ideologies have committed the most brutal acts under the slogan "the end justifies the means." No matter how noble their cause, they ended up destroying that which they were trying to create, which is some kind of happiness or social order.

To learn from history, we must analyze all the causes and conditions that contributed to the unfolding of past events. This includes the qualities of mind of the participants. A thorough analysis of the history of a violent revolution, for example, must consider not only the economic and social climate of the society, but also the emotional and intellectual makeup of the revolutionaries themselves and question the rational validity of the intellectual ideals and methods used, because all of these factors have a bearing on the outcome. With this kind of analysis, it becomes obvious that, by the natural laws of cause and effect, it is impossible to create an ideal society out of anything less than ideal means-and certainly not bloodshed and hatred.

Buddhism would say that it is not the end which justifies the means, but rather the means which *condition* the end. Thus, the result of slaughter and hatred is further violence and instability. This can be witnessed in police states and governments produced by violent revolution-there is always an aftermath of tension, the results of *kamma*, which often proves to be intolerable and social collapse soon follows. Thus the means (bloodshed and aggression) condition the end (tension and instability). Yet while ethics are subject to these natural laws, when we have to make personal ethical choices right and wrong are not always so obvious. Indeed, the question of ethics is always a highly subjective matter. Throughout our lives, we continually face-and must answer for ourselves-questions of right and wrong. Our every choice, our every intention, holds some ethical judgment.

The Buddhist teachings on matters relating to good and evil serve as guides to help us with these subjective moral choices. But while they are subjective, we should not forget that our ethical choices inevitably play themselves out in the world according to the objective principle of causes and conditions. Our ethics-and the behavior that naturally flows from our ethics-contribute to the causes and conditions that determine who we are, the kind of society we live in and the condition of our environment. One of the most profound lessons of the Buddha's teachings is the truth that internal, subjective values are directly linked to the dynamic of external objective reality.

This subtle realization is at the heart of all ethical questions. Unfortunately, most people are only vaguely aware of how their internal values condition external reality. It is easy to observe the laws of cause and effect in the physical world: ripe apples fall from trees and water runs down hill. But because people tend to think of themselves as individuals separate from the universe, they fail to see how the same laws apply to internal subjective values, such as thoughts and moral attitudes. Since ethics are "subjective," people think they are somehow unconnected to "objective" reality. According to the Buddhist view, however, ethics forms a bridge between internal and external realities.

In accordance with the law of causes and conditions, ethics act as "subjective" causes for "objective" conditions. This should be obvious when we consider that, in essence, ethical questions always ask, "Do my thoughts, words and deeds help or harm myself and those around me?" In practice, we rely on ethics to regulate the unwholesome desires of our subjective reality: anger, greed, hatred. The quality of our thoughts, though internal, constantly conditions the way we speak and act. Though subjective, our ethics determine the kind of impact our life makes on the external, objective world.

ETHICS CONDITION ECONOMICS

To be sure, the distinction between economics and ethics is easily discernible. We can look at any economic situation either from an entirely economic perspective, or from an entirely ethical one. For example, you are reading this book. From an ethical perspective, your reading is a good action; you are motivated by a desire for knowledge. This is an ethical judgment. From the economic perspective, on the other hand, this book may seem to be a waste of resources with no clear benefit. The same situation can be seen in different ways. However, the two perspectives are interconnected and do influence each other. While modern economic thinking rejects any subjective values like ethics, the influence of ethics in economic matters is all too obvious.

If a community is unsafe-if there are thieves, the threat of violence, and the roads are unsafe to travel-then it is obvious that businesses will not invest there, tourists will not want to go there, and the economy will suffer. On the other hand, if the citizens are law-abiding, well-disciplined and conscientiously help to keep their community safe and clean, businesses will have a much better chance of success and the municipal authorities will not have to spend so much on civic maintenance and security. Unethical business practices have direct economic consequences. If businesses attempt to fatten their profits by using substandard ingredients in foodstuffs, such as by using cloth-dye as a coloring in children's sweets, substituting chemicals for orange juice, or putting boric acid in meatballs (all of which have occurred in Thailand in recent years), consumers' health is endangered.

The people made ill by these practices have to pay medical costs and the government has to spend money on police investigations and prosecution of the offenders. Furthermore, the people whose health has suffered work less efficiently, causing a decline in productivity. In international trade, those who pass off shoddy goods as quality merchandise risk losing the trust of their customers and foreign markets-as well as the foreign currency obtained through those markets. Ethical qualities also influence industrial output. If workers enjoy their work and are industrious, productivity will be high. On the other hand, if they are dishonest, disgruntled or lazy, this will have a negative effect on the quality of production and the amount of productivity.

When it comes to consumption, consumers in a society with vain and fickle values will prefer flashy and ostentatious products to high quality products which are not so flashy. In a more practically-minded society, where the social values do not tend toward showiness and extravagance, consumers will choose goods on the basis of their reliability. Obviously, the goods consumed in these two different societies will lead to different social and economic results. Advertising stimulates economic activity, but often at an ethically unacceptable price.

Advertising is bound up with popular values: advertisers must draw on common aspirations, prejudices and desires in order to produce advertisements that are appealing. Employing social psychology, advertising manipulates popular values for economic ends, and because of its repercussions on the popular mind, it has considerable ethical significance. The volume of advertising may cause an increase in materialism, and unskillful images or messages may harm public morality. The vast majority of ads imbue the public with a predilection for selfish indulgence; they condition us into being perfect consumers who have no higher purpose in life than to consume the products of modern industry. In the process, we are transformed into 'hungry ghosts,' striving to feed an everlasting craving, and society becomes a seething mass of conflicting interests.

Moreover, advertising adds to the price of the product itself. Thus people tend to buy unnecessary things at prices that are unnecessarily expensive. There is much wastage and extravagance. Things are used for a short while and then replaced, even though they are still in good condition. Advertising also caters to peoples' tendency to flaunt their possessions as a way of gaining social status. When snob-appeal is the main criterion, people buy unnecessarily expensive products without considering the quality. In extreme cases, people are so driven by the need to appear stylish that they cannot wait to save the money for the latest gadget or fashion-they simply use their credit cards. Spending in excess of earnings can become a vicious cycle.

A newer model or fashion is advertised and people plunge themselves deeper and deeper into debt trying to keep up. In this way, unethical advertising can lead people to financial ruin. It is ironic that, with the vast amount of 'information technology' available, most of it is used to generate 'misinformation' or delusion. On the political plane, decisions have to be made regarding policy on advertising-should there be any control, and if so, of what kind? How is one to achieve the proper balance between moral and economic concerns? Education is also involved. Ways may have to be found to teach people to be aware of how advertising works, to reflect on it, and to consider how much of it is to be believed. Good education should seek to make people more intelligent in making decisions about buying goods.

The question of advertising demonstrates how activities prevalent in society may have to be considered from many perspectives, all of which are interrelated. Taking a wider perspective, it can be seen that the free market system itself is ultimately based on a minimum of ethics. The freedom of the free market system may be lost through businesses using unscrupulous means of competition; the creation of a monopoly through influence is one common example, the use of thugs to assassinate a competitor a more unorthodox one. The violent elimination of rivals heralds the end of the free market system, although it is a method scarcely mentioned in the economics textbooks. To be ethically sound, economic activity must take place in a way that is not harmful to the individual, society or the natural environment.

In other words, economic activity should not cause problems for oneself, agitation in society or degeneration of the ecosystem, but rather enhance well-being in these three spheres. If ethical values were factored into economic analysis, a cheap but nourishing meal would certainly be accorded more value than a bottle of whiskey. Thus, an economics inspired by Buddhism would strive to see and accept the truth of all things. It would cast a wider, more comprehensive eye on the question of ethics. Once ethics has been accepted as a legitimate subject for consideration, ethical questions then become factors to be studied within the whole causal process. But if no account is taken of ethical considerations, economics will be incapable of developing any understanding of the whole causal process, of which ethics forms an integral part.

Modern economics has been said to be the most scientific of all the social sciences. Indeed, priding themselves on their scientific methodology, economists take only measurable quantities into consideration. Some even assert that economics is purely a science of numbers, a matter of mathematical equations. In its efforts to be scientific, economics ignores all non-quantifiable, abstract values. But by considering economic activity in isolation from other forms of human activity, modern economists have fallen into the narrow specialization characteristic of the industrial age. In the manner of specialists, economists try to eliminate all non-economic factors from their considerations of human activity and concentrate on a single perspective, that of their own discipline.

In recent years, critics of economics, even a number of economists themselves, have challenged this "objective" position and asserted that economics is the most value-dependent of all the social sciences. It may be asked how it is possible for economics to be free of values when, in fact, it is rooted in the human mind. The economic process begins with want, continues with choice, and ends with satisfaction, all of which are functions of mind. Abstract values are thus the beginning, the middle and the end of economics, and so it is impossible for economics to be value-free. Yet as it stands, many economists avoid any consideration of values, ethics, or mental qualities, despite the fact that these will always have a bearing on economic concerns.

Economists' lack of ethical training and their ignorance of the workings of mental values and human desire is a major shortcoming which will prevent them from solving the problems it is their task to solve. If the world is to be saved from the ravages of overconsumption and overproduction, economists must come to an understanding of the importance of ethics to their field. Just as they might study ecology, they should also study ethics and the nature of human desire, and understand them thoroughly. Here is one area in which Buddhism can be of great help.

THE BUDDHIST VIEW OF HUMAN NATURE

According to the teachings of Buddhism, human beings are born in a state of ignorance. Ignorance is lack of knowledge, and it is this lack of knowledge that causes problems in life. Those human beings are born with ignorance, and are troubled by it right from birth, are obvious when observing the plight of a newborn baby, who cannot talk, look for food or even feed itself. Ignorance is a real limitation in life; it is a burden, a problem. In Buddhism this burden is called *dukkha* or suffering. Because human beings are born with ignorance, they do not really know how to conduct their lives. Without the guidance of knowledge or wisdom, they simply follow their desires, struggling at the directives of craving to stay alive in a hostile world. In Buddhism this blind craving is called *tanha.*

Tanha means craving, ambition, restlessness, or thirst. It arises dependent on feeling and is rooted in ignorance. Whenever a sensation of any kind is experienced, be it pleasing or displeasing-such as a beautiful or ugly sight, or a pleasant or unpleasant sound-it is followed by a feeling, pleasant, unpleasant or neutral. *Tanha* arises in correspondence with the feeling: if the feeling is pleasant, there will be a desire to hold onto it; if the feeling is unpleasant, there will be a desire to escape from or destroy it; if the feeling is neutral, there will be a subtle kind of attachment to it. These reactions are automatic; they do not require any conscious intention or any special knowledge or understanding. (On the contrary, if some reflection does interrupt the process at any time, *Tanha* may be intercepted, and the process rechanneled into a new form.)

Because *Tanha* so closely follows feeling, it tends to seek out objects which will provide pleasant feelings, which are basically the six kinds of pleasant sense objects: sights, sounds, smells, tastes, bodily feelings and mental objects. The most prominent of these are the first five, known as the five sense pleasures. The six sense objects, and particularly the five sense pleasures, are the objects that *Tanha* seeks out and fixes onto. In this context, our definition of *Tanha* might be expanded on thus: *Tanha* is the craving for sense objects which provide pleasant feeling, or craving for sense pleasures. In brief, *Tanha* could be called wanting to have or wanting to obtain.

The way *Tanha* works can be seen in the basic need for food. The biological purpose of eating is to nourish the body, to provide it with strength and well-being. Supplanted over this biological need is the desire for enjoyment, for delicious tastes. This is *Tanha*. At times, the desire of *Tanha* may be at odds with well-being, and may even be detrimental to the quality of life. If we are overwhelmed by *Tanha* when we eat, rather than eating for the purpose of nourishing the body and providing it with well-being, we eat for the experience of the pleasant taste. This kind of eating knows no end and can lead to problems in both body and mind. The food may be delicious, but we may end up suffering from indigestion or obesity. On a wider scale, the social costs of overconsumption, such as depletion of natural resources and costs incurred by health care, not to mention crime, corruption and wars, are enormous.

Modern economics and Buddhism both agree that mankind has unlimited wants. As the Buddha said, "There is no river like craving." Rivers can sometimes fill their banks, but the wants of human beings can never be filled. Even if money were to fall from the skies like rain, man's sensual desires would not be satisfied. The Buddha also said that even if one could magically transform one single mountain into two mountains of solid gold it would still not provide complete and lasting satisfaction to one person. There are numerous teachings in the Buddhist tradition describing the unlimited nature of human want. Here I would like to relate a story that appears in the *Jataka* Tales.

In the far and ancient past there lived a king called Mandhatu. He was a very powerful ruler, an emperor who is known in legend for having lived a very long life. Mandhatu had all the classic requisites of an emperor; he was an exceptional human being who had everything that anyone could wish for: he was a prince for 84,000 years, then the heir apparent for 84,000 years, and then emperor for 84,000 years. One day, after having been emperor for 84,000 years, King Mandhatu started to show signs of boredom. The great wealth that he possessed was no longer enough to satisfy him. The King's courtiers saw that something was wrong and asked what was ailing His Majesty. He replied, "The wealth and pleasure I enjoy here is trifling. Tell me; is there anywhere superior to this?" "Heaven, Your Majesty," the courtiers replied.

Now, one of the King's treasures was the *cakkaratana*, a magic wheel that could transport him anywhere he wished to go. So King Mandhatu used it to take him to the Heaven of the Four Great Kings. The Four Great Kings came out to welcome him in person, and on learning of his desire, invited him to take over the whole of their heavenly realm. King Mandhatu ruled over the Heaven of the Four Great Kings for a very long time, until one day he began to feel bored again. It was no longer enough, the pleasure that could be derived from the wealth and delights of that realm could satisfy him no more. He conferred with his attendants and was informed of the superior enjoyments of the Tavatimsa Heaven realm. So King Mandhatu picked up his magic wheel and ascended to the Tavatimsa Heaven, where he was greeted by its ruler, Lord Indra, who promptly made him a gift of half of his kingdom.

King Mandhatu ruled over the *Tavatimsa* Heaven with Lord Indra for another very long time, until Lord Indra came to the end of the merit that had sustained him in his high station, and was replaced by a new Lord Indra. The new Lord Indra ruled on until he too reached the end of his life-span. In all, thirty-six Lord Indras came and went, while King Mandhatu carried on enjoying the pleasures of his position. Then, finally, he began to feel dissatisfied-half of heaven was not enough, he wanted to rule over all of it. So King Mandhatu began to plot to kill Lord Indra and depose him. But it is impossible for a human being to kill Lord Indra, because humans cannot kill heavenly beings, and so his wish went unfulfilled. King Mandhatu's inability to satisfy this craving began to rot the very root of his being, and caused the aging process to begin.

Suddenly he fell out of Tavatimsa Heaven, down to earth, where he landed in an orchard with a resounding thump. When the workers in the orchard saw that a great king had arrived, some set off to inform the Palace and others improvised a makeshift throne for him to sit on. By now King Mandhatu was on the verge of death. The Royal Family came out to see and asked if he had any last words. King Mandhatu proclaimed his greatness. He told them of the great power and wealth he had possessed on earth and in heaven, but then finally admitted that his desires remained unfulfilled. There the story of King Mandhatu ends. It shows how Buddhism shares with economics the view that the wants of humanity are endless.

FROM CONFLICT TO HARMONY

In the struggle to feed their blind and endless desires, people do not clearly perceive what is of true benefit and what is harmful in life. They do not know what leads to true well-being and what leads away from it. With minds blinded by ignorance, people can only strive to feed their desires. In this striving they sometimes create that which is of benefit, and sometimes destroy it. If they do create some well-being, it is usually only incidental to their main objective, but in most cases the things obtained through *Tanha* harm the quality of life. As they struggle against each other and the world around them to fulfill their selfish desires, human beings live in conflict with themselves, with their societies and with the natural environment. There is a conflict of interests; a life guided by ignorance is full of conflict and disharmony.

If this were all there is to human nature, and all that needed to be taken into consideration in economic matters, then we human beings would not be much different from the animals and perhaps even worse because of our special talent for pursuing activities which are detrimental to well-being. Fortunately, there is more to human nature than this. Buddhism states that human beings are naturally endowed with a special aptitude for development. While Buddhism accepts the fact that it is natural for people to have cravings for things, it also recognizes the human desire for quality of life or well-being, the desire for self improvement and goodness. Problems arise when life is lived from ignorance and at the direction of craving. Problems can be solved by acquiring knowledge. Human development thus hinges on the development of knowledge. In Buddhism we call this kind of knowledge *pañña*, wisdom.

When ignorance is replaced with wisdom, it is possible to distinguish between what is of true benefit and what is not. With wisdom, desires will naturally be for that which is truly beneficial. In Buddhism, this desire for true well-being is called *dhammach*and*a* (desire for that which is right), *kusalach*and*a* (desire for that which is skillful), or in short, *ch*and*a*. The objective of *ch*and*a* is *dhamma* or *kusaladhamma*, truth and goodness. Truth and goodness must be obtained through effort, and so *ch*and*a* leads to action, as opposed to *Tanha*, which leads to seeking. *Ch*and*a* arises from intelligent reflection (*yoniso-manasikara*), as opposed to *Tanha*, which is part of the habitual stream of ignorant reactions.

To summarize this:

1. *Tanha* is directed toward feeling; it leads to seeking of objects which pander to self interests and is supported and nourished by ignorance.
2. *Ch*and*a* is directed toward benefit, it leads to effort and action, and is founded on intelligent reflection.

As wisdom is developed, *ch*and*a* becomes more dominant, while the blind craving of *Tanha* loses its strength. By training and developing ourselves, we live less and less at the directives of ignorance and *Tanha* and more and more under the guidance of wisdom and *ch*and*a* This leads to a more skillful life, and a much better and more fruitful relationship with the things around us. With wisdom and *ch*and*a* we no longer see life as a conflict of interests. Instead, we strive to harmonize our own interests with those of society and nature. The conflict of interests becomes a harmony of interests. This is because we understand that, in the end, a truly beneficial life is only possible when the individual, society and the environment serve each other. If there is conflict between any of these spheres, the result will be problems for all.

ETHICS AND THE TWO KINDS OF DESIRE

As we have seen, Buddhism recognizes two different kinds of wanting: (1) *Tanha*, the desire for pleasure objects; and (2) *chanda*, the desire for well-being. *Tanha* is based on ignorance, while *chanda* is based on wisdom and is thus part of the process of solving problems. *Tanha* and *chanda* both lead to satisfaction, but of different kinds. Using the example of eating, people who are driven by *Tanha* will seek to satisfy the blind craving for sensual pleasure which, in this case, is the desire for pleasant taste. Here, satisfaction results from experiencing the flavor of the food. But when guided by *chanda*, desires are directed to realizing well-being.

We are not compelled to overeat or to eat the kinds of foods that will make us sick simply because they taste good. Instead, we eat to satisfy hunger and nourish the body. Here satisfaction results from the assurance of well-being provided by the act of eating. We enjoy our food, but not in such a way that leads to remorse. *Chanda* leads to effort and action based on intelligence and clear thinking. By contrast, *Tanha* leads to blind seeking based on ignorance. Both of these internal desires motivate behavior, but with very different ethical consequences.

In Buddhism the ethical value of behavior can be judged by whether it is motivated (overtly) by *Tanha* or *chanda* and (on a deeper level) by ignorance or wisdom. When it comes to judging the ethical value of economic behavior, we must determine what kind of mental state is motivating it. When greed (*Tanha*) is driving economic decisions, behavior tends to be morally unskillful, but when desire for well-being (*chanda*) is guiding them, economic behavior will be morally skillful. By judging economic behavior in this way, we see how mental states, moral behavior and economic activity are linked in the cause and effect stream.

From the Buddhist point of view, economic activity should be a means to a good and noble life. Production, consumption and other economic activities are not ends in themselves; they are means, and the end to which they must lead is the development of well-being within the individual, within society and within the environment. Contrary to the misconception that Buddhism is only for renunciants, Buddhists recognize that acquiring wealth is one of life's fundamental activities, and the Buddha gave many teachings on the proper way to acquire wealth. But he always stressed that the purpose of wealth is to facilitate the development of highest human potential.

In Buddhism there are said to be three goals in life: the initial, medium, and ultimate goals. The initial goal is reasonable material comfort and economic security. Material security, however, is only a foundation for the two higher, more abstract goals-mental well-being and inner freedom. The major part of our lives is taken up with economic activities. If economics is to have any real part to play in the resolution of human problems, then all economic activities-production, consumption, work and spending-must contribute to well-being and help realize the potential for a good and noble life. It is something that we are capable of doing. The essence of Buddhist economics lies here, in ensuring that economic activity enhances the quality of our lives.

ETHICAL CONSIDERATIONS IN ECONOMIC ACTIVITY

A fundamental principle of modern economics states that people will only agree to part with something when they can replace it with something that affords them equal or more satisfaction. But this principle only considers the satisfaction that comes from owning material goods. Sometimes we can experience a sense of satisfaction by parting with something without getting anything tangible in return, as when parents give their children gifts: because of the love they feel for their children, they feel a more rewarding sense of satisfaction than if they had received something in return. If human beings could expand their love to all other people, rather than confining it to their own families, then they might be able to part with things without receiving anything in return, and experience more satisfaction in doing so. This satisfaction comes not from a desire to obtain things to make ourselves happy (*Tanha*), but from a desire for the well-being of others (*ch*and*a*).

Another economic principle states that the value of goods is determined by demand. This principle is classically illustrated by the story of two men shipwrecked on a desert island: one has a sack of rice and the other a hundred gold necklaces. Ordinarily, a single gold necklace would be enough, more than enough, to buy a whole sack of rice. But now the two men find themselves stranded on an island with no means of escape and no guarantee of rescue the value of the goods changes. Now the person with the rice might demand all one hundred gold necklaces for a mere portion of the rice, or he might refuse to make the exchange at all. However the question of ethics does not come into this discussion. Economists may assert that economics only concerns itself with demand, not its ethical quality, but in fact ethical considerations do affect demand.

In the example of the two shipwrecked men, there are other possibilities besides trade. The man with the gold necklaces might steal some of the rice while the owner is not watching, or he might just kill him in order to get the whole sack. On the other hand, the two men might become friends and help each other out, sharing the rice until it's all gone, so that there is no need for any buying or selling at all. In real life, it could happen in any of these ways. Factors such as personal morality or emotions such as greed and fear can and do affect economic outcome. A demand that does not stop at violence or theft will have different results from one that recognizes moral restraints.

One way to evaluate the ethical quality of economic activity is to look at the effects it has on three levels: on the individual consumer, on society and on the environment. Let us return to the example of the bottle of whiskey and the Chinese dinner. It is obvious that, though their market prices may be the same, their economic costs are not equal. The bottle of whiskey may damage the consumer's health, forcing him to spend money on medical treatment. The distillery which produced the whiskey may have released foul-smelling fumes into the air. This pollution has economic repercussions, forcing the government to spend resources on cleaning the environment.

Moreover, one who drinks and suffers from a hangover on the job will work less efficiently, or he might get drunk and crash his car, incurring more economic costs. Then there are detrimental social effects: drinking can contribute to crime, which has very high costs for society. Although ethical questions, they all have economic ramifications. They imply the necessity of looking at economic costs on a much wider scale than at present-not just in terms of market prices. There is now a trend towards including environmental costs in economic calculations. Some economists even include them in the cost of a finished product. But this is not enough. In the case of the bottle of whiskey, apart from the environmental costs, there are also the social, moral, and health costs-inefficient production, auto accidents, liver disease, crime-all of which have economic implications.

A second way to evaluate the ethical quality of economic activity is to determine which kind of desire is at its root. The most unethical economic activities are those that feed *Tanha* while undermining well-being. Trade in tobacco, drugs, and prostitution is examples of detrimental economic activities geared solely toward satisfying a craving for pleasure. The more people are driven by *Tanha* the more they destroy their true well-being. This principle applies not only to the obvious vices, but to all economic activities. Thus, in decisions dealing with consumption, production, and the use of technology, we must learn how to distinguish between the two kinds of desire and make our choices wisely.

BUDDHIST PERSPECTIVES ON ECONOMIC CONCEPTS

The basic model of economic activity is often represented in economic textbooks thus: unlimited wants are controlled by scarcity; scarcity requires choice; choice involves an opportunity cost (i.e., choosing one means foregoing the other); and the final goal is maximum satisfaction. The fundamental concepts occurring in this model-want, choice, consumption and satisfaction-describe the basic activities of our lives from an economic perspective.

These concepts are based on certain assumptions about human nature. Unfortunately, the assumptions modern economists make about human nature are somewhat confused. Buddhism, on the other hand, offers a clear and consistent picture of human nature: a view which encompasses the role of ethics and the twofold nature of human desire. Let us now take a look at some economic concepts in the light of Buddhist thinking.

Value

Given that there are two kinds of desire, it follows that there are two kinds of value, which we might term true value and artificial value. True value is created by *ch*and*a*. In other words, a commodity's true value is determined by its ability to meet the need for well-being. Conversely, artificial value is created by *Tanha*-it is a commodity's capacity to satisfy the desire for pleasure.

To assess an object's value, we must ask ourselves which kind of desire-*Tanha* or *ch*and*a*-defines it. Fashionable clothes, jewelry, luxury cars and other status-symbols contain a high degree of artificial value because they cater to people's vanity and desire for pleasure. A luxury car may serve the same function as a cheaper car, but it commands a higher price largely because of its artificial value. Many of the pleasures taken for granted in today's consumer society-the games, media thrills and untold forms of junk foods available-are created solely for the purpose of satisfying *Tanha* have no practical purpose at all and are often downright detrimental to well-being. For the most part, advertising promotes this artificial value.

Advertisers stimulate desires by projecting pleasurable images onto the products they sell. They induce us to believe, for example, that whoever can afford a luxury car will stand out from the crowd and be a member of high society, or that by drinking a certain brand of soft drink we will have lots of friends and be happy. The true value of an object is typically overshadowed by its artificial value. Craving and conceit, and the desire for the fashionable and sensually appealing, cloud any reckoning of the true value of things. How many people, for instance, reflect on the true value or reasons for eating food or wearing clothes?

CONSUMPTION

The question of consumption is similar to that of value. We must distinguish which kind of desire our consumption is intended to satisfy: is it to answer the need for things of true value, or to indulge in the pleasures afforded by artificial value? Consumption is said to be one of the goals of economic activity. However, economic theory and Buddhism define consumption differently. Consumption is the alleviation or satisfaction of desire, that much is agreed. Modern economics defines consumption as simply the use of goods and services to satisfy demand. Buddhism, however, distinguishes between two kinds of consumption, which might be termed "right" consumption and "wrong" consumption. Right consumption is the use of goods and services to satisfy the desire for true well-being.

It is consumption with a goal and a purpose. Wrong consumption arises from *Tanha;* it is the use of goods and services to satisfy the desire for pleasing sensations or ego-gratification. While the Buddhist perspective is based on a wide view of the stream of causes and effects, the specialized thinking of economics identifies only part of the stream: demand leads to consumption which leads to satisfaction. For most economists that are the end of it, there's no need to know what happens afterwards. In this view, consumption can be of anything whatsoever, so long as it results in satisfaction. There is little consideration of whether or not well-being is adversely affected by that consumption.

Consumption may satisfy sensual desires, but its true purpose is to provide well-being. For example, our body depends on food for nourishment. Consumption of food is thus a requirement for well-being. For most people, however, eating food is also a means to experience pleasure. If in consuming food one receives the experience of a delicious flavor, one is said to have satisfied one's desires. Economists tend to think in this way, holding that the experience of satisfaction is the end result of consumption. But here the crucial question is: What is the true purpose of consuming food: satisfaction of desires or the attainment of well-being? In the Buddhist view, when consumption enhances true well-being, it is said to be successful.

On the other hand, if consumption results merely in feelings of satisfaction, then it fails. At its worst, consumption through *Tanha* destroys its true objective, which is to enhance well-being. Heedlessly indulging in desires with no regard to the repercussions often leads to harmful effects and a loss of true well-being. Moreover, the compulsive consumption rampant in consumer societies breeds inherent dissatisfaction. It is a strange thing that economics, the science of human well-being and satisfaction, accepts, and indeed lauds, the kind of consumption that in effect frustrates the realization of its own objectives. By contrast, right consumption always contributes to well-being and forms a basis for the further development of human potentialities.

This is an important point often overlooked by economists. Consumption guided by *chanda* does much more than just satisfy one's desire; it contributes to well-being and spiritual development. This is also true on a global scale. If all economic activities were guided by *chanda*, the result would be much more than just a healthy economy and material progress-such activities would contribute to the whole of human development and enable humanity to lead a nobler life and enjoy a more mature kind of happiness.

MODERATION

At the very heart of Buddhism is the wisdom of moderation. When the goal of economic activity is seen to be satisfaction of desires, economic activities is open-ended and without clear definition-desires is endless. According to the Buddhist approach, economic activity must be controlled by the qualification that it is directed to the attainment of well-being rather than the "maximum satisfaction" sought after by traditional economic thinking. Well-being as an objective acts as a control on economic activity. No longer are we struggling against each other to satisfy endless desires. Instead, our activities are directed toward the attainment of well-being.

If economic activity is directed in this way, its objectives are clear and its activities are controlled. A balance or equilibrium is achieved. There is no excess, no overconsumption or overproduction. In the classical economic model, unlimited desires are controlled by scarcity, but in the Buddhist model they are controlled by an appreciation of moderation and the objective of well-being. The resulting balance will naturally eliminate the harmful effects of uncontrolled economic activity.

Buddhist monks and nuns traditionally reflect on moderation before each meal by reciting this reflection:

"Wisely reflecting, we take alms food, not for the purpose of fun, not for indulgence or the fascination of taste, but simply for the maintenance of the body, for the continuance of existence, for the cessation of painful feeling, for living the higher life. Through this eating, we subdue old painful feelings of hunger and prevent new painful feelings (of overeating) from arising. Thus do we live unhindered, blameless, and in comfort."

The goal of moderation is not restricted to monastics: whenever we use things, be it food, clothing, or even paper and electricity, we can take the time to reflect on their true purpose, rather than using them heedlessly. By reflecting in this way we can avoid heedless consumption and so understand "the right amount," the "middle way." We also come to see consumption as a means to an end, which is the development of human potential. With human development as our goal, we eat food not simply for the pleasure it affords, but to obtain the physical and mental energy necessary for intellectual and spiritual growth toward a nobler life.

NON-CONSUMPTION

Lacking a spiritual dimension, modern economic thinking encourages maximum consumption. It praises those who eat the most-three, four or more times a day. If someone were to eat ten times a day, so much the better. By contrast, a Buddhist economics understands that non-consumption can contribute to well-being. Though monks eat only one meal a day, they strive for a kind of well-being that is dependent on little. On Observance days, some Buddhist laypeople also refrain from eating after midday and, in so doing, contribute to their own well-being.

Renunciation of the evening meal allows them to spend time in meditation and reflection on the Buddha's teachings. The body is light and the mind easily calmed when the stomach is not full. Thus Buddhism recognizes that certain demands can be satisfied through non-consumption, a position which traditional economic thinking would find hard to appreciate. Refraining from eating can play a role in satisfying our nonmaterial, spiritual needs. It's not that getting down to eating one meal a day is the goal, of course. Like consumption, non-consumption is only a means to an end, not an end in itself. If abstinence did not lead to well-being, it would be pointless, just a way of mistreating ourselves. The question is not whether to consume or not to consume, but whether or not our choices lead to self-development.

OVERCONSUMPTION

Today's society encourages overconsumption. In their endless struggle to find satisfaction through consuming, a great many people damage their own health and harm others. Drinking alcohol, for instance, satisfies a desire, but is a cause of ill-health, unhappy families and fatal accidents. People who eat for taste often overeat and make them ill. Others give no thought at all to food values and waste money on junk foods. Some people even become deficient in certain vitamins and minerals despite eating large meals every day. (Incredibly, cases of malnutrition have been reported.)

Apart from doing themselves no good, their overeating deprives others of food. So we cannot say that a thing has value simply because it provides pleasure and satisfaction. If satisfaction is sought in things that do not enrich the quality of life, the result often becomes the destruction of true welfare, leading to delusion and intoxication, loss of health and well-being. A classic economic principle states that the essential value of goods lies in their ability to bring satisfaction to the consumer.

Here we may point to the examples given above where heavy consumption and strong satisfaction have both positive and negative results. The Buddhist perspective is that the benefit of goods and services lies in their ability to provide the consumer with a sense of satisfaction at having enhanced the quality of his or her life. This extra clause is essential. All definitions, whether of goods, services, or personal and social wealth, must be modified in this way.

Contentment

While not technically an economic concern and to add a few comments on the subject of contentment. Contentment is a virtue that has often been misunderstood and, as it relates to consumption and satisfaction, it seems to merit some discussion. The tacit objective of economics is a dynamic economy where every demand and desire is supplied and constantly renewed in a never-ending and ever-growing cycle. The entire mechanism is fueled by *Tanha*. From the Buddhist perspective, this tireless search to satisfy desires is itself a kind of suffering. Buddhism proposes the cessation of this kind of desire, or contentment, as a more skillful objective.

Traditional economists would probably counter that without desire, the whole economy would grind to a halt. However, this is based on a misunderstanding of the nature of contentment. People misunderstand contentment because they fail to distinguish between the two different kinds of desire, *Tanha* and *chanda*. We lump them together, and in proposing contentment, dismiss them both. A contented person comes to be seen as one who wants nothing at all. Here lies our mistake. Obviously, people who are content will have fewer wants than those who are discontent. However, a correct definition of contentment must be qualified by the stipulation that it implies only the absence of artificial want that is *Tanha*; *chanda*, the desire for true well-being, remains.

In other words, the path to true contentment involves reducing the artificial desire for sense-pleasure, while actively encouraging and supporting the desire for quality of life. These two processes-reducing *Tanha* and encouraging *chanda*-are mutually supportive.

When we are easily satisfied in material things, we save time and energy that might otherwise be wasted on seeking objects of *Tanha*. The time and energy we save can, in turn, be applied to the development of well-being, which is the objective of *chanda*. When it comes to developing skillful conditions, however, contentment is not a beneficial quality. Skillful conditions must be realized through effort. Too much contentment with regards to *chanda* easily turns into complacency and apathy. In this connection, the Buddha pointed out that his own attainment of enlightenment was largely a result of two qualities: unremitting effort, and lack of contentment with skillful conditions.

Work

Buddhist and conventional economics also have different understandings of the role of work. Modern Western economic theory is based on the view that work is something that we are compelled to do in order to obtain money for consumption. It is during the time when we are not working, or "leisure time," that we may experience happiness and satisfaction.

Work and satisfaction are considered to be separate and generally opposing principles. Buddhism, however, recognizes that work can either be satisfying or not satisfying, depending on which of the two kinds of desire is motivating it. When work stems from the desire for true well-being, there is satisfaction in the direct and immediate results of the work itself. By contrast, when work is done out of desire for pleasure-objects, then the direct results of the work itself are not so important.

With this attitude, work is simply an unavoidable necessity to obtain the desired object. The difference between these two attitudes determines whether or not work will directly contribute to well-being. In the first case, work is a potentially satisfying activity, and in the second, it is a necessary chore. As an example of these two different attitudes, let us imagine two research workers. They are both investigating natural means of pest control for agricultural use. The first researcher, Mr. Smith, desires the direct fruits of his research-knowledge and its practical application-and takes pride in his work. The discoveries and advances he makes afford him a sense of satisfaction.

The second, Mr. Jones, only works for money and promotions. Knowledge and its application, the direct results of his work, are not really what he desires; they are merely the means through which he can ultimately obtain money and position. Mr. Jones doesn't enjoy his work; he does it because he feels he has to. Work performed in order to meet the desire for well-being can provide inherent satisfaction, because it is appreciated for its own sake. Achievement and progress in the work lead to a growing sense of satisfaction at every stage of the work's development. In Buddhist terminology, this is called working with *chanda*. Conversely, working out of desire for pleasure is called working with *Tanha*. Those working with *Tanha* are motivated by the desire to consume. But since it is impossible to consume and work at the same time, the work itself affords little enjoyment or satisfaction.

It should also be pointed out that work in this case postpones the attainment of satisfaction, and as such will be seen as an impediment to it. When work is seen as an impediment to consumption it can become intolerable. In developing countries this is readily seen in the extent of hire-purchase debt and corruption, where consumers cannot tolerate the delay between working and consuming the objects of their desires. In modern industrial economies, many jobs preclude satisfaction, or make it very difficult, by their very nature. Factory jobs can be dull, undemanding, pointless, and even dangerous to health. They breed boredom, frustration, and depression, all of which have negative effects on productivity.

However, even in menial or insignificant tasks, there is a difference between working with *Tanha* and working with *chanda*. Even in the most monotonous of tasks, where one may have difficulty generating a sense of pride in the object of one's labors, a desire to perform the task well, or a sense of pride in one's own endeavors, may help to alleviate the monotony, and even contribute something of a sense of achievement to the work: even though the work may be monotonous, one feels that at least one is developing good qualities like endurance and is able to derive a certain enthusiasm for the work. As we have seen, the fulfillment of *Tanha* lies with seeking and obtaining objects which provide pleasant feelings.

While this seeking may involve action, the objective of *Tanha* is not directly related in a causal way to the action undertaken. Let's look at two different tasks and examine the cause and effect relationships involved: (1) Mr. Smith sweeps the street, and is paid $500 a month; (2) If Little Suzie finishes the book she is reading, Daddy will take her to the movies. It may seem at first glance that sweeping the street is the cause for Mr. Smith receiving his wage; that is, sweeping the street is the cause, and money is the result. But in fact, this is a mistaken conclusion. Correctly speaking, one would say: the action of sweeping the street is the cause for the street being cleaned; the cleanness of the street is a stipulation for Mr. Smith receiving his wage, based on an agreement between employer and employee.

All actions have results that arise as a natural consequence. The natural result of sweeping the street is a clean street. In the contract between employer and employee, a stipulation is added to this natural result, so that sweeping the street also brings about a payment of money. This is a man-made, or artificial, law. However, money is not the natural result of sweeping the street: some people may sweep a street and get no money for it, while many other people receive wages without having to sweep streets. Money is a socially contrived or artificial condition. Many contemporary social problems result from confusion between the natural results of actions and the human stipulations added to them. People begin to think that a payment of money really is the natural result of sweeping a street, or, to use another example, that a good wage, rather than medical knowledge, is the natural result of studying medicine.

As for Little Suzie, it may seem that completing the book is the cause, and going to the movies with Dad is the result. But in fact finishing the book is simply a stipulation on which going to the movies is based. The true result of reading the book is obtaining knowledge. Expanding on these examples, if Mr. Smith's work is directed solely by *Tanha*, all he wants is his $500, not the cleanness of the street. In fact, he doesn't want to sweep the street at all, but, since it is a condition for receiving his wage, he must. As for Little Suzie, if her true desire is to go to the movies (not to read the book), then reading will afford no satisfaction in itself; she only reads because it is a condition for going to the movies.

When people work solely out of *Tanha*, their true desire is for consumption, not action. Their actions of sweeping and reading-are seen as means of obtaining the objects of desire-the salary and a trip to the movies. When they work with *chanda*, on the other hand, Mr. Smith takes pride in (i.e., desires) the cleanness of the street and little Suzie wants the knowledge contained in the book. With *chanda*, their desire is for action and the true results of that action. Cleanness is the natural result of sweeping the street and knowledge is the natural result of reading the book. When the action is completed, the result naturally and simultaneously arises. When Mr. Smith sweeps the street, a clean street ensues, and it ensues whenever he sweeps. When Little Suzie reads a book, knowledge arises, and it arises whenever she reads the book.

With *chanda,* work is intrinsically satisfying because it is itself the achievement of the desired result. Thus, the objective of *chanda* is action and the good result which arises from it. When their actions are motivated by *chanda,* Mr. Smith applies himself to sweeping the street irrespective of his monthly wage and little Suzie will read her book even without Daddy having to promise to take her to the movies. (In reality, of course, most people do work for the wages, which are a necessity, but we also have the choice to take pride in our work and strive to do it well, which is *chanda,* or to do it perfunctorily simply for the wage. Thus, in real life situations, most people are motivated by varying degrees of both *Tanha* and *chanda.*)

As we have seen, actions motivated by *chanda* and actions motivated by *Tanha* give rise to very different results, both objectively and ethically. When we are motivated by *Tanha* and are working simply to attain an unrelated object or means of consumption, we may be tempted to attain the object of desire through other means which involve less effort. If we can obtain the objective without having to do any work at all, even better? If it is absolutely necessary to work for the objective, however, we will only do so reluctantly and perfunctorily. The extreme result of this is criminal activity. If Mr. Smith wants money but has no desire (*chanda*) to work, he may find working for the money intolerable and so resort to theft.

If Little Suzie wants to go the movies, but can't stand reading the book, she may steal money from her mother and go to the movies herself. With only *Tanha* to get their salary but no *chanda* to do their work, people will only go about the motions of performing their duties, doing just enough to get by. The result is apathy, laziness and poor workmanship. Mr. Smith simply goes through the motions of sweeping the street day by day until pay day arrives, and Little Suzie reads the book simply to let Daddy see that she has finished it, but doesn't take in anything she has read, or she may cheat, saying she has read the book when in fact she hasn't.

When sloppiness and dishonesty of this type arise within the work place, secondary checks must be established to monitor the work. These measures address the symptoms but not the cause, and only add to the complexity of the situation. For example, it may be necessary to install a supervisor to inspect Mr. Smith's work and check his hours; or Little Suzie's brother may have to look in and check that she really is reading the book. This applies to employers as well as employees: workers' tribunals must be established to prevent greedy or irresponsible employers from exploiting their workers and making them work in inhumane conditions or for unfair wages. When *Tanha* is the motivating force, workers and employers are trapped in a game of one-upmanship, with each side trying to get as much for them as they can for the least possible expense.

Tanha is escalated to a considerable extent by social influences. For instance, when the owners of the means of production are blindly motivated by a desire to get rich for as little outlay as possible, it is very unlikely that the workers will have much *chanda*. They will be more likely to follow the example of their employers, trying to get as much as they can for as little effort as possible. This tendency can be seen in the modern work place. It seems, moreover, that the more affluent a society becomes, the more this tendency is produced-the more we have, the more we want. This is a result of the unchecked growth of *Tanha* and the lack of any viable alternative. Meanwhile, the values of inner contentment and peace of mind seem to have been all but lost in modern society.

In rare cases, however, we hear of employers and employees who do work together with *chanda*. This happens when the employer is responsible, capable and considerate, thus commanding the confidence and affection of employees, who in return are harmonious, diligent, and committed to their work. There have even been cases of employers who were so caring with their employees that when their businesses failed and came close to bankruptcy, the employees sympathetically made sacrifices and worked as hard as possible to make the company profitable again. Rather than making demands for compensation, they were willing to take a cut in wages.

PRODUCTION AND NON-PRODUCTION

The word "production" is misleading. We tend to think that through production new things are created, when in fact it is merely changes of state which are effected. One substance or form of energy is converted into another. These conversions entail the creation of a new state by the destruction of an old one. Thus production is always accompanied by destruction. In some cases the destruction is acceptable, in others it is not. Production is only truly justified when the value of the thing produced outweighs the value of that which is destroyed. In some cases it may be better to refrain from production. This is invariably true for those industries whose products are for the purpose of destruction. In weapons factories, for example, non-production is always the better choice. In industries where production entails the destruction of natural resources and environmental degradation, non-production is sometimes the better choice.

To choose, we must distinguish between production with positive results and production with negative results; production that enhances well-being and that which destroys it. In this light, non-production can be a useful economic activity. A person who produces very little in materialistic terms may, at the same time, consume much less of the world's resources and lead a life that is beneficial to the world around him. Such a person is of more value than one who diligently consumes large amounts of the world's resources while manufacturing goods that are harmful to society. But modern economics could never make such a distinction; it would praise a person who produces and consumes (that is, destroys) vast amounts more than one who produces and consumes (destroys) little.

In the economics of the industrial era the term production has been given a very narrow meaning. It is taken to relate only to those things that can be bought and sold-a bull fight, where people pay money to see bulls killed, is seen as contributing to the economy, while a child helping an elderly person across the street is not; a professional comedian telling jokes on stage, relaxing his audience and giving them a good time, is taken to be economically productive because money changes hands, while an office worker with a very cheerful disposition is not considered to have produced anything by his cheerfulness toward those around him. Nor is there any accounting of the economic costs of aggressive action and speech that continually create tension in the work place, so that those affected have to find some way to alleviate it with amusements, such as going to see a comedian.

COMPETITION AND COOPERATION

Modern economics is based on the assumption that it is human nature to compete. Buddhism, on the other hand, recognizes that human beings are capable of both competition and cooperation. Competition is natural: when they are striving to satisfy the desire for pleasure-when they are motivated by *Tanha*-people will compete fiercely. At such times they want to get as much as possible for themselves and feel no sense of sufficiency or satisfaction. If they obtain the desired object without sharing it with anyone else, so much the better. Inevitably, competition is intense; this is natural for the mind driven by *Tanha*.

This competitive instinct can be redirected to induce cooperation. One might unite the members of a particular group by inciting them to compete with another group. For example, corporate managers sometimes rally their employees to work together to beat their competitors. But this cooperation is based entirely on competition. Buddhism would call this "artificial cooperation." True cooperation arises with the desire for well-being-with *ch*and*a*. Human development demands that we understand how *Tanha* and *ch*and*a* motivate us and that we shift our energies from competition towards cooperative efforts to solve the problems facing the world and to realize a nobler goal.

Choice

"Whether a given want is a true need, a fanciful desire, or a bizarre craving is of no matter to economics. Nor is it the business of economics to judge whether such wants should be satisfied," say the economics texts, but from a Buddhist perspective the choices we make are of utmost importance, and these choices require some qualitative appreciation of the options available. Choice is a function of intention, which is the heart of *kamma*, one of Buddhism's central teachings. The influence of *kamma* affects not only economics but all areas of our lives and our social and natural environment. Economic decisions, or choices, which lack ethical reflection, are bad *kamma*-they are bound to bring undesirable results.

Good economic decisions are those based on an awareness of the costs on the individual, social and environmental levels, not just in terms of production and consumption. These economic decisions are *kamma*. Every time an economic decision is made, *kamma* is made, and the process of fruition is immediately set in motion, for better or for worse, for the individual, for society and the environment. Thus it is important to recognize the qualitative difference between different courses of action and to make our choices wisely.

We have discussed the various economic activities. We may now ask: what is the purpose of these activities? What are we striving for in all this buying and selling, producing and consuming? Or we may ask an even grander question: What indeed is the purpose of life? Everybody holds views on these matters, although most of us are unconscious of them. Buddhist teachings stress that these views exert a tremendous influence on our lives. The Pali word for view is *ditthi*. This term covers all kinds of views on many different levels-our personal opinions and beliefs; the ideologies, religious and political views espoused by groups; and the attitudes and world-views held by whole cultures and societies.

Views lead to ramifications far beyond the realm of mental states and intellectual discourse. Like ethics, views are linked to the stream of causes and conditions. They are "subjective" mental formations that inevitably condition events in "objective" reality. On a personal level, one's world-view affects the events of life. On a national level, political views and social mores condition society and the quality of day-to-day life. The Buddha warned that views are potentially the most dangerous of all mental conditions. Unskillful views can wreak unimaginable damage.

The violence of the Crusades, Nazism and Communism, to name just three disastrous fanatical movements, were fueled by extremely unskillful views.

Skillful views, on the other hand, are the most beneficial of mental conditions. As the Buddha said: "Monks, I see no other condition which is so much a cause for the arising of as yet unarisen unskillful conditions, and for the development and fruition of unskillful conditions already arisen, as wrong view..."

This begs the question: what view of life is behind modern economics? Is it a skillful or an unskillful one? At the risk of oversimplifying, let us say that the goal of modern life is to find happiness. This view is so pervasive in modern societies that it is rarely even recognized, let alone examined or questioned. The very concept of "progress"-social, economic, scientific and political-assumes that society's highest goal is to reach a state where everyone will be happy. The United States Declaration of Independence poetically embodies this ideal by asserting mankind's right to "life, liberty and the pursuit of happiness."

While certainly a good-hearted aspiration, the view that happiness is the goal of life betrays a fundamental confusion about the truth of life. "Happiness" is never more than an ill-defined, elusive quality. Many people equate happiness with sense pleasure and the satisfaction of their desires. For these people, happiness remains a remote condition, something outside them, a future prize that must be pursued and captured. But happiness cannot be obtained through seeking, only through bringing about the causes and conditions which lead to it, and these are personal and mental development.

From the Buddhist point of view, people often confuse *Tanha*-their restless craving for satisfaction and pleasure-with the pursuit of happiness. This is indeed an unskillful view, because the craving of *Tanha* can never be satisfied. If the pursuit of happiness equals the pursuit of the objects of *Tanha*, then life itself becomes a misery. To see the consequences of this unfortunate view, one need only witness the depression and angst of the citizens in so many modern cities filled with limitless distractions and pleasure centers.

Rather than leading to contentment and well-being, the pursuit of happiness so often leads to restlessness and exhaustion in the individual, strife in society and unsustainable consumption of the environment. By contrast, the Buddhist view of life is much less idealistic but much more practical. The Buddha said simply, "There is suffering." This was the first of his Four Noble Truths, the central tenets of Buddhism. He went on to describe what suffering is: "Birth is suffering; old age is suffering; sickness is suffering; death is suffering; sorrow, lamentation, pain, grief and despair are suffering; separation from the loved is suffering; getting what you don't want is suffering; not getting what you want is suffering..."

There is little question that these things exist in life and they are all unpleasant, but the tendency of our society is to deny them. Death, in particular, is rarely thought or spoken about as a personal inevitability. Denying these things, however, does not make them go away. This is why the Buddha said that suffering is something that should be recognized. The first Noble Truth is the recognition that all things must pass and that ultimately there is no security to be had within the material world. This is the kind of truth the Buddha urged people to face-the painfully obvious and fundamental facts of life. The second Noble Truth explains the cause of suffering. The Buddha said that suffering is caused by craving based on ignorance (that is, *Tanha*).

In other words, the cause of suffering is an internal condition. We may ask, "Does craving cause old age?" it is not craving that causes old age, but rather craving for youth which makes old age a cause of suffering. Old age is inevitable; craving is not. The Buddha said that craving can be eliminated, which brings us to the third Noble Truth, which concerns the cessation of suffering. With the complete and utter abandonment of craving, suffering ceases. In the fourth Noble Truth the Buddha tells how. It is the Noble Eightfold Path for the cessation of suffering, through training of body, speech and mind in accordance with the Buddhist code of Right View, Right Thought, Right Speech, Right Action, Right Livelihood, Right Effort, Right Mindfulness and Right Concentration.

It is fairly obvious from the Four Noble Truths that the Buddhist view of life is very much at odds with the view common to modern societies. Whereas Buddhism says "There is suffering," modern societies say, "There is happiness, and I want it now!" The implications of this simple shift in perception are enormous. A society that views the purpose of life as the pursuit of happiness is one that is recklessly pursuing some future dream. Happiness is seen as something that is inherently lacking and must be found somewhere else. Along with this view comes dissatisfaction, impatience, contention, an inability to deal with suffering, and a lack of attention to the present moment.

On the other hand, with a view of life that appreciates the reality of suffering, we pay more attention to the present moment so that we can recognize problems when they arise. We cooperate with others to solve problems, rather than competing with them to win happiness. Such a view also influences our economic choices.

Our production and consumption are geared less toward the pursuit of sense gratification (*Tanha*) and more toward relieving suffering (*chanda*). If this Buddhist view were taken up on a national or global scale, rather than seeking to satisfy every demand, our economies would strive to create a state free of suffering, or a state which is primed for the enjoyment of happiness (just as a healthy body is one which is primed to enjoy happiness).

Only through understanding suffering can we realize the possibility of happiness. Here Buddhism makes a distinction between two kinds of happiness: dependent happiness and independent happiness. Dependent happiness is happiness that requires an external object. It includes any happiness contingent on the material world, including wealth, family, honor and fame. Dependent happiness, being dependent on things that can never be ours in an ultimate sense, is fickle and uncertain. Independent happiness, on the other hand, is the happiness that arises from within a mind that has been trained and has attained some degree of inner peace. Such happiness is not dependent on externals and is much more stable than dependent happiness.

Dependent happiness leads to competition and conflict in the struggle to acquire material goods. Any happiness arising from such activity is a contentious kind of happiness. There is, however, a third kind of happiness which, while not as exalted as the truly independent kind, is nevertheless more skillful than the contentious kind. It is a happiness that is more altruistically based, directed toward well-being and motivated by goodwill and compassion. Through personal development, people can appreciate this truer kind of happiness-the desire to bring happiness to others (which in Buddhism we call *metta*). With this kind of happiness, we can experience gladness at the happiness of others, just as parents feel glad at the happiness of their children.

This kind of happiness might be called "harmonious happiness," as distinct from the contentious kind of happiness. It is less dependent on the acquisition of material goods and arises more from giving than receiving. Although such happiness is not truly independent, it is much more skillful than the happiness resulting from selfish acquisition. The most assured level of happiness is the liberation resulting from enlightenment, which is irreversible. But even to train the mind, through study and meditation practice, to achieve some inner contentment is a powerful antidote to the dissatisfaction of the consumer society. And with the clarity of inner calm comes an insight into one of life's profound ironies: striving for happiness, we create suffering; understanding suffering, we find peace.

THE ROLE OF WEALTH IN BUDDHISM

Although Buddhism has been characterized as an ascetic religion, asceticism was in fact experimented with and rejected by the Buddha before he attained enlightenment. As far as Buddhism is concerned, the meaning of the word 'asceticism' is ambiguous and should not be used without qualification. The term 'poverty' is also misleading. The familiar Buddhist concepts are rather contentment (*santutthi*) or limited desires (*appicchata*). Poverty (*dadiddiya*) is in no place praised or encouraged in Buddhism. As the Buddha said, "For householders in this world, poverty is suffering"; "Woeful in the world is poverty and debt."

In fact, the possession of wealth by certain people is often praised and encouraged in the Pali Canon, indicating that wealth is something to be sought after. Among the Buddha's lay disciples, the better known, the most helpful, and the most often praised were in large part wealthy persons, such as Anathapindika. Even for the monks, who are not expected to seek wealth, to be a frequent recipient of offerings was sometimes regarded as a good quality. The monk Sivali, for example, was praised by the Buddha as the foremost of those "who are obtainers of offerings." However, these remarks must be qualified.

The main theme in the Scriptures is that it is not wealth as such that is praised or blamed but the way it is acquired and used. For the monks, as mentioned above, it is not acquisition as such that is blamed, or poverty that is praised. Blameworthy qualities are greed for gain, stinginess, grasping, attachment to gain and hoarding of wealth. Acquisition is acceptable if it is helpful in the practice of the Noble Path or if it benefits fellow members of the Order. On the other hand, this does not mean that monks are encouraged to own possessions. As long as it is allowed by the *Vinaya,* or monastic code, gain is justifiable if the possessions belong to the monastic community, but if a monk is rich in personal possessions, it is evidence of his greed and attachment and he cannot be said to conform to Buddhist principles.

The right practice for monks is to own nothing except the basic requisites of life. Here the question is not one of being rich or poor, but of having few personal cares, easy mobility, the spirit of contentment and few wishes and, as the monk's life is dependent for material support on other people, of making one easy to support. With high mobility and almost no personal cares, monks are able to devote most of their time and energy to their work, whether for their individual perfection or for the social good. "The monk is content with sufficient robes to protect the body and sufficient alms food for his body's needs. Wherever he goes he takes just these with him, just as a bird on the wing, wherever it may fly, flies only with the load of its wings."

Thus, it is contentment and paucity of wishes accompanied by commitment to the development of the good and the abandonment of evil that are praised. Even contentment and paucity of wishes are to be qualified, that is, they must be accompanied by effort and diligence, not by complacency and idleness. The monk contents himself with whatever he gets so that he can devote more of his time and energy to his own personal development and the welfare of others. In other words, while it may be good for a monk to gain many possessions, it is not good to own or to hoard them. It is good rather to gain much, and give much away.

"Furthermore, monks, he is content with whatever necessities, be it robes, alms food, shelter or medicines, he obtains. Furthermore, monks, he is continually stirring up effort to eliminate bad qualities, making dogged and vigorous progress in good things, and never throwing off his obligations."

"One is the road that leads to wealth, another road that leads to Nibbana. If a monk, disciple of the Buddha, has learned this, he will yearn not for honor, but will foster solitude."

For the laity, as mentioned above, there is no instance in which poverty is encouraged. On the contrary, many passages in the Scriptures exhort lay people to seek and amass wealth in rightful ways. Among the good results of good *kamma,* one is to be wealthy. What is blamed in connection with wealth is to earn it in dishonest ways. Worthy of blame also is the one who, having earned wealth becomes enslaved by it and creates suffering as a result of it. No less evil and blameworthy and the unlawful earning of wealth is to accumulate riches out of stinginess, and not to spend it for the benefit and well-being of oneself, one's dependents, or other people. Again, squandering wealth foolishly or indulgently, or using it to cause suffering to other people, is also criticized:

"Monks, if people knew, as I know, the fruits of sharing gifts, they would not enjoy their use without sharing them, nor would the taint of stinginess obsess the heart. Even if it were their last bit, their last morsel of food, they would not enjoy its use without sharing it if there was someone else to share it with."

Good and praiseworthy wealthy people are those who seek wealth in rightful ways and use it for the good and happiness of both themselves and others. Accordingly, many of the Buddha's lay disciples, being wealthy, liberally devoted much or most of their wealth to the support of the *Sangha* and to the alleviation of poverty and suffering. For example, the millionaire Anathapindika is said in the Commentary on the *Dhammapada* to have spent a large amount of money every day to feed hundreds of monks as well as hundreds of the poor. Of course, in an ideal society, under an able and righteous ruler or under a righteous and effective administration, there would be no poor people, as all people would be at least self-sufficient, and monks would be the only community set apart to be sustained by the material surplus of the lay society.

Thus, contrary to the popular image of Buddhism as a religion of austerity, Buddhist teachings do acknowledge the role of material comfort in the creation of happiness. However, Buddhism aims at the development of human potential and, in this regard, material wealth is considered secondary. A lucrative economic activity that is conducive to well-being can contribute to human development-the accumulation of wealth for its own sake cannot.

RIGHT LIVELIHOOD

Right Livelihood is one factor on the Noble Eightfold Path. It is not determined by the amount of material wealth it produces, but rather by the well-being it generates. Many livelihoods which produce a surplus of wealth simply cater to desires rather than providing for any true need. For the individual, the objective of livelihood is to acquire the four necessities or requisites of human existence: food, clothing, shelter, and medicine. Again, the acquisition of these four requisites is it in sufficient amount or in surplus is not the ultimate objective. The four requisites are merely a foundation upon which efforts to realize higher objectives can be based.

Some people are content with few possessions and need only a minimum to devote their energies to mental and spiritual development. Others cannot live happily on such a small amount; they are more dependent on material goods. As long as their livelihood does not exploit others, however, Buddhism does not condemn their wealth. Moreover, people who are charitably inclined can use their wealth in ways that are beneficial for society as a whole. In opposition to contemporary urban values, Buddhism does not measure a person's or nation's worth by material wealth. Nor does it go to the opposite extreme, as do Marxist thinkers, and condemn the accumulation of wealth as an evil in and of itself. Instead, Buddhism judges the ethical value of wealth by the ways in which it is obtained, and the uses to which it is put.

Miserliness

Obtaining wealth in immoral ways and using it to harmful ends are two evils associated with wealth. A third is hoarding wealth-refusing to either share one's wealth or put it to good use. In this story, the Buddha recounts the evils of miserliness:

At one time, King Pasenadi of Kosala visited the Buddha. The King told the Buddha that a rich old miser had recently died leaving no heir to his huge fortune, and the King had gone to oversee the transfer of the miser's wealth into the kingdom's treasury.

King Pasenadi described the amount of wealth he had to haul away: eight million gold coins, not to mention the silver ones, which were innumerable. And, he said, when the old miser was alive he had lived on broken rice and vinegar, dressed in three coarse cloths sewn together, used a broken-down chariot for transport and shaded himself with a sunshade made of leaves.

The Buddha remarked:

"That is how it is, Your Majesty. The foolish man, obtaining fine requisites, supports neither himself nor his dependents, his father and mother, wife and children, his servants and employees, his friends and associates, in comfort. He does not make offerings, which are of great fruit, and which are conducive to mental well-being, happiness and heaven, to religious mendicants. That wealth unconsumed and unused by him is confiscated by Kings, stolen by thieves, burnt by fire, swept aside by floods, or inherited by unfavored relatives. His wealth, accumulated and not used, disappears to no purpose. His wealth is like a forest pool, clear, cool and fresh, with good approaches and shady setting, in a forest of ogres. No-one can drink, bathe in or make use of that water.

"As for the wise man, having obtained fine requisites, he supports himself, his mother and father, his wife and children, his servants and employees, and his friends and associates comfortably, sufficiently. He makes offerings, which are of great fruit, and which are conducive to mental well-being, happiness and heaven, to religious mendicants. The wealth that he has so rightly used is not confiscated by Kings, thieves cannot steal it, fire cannot burn it, floods cannot carry it away, and unfavored relatives cannot appropriate it. The wealth rightly used by him is put to use, it does not disappear in vain. His wealth is like a forest pool not far from a village or town, with cool, clear, fresh water, good approaches and shady setting. People can freely drink of that water, carry it away, bathe in it, or use it as they please.

"The evil person, obtaining wealth, neither uses it nor lets others use it, like a forest pool in a haunted forest-the water cannot be drunk and nobody dares to use it. The wise man, obtaining wealth, both uses it and puts it to use. Such a person is exemplary; he supports his relatives and is blameless. He attains to heaven."

"Your Majesty, those people who, having obtained vast wealth, are not intoxicated by it, are not led into heedlessness and reckless indulgence which endangers others, are very rare in this world. Those whoobtained much wealth, are intoxicated by it, led into heedlessness and reckless indulgence which endangers others, are truly of far greater number."

Elsewhere in the Scriptures, the miserly person is likened to a bird called the "mayhaka" bird, which lives in the fig tree. While all the other birds flock to the tree and eat its fruits, all the *mayhaka* bird can do is standing there calling out "*mayham, mayham*" ("mine, mine"). To sum up, harmful actions associated with wealth can appear in three forms: seeking wealth in dishonest or unethical ways; hoarding wealth for its own sake; and using wealth in ways that are harmful.

KNOWING WEALTH'S LIMITATIONS

Wealthy people with virtue use their wealth to perform good works for themselves and others, but the truly wise also understand that wealth alone cannot make them free. In the passages below, the Buddha expounds on the limitations of wealth and exhorts us to strive for that which is higher than material possessions.

"Actions, knowledge, qualities, morality and an ideal life: these are the gauges of a being's purity, not wealth or name."

"I see beings in this world that are wealthy: instead of sharing their wealth around, they become enslaved by it; they hoard it and demand more and more sensual gratification.

"Kings conquer whole lands, reigning over realms that stretch from ocean to ocean, yet they are not content with simply this shore -they want the other side as well. Both Kings and ordinary people must die in the midst of want, never reaching an end to desire and craving. With craving unfulfilled, they cast off the body. There is no satisfying the desires for sense objects in this world.

"Relatives let down their hair and grieve over deceased loved ones, wailing, 'Oh, our loved one has passed away from us.' They wrap the body in a cloth, set it upon the funeral pyre and cremate it; the undertakers take sticks and poke the body until it is wholly burnt. All the deceased can take with them is a single cloth, all wealth is left behind.

"When it is time to die, no-one, neither relative nor friend, can forestall the inevitable. Possessions are carried off by the heirs while the deceased fares according to his *kamma*. When it is time to die, not one thing can you take with you, not even children, wife (or husband), wealth or land. Longevity cannot be obtained through wealth, and old age cannot be bought off with it. The wise say that life is short, uncertain and constantly changing.

"Both the rich and the poor experience contact with the realm of senses; both the foolish and the wise experience contact also. But the foolish person, through lack of wisdom, is overwhelmed and stricken by it. As for the wise man, even though he experiences contact he is not upset. Thus, wisdom is better than wealth, because it leads to the highest goal in this life."

MENTAL ATTITUDE TO WEALTH

A true Buddhist lay person not only seeks wealth lawfully and spends it for constructive purposes, but also enjoys spiritual freedom, not being attached to it, infatuated with it or enslaved by it. This is the point where the mundane and the transcendent meet. The Buddha classifies lay people (*kamabhogi*, those who partake in sense pleasures) into various levels according to lawful and unlawful means of seeking wealth, spending or not spending wealth for the happiness of oneself and others, and the attitude of greed and attachment or wisdom and spiritual freedom in dealing with wealth. The highest kind of person enjoys life on both the mundane and the transcendent planes as follows:

Mundane:

1. Seeking wealth lawfully and honestly.
2. Seeing to one's own needs.
3. Sharing with others and performing meritorious deeds.

Transcendent:

4. Making use of one's wealth without greed, longing or infatuation, heedful of the dangers and possessed of the insight that sustains spiritual freedom.

Such a person is said to be a Noble Disciple, one who is progressing toward individual perfection. Of particular note here is the compatibility between the mundane and the transcendent spheres of life, which combine to form the integral whole of Buddhist ethics, which is only perfected when the transcendent sphere is incorporated.

In spite of its great utility, then, too much importance should not be given to wealth. Its limitations in relation to the realization of the goal of *Nibbana*, furthermore, should also be recognized. Though on the mundane level poverty is something to be avoided, a poor person is not completely deprived of means to do good for him or society. The ten ways of making merit may begin with giving, but they also include moral conduct, the development of mental qualities, the rendering of service, and the teaching of the *Dhamma*. Because of poverty, people may be too preoccupied with the struggle for survival to do anything for their own perfection, but when basic living needs are satisfied, if one is mentally qualified and motivated, there is no reason why one cannot realize individual perfection.

While wealth as a resource for achieving social good can help create favorable circumstances for realizing individual perfection, ultimately it is mental maturity and wisdom, not wealth, that bring about its realization. Wealth mistreated and abused not only obstructs individual development, but can also be detrimental to the social good.

"Wealth destroys the foolish, but not those who search for the Goal." [Dh.355]

A life that is free-one that is not overly reliant on material things-is a life that is not deluded by them. This demands a clear knowledge of the benefits and limitations of material possessions. Without such wisdom, we invest all our happiness in material things, even though they can never lead to higher qualities of mind. In fact, as long as we remain attached to them, possessions will hinder even simple peace of mind. By their very nature, material things lack the ability to completely satisfy: they are impermanent and unstable; they cannot be ultimately controlled and must inevitably go to dissolution. Clinging onto them, we suffer needlessly. When we were born they were not born with us, and when we die we cannot take them along.

Used with wisdom, material goods can help relieve suffering, but used without wisdom, they only increase the burden. By consuming material goods with discrimination we can derive true value from them.

One who gains riches by diligent application to livelihood, and who puts that wealth to good use for himself and others, is said in Buddhism to be victorious in both this world and the next. [*Digha Nikaya*. III.181] When he is also possessed of the wisdom that leads to detachment (*nissarana-pañña*), when he neither becomes enslaved by possessions nor carries them as a burden, when he can live cheerfully and unconfused without being spoiled by worldly wealth, he is even more commendable.

THE MAJOR CHARACTERISTICS OF BUDDHIST ECONOMICS

Middle Way Economics: Realization of true Well-being

Buddhism is full of teachings referring to the Middle Way, the right amount and knowing moderation, and all of these terms may be considered as synonyms for the idea of balance or equilibrium. Knowing moderation is referred to in the Buddhist scriptures as *mattaññuta*. *Mattaññuta* is the defining characteristic of Buddhist economics. Knowing moderation means knowing the optimum amount, how much is "just right." It is an awareness of that optimum point where the enhancement of true well-being coincides with the experience of satisfaction.

This optimum point, or point of balance, is attained when we experience satisfaction at having answered the need for quality of life or well-being. Consumption, for example, which is attuned to the Middle Way, must be balanced to an amount appropriate to the attainment of well-being rather than the satisfaction of desires. Thus, in contrast to the classical economic equation of maximum consumption leading to maximum satisfaction, we have moderate or wise consumption, leading to well-being.

Middle Way Economics: Not Harming Oneself or Others

A further meaning of the term "just the right amount" is of not harming oneself or others. This is another important principle and one that is used in Buddhism as the basic criterion of human action, not only in relation to consumption, but for all human activity. Here it may be noted that in Buddhism "not harming others" applies not only to human beings but to all that lives.

From a Buddhist perspective, economic principles are related to the three interconnected aspects of human existence: human beings, society and the natural environment. Buddhist economics must be in concord with the whole causal process and to do that it must have a proper relationship with all three of those areas, and they in turn must be in harmony and mutually supportive. Economic activity must take place in such a way that it doesn't harm oneself (by causing a decline in the quality of life) and does not harm others (by causing problems in society or imbalance in the environment).

At the present time there is a growing awareness in developing countries of environmental issues. People are anxious about economic activities that entail the use of toxic chemicals and fossil fuels. Such activities are harmful to the health of individuals and to the welfare of society and the environment. They may be included in the phrase "harming oneself and harming others," and are a major problem for mankind.

TEACHINGS ON ECONOMICS FROM THE BUDDHIST SCRIPTURES

The Buddhist teachings on economics are scattered throughout the Scriptures among teachings on other subjects. A teaching on mental training, for example, may include guidelines for economic activity, because in real life these things are all interconnected. Thus, if we want to find the Buddhist teachings on economics, we must extract them from teachings on other subjects. Although the Buddha never specifically taught about the subject of economics, teachings about the four requisites-foods, clothing, shelter and medicine-occur throughout the Pali Canon. In essence, all of the teachings concerning the four requisites are teachings on economics.

THE MONASTIC ORDER

The Books of Discipline for the monastic order stipulate the attitude and conduct Buddhist monks and nuns are to adopt toward the four requisites. As mendicants, monks and nuns depend entirely on donations for their material needs. The Discipline lays down guidelines for a blameless life that is worthy of the support of the laity. A life dedicated to *Dhamma* study, meditation and teaching is Right Livelihood for monks and nuns. The Discipline also contains standards and regulations for ensuring that the four requisites, once supplied to the Order, will be consumed in peace and harmony rather than contention and strife.

Buddhist monks are forbidden from demanding special food or requisites. A monk must be content with little. In this passage, the Buddha instructs monks on the proper attitudes toward the four requisites. A monk in this teaching and discipline is content with whatever robes he is given and praises contentment with whatever robes are given. He does not greedily seek robes in unscrupulous ways. If he does not obtain a robe, he is not vexed; if he obtains a robe, he is not attached, not enamored of it and not pleased over it. He uses that robe with full awareness of its benefits and its dangers. He has wisdom which frees him from attachment. Moreover, he does not exalt himself or disparage others on account of his contentment with whatever robes are offered. Any monk who is diligent, ardent, not given to laziness, who is fully aware and recollected in contentment with robes, is said to be stationed in the time-honored lineage.

Moreover, a monk is one who delights in developing skillful qualities and praises their development; he delights in abandoning unskillful qualities and praises their abandoning; he does not exalt himself nor disparage others on account of his delighting in skillful qualities and praising their development, nor on account of his abandoning of unskillful qualities and praising their abandoning. A monk who is diligent, ardent, not given to laziness, but fully aware and recollected in such development (*bhavana*) and abandoning (*pahana*) is said to be stationed in the time-honored lineage. [*Anguttara Nikaya*. II.27]

This passage shows the relationship between contentment with material possessions and effort-material requisites are used as foundation for human development.

The monastic discipline exemplifies a life-style which makes use of the least possible amount of material goods. This is partly for practical reasons, to enable the Order to live in a way that does not overtax the community, and partly so that the monks can devote as much of their time and energy as possible in the study, practice and teaching of the *Dhamma*. It also enables them to live a live that is as independent of the social mainstream as possible, so that their livelihood is not all geared to any socially valued gain. All Buddhist monks, be they *Arahants* (completely enlightened beings) or newly ordained monks, live their lives according to this same basic principle of a minimal amount of material possessions and an optimum of devotion to *Dhamma* practice.

To live happily without an abundance of material possession, monks rely on *sila*, morality or good conduct. Note that each of the four types of good conduct mentioned below [*Visuddhimagga*.16] calls upon another spiritual quality to perfect it:

Restraint of behavior (*patimokkha samvara sila*) means to live within the restraint of the Monastic Code of Discipline (*Patimokkha*); to refrain from that which is forbidden, and to practice according to that which is specified, to diligently follow in all the training rules. This kind of *sila* is perfected through *saddha*, faith.

Restraint of the senses (*indriya samvara sila*) is accomplished by guarding over the mind so as not to let unskillful conditions, such as like, dislike, attachment or aversion, overwhelm it when experiencing any of the six kinds of sense impressions: sight, sound, smell, taste, sensation in the body or thought in the mind. This kind of *sila* is perfected through *sati*, mindfulness or recollection. Purity of livelihood (*ajiva parisuddhi sila*) demands that one conduct one's livelihood honestly, avoiding ways of livelihood that are wrong.

For a monk, this includes not bragging about superhuman attainments, such as meditation accomplishments or stages of enlightenment, or asking for special food when one is not sick; refraining from extortion, such as putting on a display of austerity to impress people into giving offerings; not fawning or sweet talking supporters; not hinting or making signs to get householders to make offerings; not threatening them or bullying them into making offerings; and not bartering with them, such as in giving something little and expecting much in exchange. This kind of *sila*, or purity, is perfected through *viriya*, effort.

Morality connected with requisites (*paccaya sannisita sila*) means using the four requisites with circumspection, with an awareness of their true use and value, rather than using them out of desire. At meal time, this means eating food for the sake of good health, so that one is able to live comfortably enough to practice the *Dhamma* conveniently, not eating to indulge in the sensual pleasure of eating. This kind of *sila* is perfected through *pañña,* wisdom.

Householders

While much of the Buddha's teachings were directed towards monks, there is no indication anywhere in the Scriptures that the Buddha wanted householders to live like monks. Nor is there any indication that the Buddha wanted everybody to become monks and nuns. In establishing the order of monks and nuns, the Buddha created an independent community as an example of righteousness, and community that could nourish society with the *Dhamma* and provide a refuge for those who wished to live a life dedicated to *Dhamma* study.

Within this community there are both formal members and true members. The formal members are those who are ordained into the Buddhist Order as monks and nuns and who live super-imposed, as it were, onto normal "householder society." The truly free members, however, are those of Noble Order, both ordained and householders, who have experienced transcendent insight and are scattered throughout the regular society of unenlightened beings. While the teachings in the Books of Discipline can be applied to the lives of householders, they are more directly related to monks. The monastic life is designed to be comfortable even when the four requisites are in low supply. In this regard, monks and nuns serve as living examples that life can be happy and fulfilling even when the four requisites are not plentiful.

Most lay people, however, see the four requisites as basis on which to build more wealth and comfort. While householders may seem to require more material goods than monks and nuns because of their demanding responsibilities, such as raising children and running a business, the fact remains that all of life's basic needs can be met by the four requisites. Practical teachings on economic matters for householders are contained in the Books of Discourses, or

Suttas. The Suttas recount the advice the Buddha gave to various people in various stations throughout his life. In the Suttas, the Buddha stresses four areas in which householders may relate skillfully to wealth:

- Acquisition-Wealth should not be acquired by exploitation, but through effort and intelligent action; it should be acquired in a morally sound way.
- Safekeeping-Wealth should be saved and protected as an investment for the further development of livelihood and as an insurance against future adversity. When accumulated wealth exceeds these two needs, it may be used for creating social benefit by supporting community works.
- Use-Wealth should be put to the following uses: (1) to support oneself and one's family; (2) to support the interests of fellowship and social harmony, such as in receiving guests, or in activities of one's friends or relatives; (3) to support good works, such as community welfare projects.
- Mental attitude-Wealth should not become an obsession, a cause for worry and anxiety. It should rather be related to with an understanding of its true benefits and limitations, and dealt with in a way that leads to personal development.

The Buddha praised only those wealthy people who have obtained their wealth through their own honest labor and used it wisely, to beneficial ends.

That is, the Buddha praised the quality of goodness and benefit more than wealth itself. The common tendency (in Thailand) to praise people simply because they are rich, based on the belief that their riches are a result of accumulated merit from previous lives, without due consideration of the factors from the present life, contradicts the teachings of Buddhism on two counts: Firstly, it does not exemplify the Buddha's example of praising goodness above wealth; secondly it does not make use of reasoned consideration of the entire range of factors involved.

The present life is much more immediate and as such must be afforded more importance. Previous *kamma* determines the conditions of one's birth, including physical attributes, talents, intelligence and certain personality traits. While it is said to be a determining factor for people who are born into wealthy families, the Buddha did not consider birth into a wealthy family as such to be worthy of praise, and Buddhism does not place much importance on birth station. The Buddha might praise the good *kamma* which enabled a person to attain such a favorable birth, but since their birth into a wealthy station is the fruition of good past *kamma*, such people have been duly rewarded and it is not necessary to praise them further.

A favorable birth is said to be a good capital foundation which affords some people better opportunities than others. As for the unfolding of the present life, the results of previous *kamma* stop at birth, and a new beginning is made. A good "capital foundation" can easily degenerate. If it is used with care and intelligence it will lead to benefit for all concerned, but if one is deluded by one's capital foundation, or favorable situation, one will use it in a way that not only wastes one's valuable opportunities, but leads to harm for all concerned. The important question for Buddhism is how people use their initial capital. The Buddha did not praise or criticize wealth; he was concerned with actions. According to the Buddhist teachings, wealth should be used for the purpose of helping others; it should support a life of good conduct and human development.

According to this principle, when wealth arises for one person, the whole of society benefits, and although it belongs to one person, it is just as if it belonged to the whole community. A wealthy person who uses wealth in this manner is likened to a fertile field in which rice grows abundantly for the benefit of all. Such people generate great benefit for those around them. Without them, the wealth they create would not come to be, and neither would the benefit resulting from it. Guided by generosity, these people feel moved to represent the whole of society, and in return they gain the respect and trust of the community to use their wealth for beneficial purposes. The Buddha taught that a householder who shares his wealth with others is following the path of the Noble Ones:

"If you have little, give little; if you own a middling amount, give a middling amount; if you have much, give much. It is not fitting not to give at all. Kosiya, I say to you, 'Share your wealth, use it. Tread the path of the noble ones. One who eats alone eats not happily."

Some people adhere to the daily practice of not eating until they have given something to others. This practice was adopted by a reformed miser in the time of the Buddha, who said, "As long as I have not first given to others each day, I will not even drink water."

When the wealth of a virtuous person grows, other people stand to gain. But the wealth of a mean person grows at the expense of misery for those around him. People who get richer and richer while society degenerates and poverty spreads are using their wealth wrongly. Such wealth does not fulfill its true function. It is only a matter of time before something breaks down-either the rich, or the society, or both, must go. The community may strip the wealthy of their privileges and redistribute the wealth in the hands of new "stewards," for better or for worse. If people use wealth wrongly, it ceases to be a benefit and becomes a bane, destroying human dignity, individual welfare and the community.

Buddhism stress that our relationship with wealth be guided by wisdom and a clear understanding of its true value and limitations. We should not be burdened or enslaved by it. Rather, we should be masters of our wealth and use it in ways that are beneficial to others. Wealth should be used to create benefit in society, rather than contention and strife. It should be spent in ways that relieve problems and lead to happiness rather than to tension, suffering and mental disorder. Here is a passage from the Scriptures illustrating the proper Buddhist attitude to wealth:

- "Bhikkhus, there are these three groups of people in this world. What are the three? They are the blind, the one-eyed, and the two-eyed.
- "Who is the blind person? There are some in this world who do not have the vision which leads to acquisition of wealth or to the increase of wealth already gained. Moreover, they do not have the vision which enables them to know what is skillful and what is unskillful... what is blameworthy and what is not... what is coarse and what is refined... good and evil. This is what I mean by one who is blind.
- "And who is the one-eyed person? Some people in this world have the vision which leads to the acquisition of wealth, or to the increase of wealth already obtained, but they do not have the vision that enables them to know what is skillful and what is not... what is blameworthy and what is not... what is coarse and what is refined... good and evil. This I call a one-eyed person.
- "And who is the two-eyed person? Some people in this world possess both the vision that enables them to acquire wealth and to capitalize on it, and the vision that enables them to know what is skillful and what is not... what is blameworthy and what is not... what is coarse and what is refined... good and evil. This I call one with two eyes...
- "One who is blind is hounded by misfortune on two counts: he has no wealth, and he performs no good works. The second kind of the person, the one-eyed, looks about for wealth irrespective of whether it is right or wrong. It may be obtained through theft, cheating, or fraud. He enjoys pleasures of the sense obtained from his ability to acquire wealth, but as a result he goes to hell. The one eyed person suffers according to his deeds.
- "The two eyed person is a fine human being, one who shares out a portion of the wealth obtained through his diligent labor. He has noble thoughts, a resolute mind, and attains to a good bourn, free of suffering. Avoid the blind and the one-eyed, and associate with the two-eyed."

Government

The Buddha said "poverty is suffering in this world." Here he speaks to the use of wealthy by governments. Poverty and want, like greed (to which they are closely related) contribute to crime and social discontent. Buddhism maintains that it is the duty of the government or the administrators of a country to see to the needs of those who are in want and to strive to banish poverty from the land. At the very least, honest work should be available to all people, trade and commerce should be encouraged, capital should be organized and industries monitored to guard against dishonest or exploitive practices. By these criteria, the absence of poverty is a better gauge of government's success than the presence of millionaires.

It is often asked which economic or political system is most compatible with Buddhism. Buddhism does not answer such a question directly. One might say Buddhism would endorse whatever system is most compatible with it, but economic and political systems are a question of method, and methods, according to Buddhism, should be attuned to time and place. What is the purpose of a government's wealth? Essentially, a government's wealth is for the purpose of supporting and organizing its citizens' lives in the most efficient and beneficial way possible. Wealth enables us to practice and to attain progressively higher levels of well-being. Wealth should support the community in such a way that people who live in it conduct good lives and are motivated to a higher good.

A political or economic system that uses wealth to these ends is compatible with Buddhism (subject to the stipulation that it is a voluntary or free system rather than an authoritarian one). Specific systems are simply methods dependent on time and place, and can vary accordingly. For example, when the Buddha established the Order of monks as a specialized community, he set up rules limiting a monk's personal possessions. Most requisites were to be regarded as communal property of the Order. The Buddha gave different teachings regarding wealth for householders or worldly society.

In his day, there were two main political systems in India: some parts of the country were ruled by absolute monarchies, others were ruled by republican states. The Buddha gave separate teachings for each. This is characteristic of his teachings. Buddhism is not a religion of ideals and philosophy, but a religion of practice. The Buddha made his teaching applicable to the real life of the people in the society of the time. If the Buddha had waited until he had designed a perfect society before he taught, he would have fallen into idealism and romanticism. Since the perfect society will always be a "hoped-for" society, the Buddha gave teachings that could be put to effect in the present time, or, in his words, "those truths which are truly useful."

For the monarchies, the Buddha taught the duties of a Wheel-Turning Emperor, exhorting rulers to use their absolute power as a tool for generating benefit in the community rather than a tool for seeking personal happiness. For the republican states, he taught the *aparihaniyadhamma*-principles and methods for encouraging social harmony and preventing decline. In separate ways both these teaching show how a people can live happily under different political systems.

When the absolute monarchy reached its highest perfection in India, the Emperor Ashoka used these Buddhist principles to govern his empire. He wrote in the Edicts, "His Highness, Priyadassi, loved by the devas, does not see rank or glory as being of much merit, except if that rank or glory is used to realize the following aim: 'Both now and in the future, may the people listen to my teaching and practice according to the principles of *Dhamma*.'"

The ideal society is not one in which all people occupy the same station; such a society is in fact not possible. The ideal society is one in which human beings, training themselves in mind and intellect, although possessing differences, are nevertheless striving for the same objectives. Even though they are different they live together harmoniously. At the same time, it is a society which has a noble choice, a noble way out, for those so inclined, in the form of a religious life.

While absolute equality is impossible, governments should ensure that the four requisites are distributed so all citizens have enough to live on comfortably and can find honest work. Moreover, the economic system in general should lead to a harmonious community rather than to contention and strife, and material possessions used as a base for beneficial human development rather than as an end in themselves.

In one Sutta, the Buddha admonishes the Universal Emperor to apportion some of his wealth to the poor. The emperor is told to watch over his subjects and prevent abject poverty from arising. Here we see that ethical economic management for a ruler or governor is determined by the absence of poverty in his domain, rather than by a surplus of wealth in his coffers or in the hands of a select portion of the population. When this basic standard is met, the teachings do not prohibit the accumulation of wealth or stipulate that it should be distributed equally. With an understanding of the Buddhist perspective on social practice, those involved in such matters can debate which system is not compatible with Buddhism? Or they may opt to devise a new, more effective system. This might be the best alternative. However, it is a matter of practical application which is beyond the scope of this book.

THE INNER PERSPECTIVE

The Abhidhamma Pitaka contains the Buddha's more esoteric teaching. While the Abhidhamma does not directly address economics, it does have a strong indirect connection because it analyses the mind and its constituents in minute detail. These mental factors are the root of all human behavior, including, of course, economic activity. Negative mental constituents such as greed, aversion, delusion and pride motivate economic activity as do the positive constituents such as non-greed, non-aversion and non-delusion, faith, generosity, and goodwill. In this respect, the Abhidhamma is a study of economics on its most fundamental level.

In a similar connection, the more esoteric practices of Buddhism, meditation in particular, relate indirectly but fundamentally to economics. Through meditation and mental training, we come to witness the stream of causes and conditions that begin as mental conditions and lead to economic activity. With this insight, we can investigate our mental process and make sound ethical judgments.

Meditation helps us to see how ethical and unethical behaviors are the natural consequence of the mental conditions which motivate them. Individual people, classes, races and nationalities are neither intrinsically good nor evil. It is rather our mental qualities that guide our behavior toward the ethical and the unethical. Greed, hatred and delusion drive us to unethical acts. Wisdom and a desire for true well-being guide us to ethical behavior and a good life.

With meditation, we gain perspective on our motivations: we sharpen our awareness and strengthen free will. Thus, when it comes to making economic decisions, decision about our livelihood and consumption, we can better resist compulsions driven by fear, craving, and pride and choose instead a moral course that aims at true well-being. In this way, we begin to see how mental factors form the basis of all economic matters, and we realize that the development of this kind of mental discernment leads the way to true economic and human development. Perhaps more importantly, through meditation training it is possible to realize a higher kind of happiness-inner peace, the independent kind of happiness. When we have the ability to find peace within ourselves we can use wealth, which is no longer necessary for our own happiness, freely for the social good.

SEEKING AND PROTECTING WEALTH

The following Sutta offers teachings on livelihood for a householder with an emphasis on the benefits that arise from right livelihood. At one time, the Brahmin Ujjaya went to visit the Buddha to ask his advice on how to gain prosperity through right livelihood. The Buddha answered by explaining the conditions that would lead to happiness in the present and in the future:

"Brahmin, these four conditions lead to happiness and benefit in the present. They are industriousness, watchfulness, good company and balanced livelihood.

"And what is the endowment of industriousness (*utthanasampada*)? A son of good family supports himself through diligent effort. Be it through farming, commerce, raising livestock, a military career, or the arts, he is diligent, he applies himself, and he is skilled. He is not lazy in his work, but clever, interested. He knows how to manage his work, he is able and responsible: this is called endowment of industriousness.

"And what is the endowment of watchfulness (*arakkhasampada*)? A son of good family has wealth, the fruit of his own sweat and labor, rightly obtained by him. He applies himself to protecting that wealth, thinking, 'How can I prevent this wealth from being confiscated by the King, stolen by thieves, burnt from fire, swept away from floods or appropriated by unfavored relatives?' This is called the endowment of watchfulness.

"And what is good company (*kalyanamittata*)? Herein, a son of good family, residing in a town or village, befriends, has discourse with, and seek advice from, those householders, sons of householders, young people who are mature and older people who are venerable, who are possessed of faith, morality, generosity, and wisdom. He studies and emulates the faith of those with faith; he studies and emulates the morality of those with morality; he studies and emulates the generosity of those who are generous; he studies and emulates the wisdom of those who are wise. This is to have good company.

"And what is balanced livelihood (*samajivita*)? A son of good family supports himself in moderation, neither extravagantly nor stintingly. He knows the causes of increase and decrease of wealth; he knows which undertakings will yield an income higher than the expenditure rather than the expenditure exceeding the income. Like a person weighing things on a scale, he knows the balance either way... If this young man had only a small income but lived extravagantly, it could be said of him that he consumed his wealth as if it were peanuts. If he had a large income but used it stintingly, it could be said of him that he will die like a pauper. But because he supports himself in moderation, it is said that he has balanced livelihood.

"Brahmin, the wealth rightly gained in this way has four pathways of decline. They are to be given to debauchery, drink, gambling, and association with evil friends. It is like a large reservoir with four channels going into it and four channels going out opened up, and the rain does not fall in due season, that large reservoir can be expected only to decrease, not to increase...

"Brahmin, wealth so gained rightly has four pathways of prosperity. They are to refrain from debauchery, drink and gambling, and to associate with good friends, to be drawn to good people. It is like a large reservoir with four channels leading into it and four channels leading out. If the channels leading into it are opened up, and the channels leading out are closed off, and rain falls in due season, it can be expected that for this reservoir there will be only increase, not decrease... Brahmin, these four conditions are for the happiness and benefit of a young man in the present moment." [*Anguttara Nikaya*. IV.241]

The Buddha then went on to describe four conditions which lead to happiness and benefit in the future. In short, they are to possess the spiritual qualities of faith, morality, generosity and wisdom.

The Happiness of a Householder

The following teaching was given to the merchant Anathapindika. It is known simply as the four kinds of happiness for a householder:

"Herein, householder, these four kinds of happiness are appropriate for one who leads the household life and enjoys the pleasures of the senses. They are the happiness of ownership, the happiness of enjoyment, the happiness of freedom from debt, and the happiness of blamelessness.

"What is the happiness of ownership (*atthisukha*)? A son of good family possesses wealth that has been obtained by his own diligent labor, acquired through the strength of his own arms and the sweat of his own brow, rightly acquired, rightly gained. He experiences pleasure, he experiences happiness, thinking, 'I possess this wealth that has been obtained by my own diligent labor, acquired through the strength of my own arms and the sweat of my own brow, rightly acquired, rightly gained.' This is the happiness of ownership.

"And what is the happiness of enjoyment (*bhogasukha*)? Herein, a son of good family consumes, puts to use, and derives benefit from the wealth that has been obtained by his own diligent labor, acquired through the strength of his own arms and the sweat of his own brow, rightly acquired, rightly gained. He experiences pleasure, he experiences happiness, thinking, 'Through this wealth that has been obtained by my own diligent labor, acquired through the strength of my own arms and the sweat of my own brow, rightly acquired, rightly gained, I have derived benefit and performed good works.' This is called the happiness of enjoyment.

"And what is the happiness of freedom from debt (*ananasukha*)? Herein, a son of good family owes no debt, be it great or small, to anyone at all. He experiences pleasure and happiness, reflecting. 'I owe no debts, be they great or small, to anyone at all.' This is called the happiness of freedom from debt.

"And what is the happiness of blamelessness (*anavajjasukha*)? Herein, a noble disciple is possessed of blameless bodily actions, blameless speech, and blameless thoughts. He experiences pleasure and happiness, thinking, 'I am possessed of blameless bodily actions, blameless speech, and blameless thoughts.' This is called the happiness of blamelessness.

"When he realizes the happiness of being free from debt, he is in a position to appreciate the happiness of owning possessions. As he uses his possessions, he experiences the happiness of enjoyment. Clearly seeing this, the wise man, comparing the first three kinds of happiness with the last, sees that they are not worth a sixteenth part of the happiness that arises from blameless behavior."

THE BENEFITS OF WEALTH

In this passage, the Buddha explains to the merchant Anathapindika some of the benefits that can arise from wealth. Since the teachings are specific to an earlier time, the reader is advised to glean the gist of them and apply it to the modern day:

"Herein, householder, there are five uses to which wealth can be put. They are:

"With the wealth that has been obtained by his own diligent labor, acquired through the strength of his own arms and the sweat of his own brow, rightly acquired, rightly gained, the noble disciple supports himself comfortably, sufficiently, he applies himself to seeing to his own happiness in rightful ways. He supports his father and mother... wife and children, servants and workers comfortably, to a sufficiency, applying himself to their needs and their happiness as is proper. This is the first benefit to obtain from wealth.

"Moreover, with the wealth that has been obtained by his own diligent labor, acquired through the strength of his own arms and the sweat of his own brow, rightly acquired, rightly gained, the noble disciple supports his friends and associates comfortably, to a sufficiency, taking an interest in their happiness as is proper. This is the second benefit to be derived from wealth.

"Moreover, with the wealth that has been obtained by his own diligent labor, acquired through the strength of his own arms and the sweat of his own brow, rightly acquired, rightly gained, the noble disciple protects his wealth from the dangers of confiscation by kings, theft, fire, flood, and appropriation by unfavored relatives. He sees to his own security. This is the third benefit to be derived from wealth.

"Moreover, with the wealth that has been obtained by his own diligent labor, acquired through the strength of his own arms and the sweat of his own brow, rightly acquired, rightly gained, the noble disciple makes the five kinds of sacrifice. They are: to relatives (supporting relatives); to visitors (receiving guests); to ancestors (offerings made in the name of ancestors); to the king (for taxes and public works); and to the gods (that is, he supports religion). This is another benefit to be derived from wealth.

"Moreover, with the wealth that has been obtained by his own diligent labor, acquired through the strength of his own arms and the sweat of his own brow, rightly acquired, rightly gained, the noble disciple makes offerings which are of the highest merit, which are conducive to mental well-being, happiness and heaven, to religious mendicants, those who live devoted to heedfulness, are established in patience and gentleness, are trained, calmed, and cooled of defilements. This is the fifth benefit to be obtained from wealth.

"Householder, there are these five benefits to be obtained from wealth. If wealth is used by a noble disciple in such a way that these five benefits are fulfilled, and if it should then become spent, that noble disciple can reflect thus: 'Whatever benefit is to be obtained from wealth, I have obtained. Now my wealth is spent.' That noble disciple experiences no distress on that account. And if, after that noble disciple has used his wealth to provide these five benefits, that wealth should increase, that noble disciple reflects thus: 'Whatever benefit is to be obtained from my wealth I have already obtained. And now my wealth has increased.' That noble disciple is also not distressed on that account; he is distressed in neither case."

Wealth and Spiritual Development

The Buddha taught that basic material needs must be met before spiritual development can begin. The following story [Dh.A.III.262] illustrates how hunger is both a cause of physical suffering and an obstacle to spiritual progress:

One morning while the Buddha was residing in the Jetavana monastery near the city of Savatthi, he sensed with his psychic powers that the spiritual faculties of a certain poor peasant living near the city of Alavi were mature enough for him to understand the teaching, and that he was ripe for enlightenment. So, later that morning, the Buddha set off walking to Alavi, some 30 *yojanas* (about 48 km) away.

The inhabitants of Alavi held the Buddha in great respect, and on his arrival warmly welcomed him. Eventually a place was prepared for everyone to gather together and listen to a discourse. However, as the Buddha's particular purpose in going to Alavi was to enlighten this one poor peasant, he waited for him to arrive before starting to talk. The peasant heard the news of the Buddha's visit and, since he had been interested in the Buddha's teaching for some time, he decided to go to listen to the discourse. But it so happened and one of his cows had just disappeared and he wondered whether he should go and listen to the Buddha first and look for his cow afterwards, or to look for the cow first. He decided that he should look for the cow first and quickly set off into the forest to search for it.

Eventually the peasant found his cow and drove it back to the herd, but by the time everything was as it should be, he was very tired. The peasant thought to himself, "Time is getting on, if I go back home first it will take up even more time. I'll just go straight into the city to listen to the Buddha's discourse." Having made up his mind, the poor peasant started walking into Alavi. By the time he arrived at the place set up for the talk, he was exhausted and very hungry. When the Buddha saw the peasant's condition, he asked the city elders to arrange some food for the poor man, and only when the peasant had eaten his fill and was refreshed did the Buddha start to teach. While listening to the discourse the peasant realized the fruit of 'Stream Entry,' the first stage of enlightenment. The Buddha had fulfilled his purpose in traveling to Alavi.

After the talk was over, the Buddha bade farewell to the people of Alavi and set off back to the Jetavana monastery. During the walk back, the monks who were accompanying him started to discuss the day's events: "What was that all about? The Lord didn't quite seem himself today. I wonder why he got them to arrange food for the peasant like that, before he would agree to give his discourse." The Buddha, knowing the subject of the monks' discussion, turned back towards them and started to explain his reason, saying, "When people are overwhelmed and in pain through suffering, they are incapable of understanding religious teaching." The Buddha went on to sat that hunger is the most severe of all illnesses and that conditioned phenomena provide the basis for the most ingrained suffering. Only when one understands these truths will one realize the supreme happiness of *Nibbana*.

Buddhism considers economics to be of great significance-this is demonstrated by the Buddha having the peasant eat something before teaching him. Economists might differ as to whether the Buddha's investment of a 45 kilometer walk was worth the enlightenment of one single person, but the point is that not only is Right Livelihood one of the factors of the Eightfold Path, but that hungry people cannot appreciate the *Dhamma*. Although consumption and economic wealth are important, they are not goals in themselves, but are merely the foundations for human development and the enhancement of the quality of life. They allow us to realize the profound: after eating, the peasant listened to *Dhamma* and became enlightened. Buddhist economics ensures that the creation of wealth leads to a life in which people can develop their potentials and increase in goodness. Quality of life, rather than wealth for its own sake, is the goal.

Bibliography

Akira, Hirakawa, The Formation of the Panca-Sila in Early Buddhism, *World Fellowship of Buddhists Review* 32 (3): 8–23, 1995.

Barua, Dipak Kumar, *Viharas in Ancient India: A Survey of Buddhist Monasteries,* Calcutta: Indian Publications, 1969.

Cousins, L. S., Ethical Standards in World Religions: III. Buddhism, *The Exository Times* Vol. LXXXV, pp. 100–104, 1974.

Cousins, L. S., Good or Skilful? Kusala in Canon and Commentary, *Journal of Buddhist Ethics* 3:136–64, 1996.

Dharmasiri, G., *Fundamentals of Buddhist Ethics,* Antioch, CA.: Golden Leaves Publ. Co., 1989.

Frauwallner, E., *The Earliest Vinaya and the Beginnings of Buddhist Literature,* Rome: Istituto Italiano per il Medio ed Estremo Oriente, 1956.

Fu, C. W., and S. A. Wawrytko, eds., *Buddhist Ethics and Modern Society: an International Symposium*, New York: Greenwood Press, 1991.

Guenther, Herbert V., *Philosophy and Psychology in the Abhidharma,* Berkeley, Calif.: Shambhala, 1976.

Harvey, P., *An Introduction to Buddhism: Teachings, History and Practices,* Cambridge: Cambridge University Press, chap. 9, 1990.

Harvey, P., *An Introduction to Buddhist Ethics: Foundations, Values and Issues,* Cambridge: Cambridge University Press, 2000.

Harvey, P., *An Introduction to Buddhist Ethics: Foundations, Values and Issues*, Cambridge: Cambridge University Press, pp. 11-31, 2000.

Hinderey, R., *Comparative Ethics in Hindu and Buddhist Traditions*, Delhi: Motilal Banarsidass, 1978.

Jacobson, Nolan Pliny, *Buddhism, the Religion of Analysis*. London: Feffer & Simons, 1974.

Jayatilleke, K. N., *Ethics in Buddhist Perspective: Wheel Booklet no,*175/176. Kandy, Sri Lanka: Buddhist Publication Society, 1972.

Keown, D. (ed), *Contemporary Buddhist Ethics*, London: Curzon Press, 2000.

Keown, D., *The Nature of Buddhist Ethics*, London: Macmillan, 1992.

Keown, D., *Buddhism and Bioethics*, London: Macmillan; New York: St. Martin's Press, chap. 1, 1995.

Little, D. and S. B. Twiss., *Comparative Religious Ethics: A New Method,* New York: Harper and Row, 1978.

Mahasi Sayadaw, *Sallekha Sutta: A Discourse on the Refinement of Character*, Hinsdale, Il.: Buddhadharma Meditation Center, 1981.

McDermott, J. P., *Development in the Early Buddhist Concept of Kamma/Karma*, New Delhi: Munshiram Manoharlal, 1984.

Misra, G. S. P., *Development of Buddhist Ethics*, New Delhi: Munshiram Manoharlal, 1984.

Nhat Hanh, Thich, et al., *For a Future to be Possible: Commentaries on the Five Wonderful Precepts*, Berkeley, CA.: Parallax Press, 1993.

Nyanaponika, *The Roots of Good and Evil: Wheel booklet no,* 251/253. Kandy, Sri Lanka: Buddhist Publication Society, 1978.

Pardue, Peter, *Buddhism: A Brief Account*. New York: Macmillan, Social history, 1971.

Prebish, C. S., ed., *Buddhist Ethics: A Cross-cultural Approach*, Kendall/Hunt, 1992.

Whitehill, James, "Buddhism and the Virtues" in Keown, D. (ed) *Contemporary Buddhist Ethics*, London: Curzon Press, 17-36, 2000.

Saddhatissa, H., *Buddhist Ethics: Essence of Buddhism*, London: George Allen and Unwin, 1970.

Saddhatissa, H., *The Buddha's Way*, New York: Brazillier, Reprint, London: Allen and Unwin, 1985.

Varma, Vishvanath Prasad, *Early Buddhism and Its Origins.* Delhi: Munshiram Monaharlal, 1973.

Index

L

M

N

O

R

S

T

U